THE
NELSON
COMPANION

'His Name is a monument, that will exist undiminished throughout all ages and be warmly cherished in the remembrance of Britons'

from a sermon preached by the Revd Thomas Wood
in aid of the Patriotic Fund, 5 December 1805

THE
NELSON
COMPANION

Edited by
COLIN WHITE

Bramley Books

First published in 1995 by Alan Sutton Publishing Limited, an imprint of Sutton Publishing Limited in association with the Royal Naval Museum

This edition published in 1997 by Bramley Books, an imprint of Quadrillion Publishing

British Library Cataloguing in Publication Data

Nelson Companion
  I. White, Colin
  359.331092

ISBN 1-85833-765-8

This book was designed and produced by
Sutton Publishing Limited · Phoenix Mill · Thrupp · Stroud · Gloucestershire

Endpapers, front: A First World War souvenir handkerchief attempting to invoke the spirit of Nelson; back: HMS Victory *during the great restoration of 1922 to 1927.*

Typeset in 10/13 Sabon.
Typesetting and origination by
Sutton Publishing Limited.
Printed in Great Britain by
WBC Limited, Bridgend.

Contents

List of Illustrations

Sources

RNM	Royal Naval Museum	Mon	Nelson Museum, Monmouth
RNM/MC	RNM: McCarthy Collection	MNA	Michael Nash Archive
NMM	National Maritime Museum		(private)
NPG	National Portrait Gallery	TP	Tom Pocock Archive (private)
BL	British Library		

Acknowledgements

My first, and principal, thanks go to my fellow-authors. A joint project such as this is fertile ground for potential disagreements – especially when each participant is an expert in their own field. Yet all my colleagues have been unstinting of their time and expertise – and, most important, of their support. It has been a most enjoyable exchange of ideas and information, enlivened by some robust debates. For example, we *still* cannot agree on whether the portrait by Charles Lucy (see page 152) is a good likeness!

One of the many rewards of a career as a museum curator is the opportunities it offers for meeting private collectors and enthusiasts – and in the Nelson field, they are legion. I would like to thank particularly a lady whose name appears continuously in the pages that follow – and rightly for she is the undisputed Queen of Nelsonians – Mrs Lily McCarthy CBE, who has generously allowed items from her remarkable collection to be featured throughout the book. I am also indebted to Clive Richards for allowing me access to his private collection; Ben Burgess, with whom I have maintained a long and fruitful correspondence on the subject of Samuel Drummond's paintings of the death of Nelson; Dr and Mrs Emmanuel for help and advice; Jean Kislak, the donor of the monument to Emma Hamilton in Calais; David Shannon of the Nelson Society and my fellow-members of The 1805 Club, with whom I have enjoyed so many convivial discussions about the Admiral. Preparing this book has made me powerfully aware of the strong influence that Nelson still exercises over the lives of very many people – not least mine!

I have also received much help from professional colleagues. At the Royal Naval Museum: from the Head of Publications, Dr Chris Howard Bailey, who has been most generous with her considerable knowledge of editing and publishing; Chris Brindle, General Manager of our Trading Company, who provided the 'pump-priming' finance for the project; Lesley Thomas, Head of Exhibits; Melanie McKeown, Public Relations Officer; and curators Andrew Trotman (printed books), Richard Noyce (artefacts), Matthew Sheldon (manuscripts) and Assunta del Priore (visual image). I have also benefited greatly from the advice and expertise of our consultant designer, Michael O'Callaghan. Colleagues at other institutions have been equally generous with their assistance: at the National Maritime Museum, Greenwich, Dr Roger Knight, Caroline Roberts and David Spence; at the Nelson Museum, Monmouth, Andrew Helme, and at the Australian National Maritime Museum in Sydney, Lindsey Shaw. At Alan Sutton Publishing, I have leant heavily on the advice and expertise of Roger Thorp and Rosemary Prudden, and thanks are also due to the staff of Christie's, Phillips and Sotheby's for assistance with the illustrations for Chapter Seven. Also, a special word of gratitude to Ross Young of Ross Young Photographers, Portsmouth, who has so splendidly photographed objects from the Royal Naval Museum's collections especially for this book.

Finally, I would like to thank five people 'without whom this book could not have been written' – a well-worn phrase which, in this case, is simply true. They are: the RNM's Director, Campbell McMurray, who has enthusiastically supported the project from its inception in early 1993 and has allowed me the time in which to complete it; Tom Pocock – widely acknowledged as our leading Nelson expert – who has been characteristically generous with his advice and expertise; Michael Nash, whose personal knowledge about Nelson is encyclopaedic and who has allowed me unrestricted access to his remarkable Nelson Archive; John May, who has provided just the right blend of robust encouragement whenever difficulties were encountered; and finally my PA, Helen Gooding, who has dealt with all the extra correspondence, meetings and telephone calls engendered by the project – and yet has *still* managed to keep me abreast of all my other Museum duties.

Palmam qui meruit ferat, Nelson's personal motto, sums up my feelings very neatly: 'Let him (or her) who has deserved it bear the palm.' The brickbats for any errors, however, should be reserved for me alone!

COLIN WHITE
Royal Naval Museum, May 1995

Editor's Introduction

On 7 January 1806 John Evans visited HMS *Victory* in the Medway, where she lay awaiting refit in Chatham Dockyard, following the heavy damage she had suffered at Trafalgar. He and his party were shown all over the ship and their eager questions were patiently answered. Reporting on his visit in a letter to a friend, he noted: 'You may perceive that everything that has the remotest reference to the departed hero is held in veneration. Even a lock of hair, preserved in a breast pin, was shown to us as a precious relic.'

Evans had witnessed the early stages of the Nelson cult and, as with all cults, it had two distinctive characteristics: the impulse to visit a location associated with the hero, and the longing to possess some item associated with him. This book studies these two phenomena in some depth and offers itself as a companion for the Admiral's modern enthusiasts as 'The Nelson Decade' gets under way. For those who have the visiting urge, Tom Pocock introduces the worldwide Nelsonian sites and Flora Fraser the extraordinary variety of monuments. For those who prefer collecting, John Munday examines the rich store of Nelson relics, John May the diverse field of Nelson commemoratives and Michael Nash some of the best biographies.

The book also deals with the phenomenon of Nelson The Hero – with what I have called, in my opening, contextual essay, 'The Nelson Legend'. But legend has no power unless it is rooted in reality. So we have also included essays on two key ways the 'real' Nelson may be encountered: through the many surviving portraits, examined by Richard Walker, and through the rich legacy of his letters and despatches, analysed by Felix Pryor.

The Nelson Legend is too vast a subject to be contained within a single book and so what follows is intended only as an introduction, and a guide to further, more detailed study. Certainly, *The Nelson Companion* makes no claim to be either exhaustive or definitive and it is inevitable that other Nelson experts will be able to fill gaps and identify errors. I regard this book, therefore, as the opening stage in a long-term project and hope that other studies will follow, looking in more depth at the different aspects of the story told here.

CHAPTER I

The Immortal Memory
by Colin White

A round four o'clock on the afternoon of Monday 21 October 1805 the
heavy cannonade off Cape Trafalgar began to slacken. As the gunsmoke
began to drift sluggishly eastwards towards the distant coastline of Spain,
breaking up as it did so, the ship's company of HMS *Agamemnon*, a 64-gun
British battleship, caught a glimpse of the fleet flagship, HMS *Victory*, some half a
mile away to the south. Despite extensive damage from the concentrated
broadsides of the allied fleet's centre division in the opening stages of the action,
she was still proudly sporting the extra battle ensigns ordered by the commander-
in-chief; and his white flag, with its blood-red cross of St George, was still flying
from her obviously unstable foretopmast.

Yet as the *Agamemnon*'s captain, Sir Edward Berry, looked across the
wreckage-strewn water, premonition gripped his heart. He was particularly close
to Vice Admiral Lord Nelson, one of the famous 'band of brothers', and now he
sensed that something was wrong. Calling urgently for his barge, he left his ship
and was rowed across to the *Victory*.

His departure was noted by one of his young midshipmen, Joseph Woollnough,
who was in command of the fo'c'sle guns. He was also around to watch Berry's
return and, to his consternation, saw that tears were pouring down the captain's face
as, without pausing to speak to anyone, he went straight down to his cabin. By now
rumours were spreading. The barge's crew had been told by their comrades in the
Victory that the Admiral had been wounded earlier in the battle and carried off the
quarter-deck; but no one knew for certain whether, as so often before, he had
managed to survive yet another severe wound. Eventually, the first lieutenant, Hugh
Cook, decided to go below and ask the captain for definite news. Moments later he
returned with the tidings they had all been fearing: Berry had arrived on board the
Victory just too late to say his last farewells to his friend; Nelson was dead.

Midshipman Woollnough noted how the tidings cast an immediate dampener on the spirit of the victors: 'A stranger might have supposed from the gloom that spread among them that they had been beaten instead of being conquerors.'[1] The mood was most eloquently summed up by the fleet second-in-command, Vice Admiral Cuthbert Collingwood. He had been among the first to know the worst for, as soon as he was wounded, Nelson had sent an officer to his old friend, bearing the news and his love. Later Collingwood was to recall that moment vividly: 'I asked the officer if the wound was dangerous, and he by his look told me what he could not speak, nor I reflect upon now, without suffering again the anguish of that moment.' [2] The day after the battle, worn out with the fighting and by the opening stages of the great storm which was even then breaking over the shattered ships, he sat down to write his official dispatch. And the words that came to him first were not of success or victory, but of personal loss: 'The ever-to-be-lamented death of Vice Admiral Lord Viscount Nelson, who, in the late conflict with the enemy, fell in the hour of victory. . . .'

Slowly, the news spread wider. It reached Gibraltar on 24 October, and the *Gibraltar Chronicle* rushed out a special edition which contained a letter

The End of the Day *by Harold Wyllie. As the storm clouds gather on the evening of 21 October the crew of HMS* Victory *struggle to repair the damage to their shattered ship. The windows of Nelson's cabin are dark and his flag flies at half-mast – the first indication to many in the fleet that he is dead.*

Collingwood had written to the military commander-in-chief, with a French translation for propaganda purposes. It reached England in the early morning of 4 November, when the schooner HMS *Pickle*, carrying Collingwood's dispatch, encountered the Mousehole fishing fleet in the Channel. Leaving their work, the fishermen returned to port and hurried with the news to Penzance, where they found the mayor attending a reception at the Union Hotel. He announced the news from a balcony in the assembly rooms. Meanwhile, Lieutenant Lapenotière of the *Pickle* landed at Falmouth (which still vies with Penzance for the honour of being the place where the news was first announced in England) and tore in a post-chaise up the turnpike road to London, through Truro, Tavistock, Exeter, Axminster and Basingstoke, spreading the news wherever he stopped to change his horses. Arriving in the fog-bound capital at about one o'clock in the early hours of 6 November, he burst into the Board Room at the Admiralty, where the Secretary to the Admiralty Board, William Marsden, was still working by flickering candlelight, and announced dramatically: 'Sir: we have gained a great victory; but we have lost Lord Nelson!'

At once, the news-spreading machinery was set in motion. It is often thought that news travelled slowly in those days before television and fax machines, but there was in fact a sophisticated system of communication. From the Admiralty, messengers went out to the King at Windsor and the Prime Minister, William Pitt, at Downing Street. Meanwhile, copies of the dispatch were made by hastily summoned clerks and rushed to the printers. By late afternoon a special edition of the *London Gazette* was available on the streets; while three thousand copies had been sent off by coach to Great Yarmouth, there to be loaded on a fast packet-boat to carry the news to the Continent. As soon as it was light enough, the telegraph on the Admiralty roof began transmitting the news to the chief naval ports and orders went out for the firing of a victory salute by the guns at the Tower.

At around ten o'clock that morning Emma Hamilton was lying in bed at Merton Place in Surrey (the house she had shared with Nelson), suffering from the nervous eczema which often afflicted her. With her was one of Nelson's sisters, Mrs Susannah Bolton. Suddenly, Emma thought she heard the distant thud of guns. Mrs Bolton suggested they might be firing in celebration of another victory by her brother, but Emma dismissed the possibility: it was too early; he had only been gone for six weeks. Five minutes later a carriage drew up bearing Captain Whitby from the Admiralty. As Emma recalled:

> He came in and with a pale countenance and faint voice said, 'We have gained a great victory.' 'Never mind your victory,' I said, 'My letters – give me my letters!' Capt. Whitby was unable to speak – tears in his eyes and a deathly paleness over his face made me comprehend him. I believe I gave a scream and fell back, and for ten hours after I could neither speak nor shed a tear.[3]

The messenger to the King had reached Windsor at half past six and the King was so shocked by the news that he remained silent for a full five minutes before going with his family to St George's Chapel to give thanks for the victory. Later in the day the news reached Henley-on-Thames, sent there by one of Pitt's colleagues, Lord Malmesbury, who had written to a printer he knew called George Norton. Reporting to his patron early in the morning of 7 November, Norton wrote that he had run off five hundred copies of a special 'flyer' and put them in the mailbags for towns throughout the Thames Valley, and even as far afield as Gloucester and Worcester, adding: 'I shall also give some to the Mail Guards [on the mail coaches] to circulate through all the villages they pass to and from London.'[4] Warwick received the news the same day and the churchwarden's accounts record that the ringers were paid a guinea for ringing a victory peal. It reached both the south of Ireland and the north of Scotland by 9 November for, on 10 November, one of Nelson's close civilian friends, Lord Minto, wrote from Perth: 'My sense of his irreparable loss, as well as my sincere and deep regret for so kind a friend have hardly left room for other feelings.' Even as he wrote, in Castletownshend, near Cork, Captain Joshua Rowley Watson of the Royal Navy together with two hundred men of the Sea Fencibles under his command, assisted by eight masons, were erecting a memorial arch. Completed in just five hours, it stood some 30 feet tall and lasted until 1920 when it was finally pulled down. It was re-erected in 1926, only to be blown up by nationalists in 1966, at the same time as the more famous Nelson pillar in Dublin (see Chapter Six).

Still the ripples went on spreading. Barbados learned the news on 20 December and held official celebrations three days later; but an eyewitness noted the 'gloomy effect which shaded their brightness'. In South Africa a British force had captured Capetown on 12 January 1806, and so when the unofficial news arrived in a ship from England it was published in a special edition of the *Cape Town Gazette and African Advertiser* on Sunday 26 January, followed by Collingwood's official dispatch on Tuesday 18 February when copies arrived. Among the last places of all, news reached the penal colony of New South Wales, Australia, in mid-April 1806. On 13 April the *Sydney Gazette* reported that the following Sunday, 20 April, had been appointed a Day of General Thanksgiving, adding peremptorily: 'All persons not prevented by sickness or the necessary care of their dwellings are expected to attend.'[5] The Bowman family, free emigrants who had arrived in 1798, made a special flag and flew it outside their house at Archerfield, near Richmond, NSW. Designed by Mary Bowman, a talented painter, the flag consisted of a shield bearing an entwined rose, shamrock and thistle with the motto, 'England Expects Every Man Will Do His Duty'. The shield was flanked by an emu and a kangaroo – the first known appearance in heraldry of those now familiar supporters of the Australian arms.

In England, the peculiar mixture of elation and sorrow which greeted the first news continued throughout November and December, culminating in the ceremonial expression of national sorrow in the State Funeral in early January 1806. And out of that intense period of corporate grief was born the Nelson Legend.

The word 'legend' has become debased of late, and so it is important to emphasize that it is used here in its older sense, meaning something larger than life which, at the same time, strikes deep and ancient chords in the human psyche. And that is what Nelson does: each generation has managed to find in him qualities that are both reassuringly familiar and yet also inspiring. This chapter will trace the extraordinary way in which he has ceased to be merely a creature of his own time and has become a hero for all ages.

To his contemporaries his heroism was unquestioned. Indeed, as the succeeding chapters show, he had become a hero in his own lifetime – especially after the resounding victory of the Nile. But his death, in the very moment of victory, transformed him from a hero among many, to *the* Hero. As soon as the news of Trafalgar began to spread, the London theatres vied with each other to mount increasingly spectacular tributes – and all of them concentrated on Nelson's death. On the evening of 6 November the Theatre Royal Drury Lane presented a brief interlude featuring 'Rule Britannia', led by the famous tenor John Braham (who, in happier times had sung duets with Emma Hamilton at Merton) and some hurriedly written verses lamenting Nelson: 'His dirge our groans – his monument our praise.' But at Covent Garden the management was even more enterprising. After the last play of the evening, the audience were treated to 'a view of the English fleet riding triumphantly' while a group of naval officers were discovered 'in attitudes of admiration'. As they gazed heavenwards, a medallion was lowered bearing a portrait of Nelson surrounded by rays of glory. The whole company then led the audience in singing 'Rule Britannia', including a new verse written specially for the occasion which ended:

> Rule, brave Britons, rule the main,
> Avenge the god-like hero slain!

Not to be outdone, Drury Lane responded the next night with a short sketch, mounted with still more impressive scenic effects. This time it was the figure of Fame who descended from the skies, carrying the first of many misquotations of 'England expects'. Such theatricality extended even to the Lord Mayor's Banquet on 9 November, when Prime Minister William Pitt made his ringing claim: 'England has saved herself by her exertions; and will, as I trust, save Europe by her example.' The mayor and his chief guest sat under an illuminated arch bearing the words 'Nelson and Victory', with behind them a portrait of Nelson. Also on display was a sword, beside which was the legend: 'The sword of the French

The Hero of the Nile: the designs for the elaborate stage effects of the special commemorative theatrical pieces have long vanished but this engraving of 1798 gives some idea of their style.

Admiral Blanquet, the gift of Lord Nelson to the City of London in the year 1798.'

A month later, on Tuesday 5 December, the whole nation observed a Day of Thanksgiving for the victory. The tone was set by a special collect written for the occasion: 'Let not Thy gracious goodness towards us, in the signal Victory which Thou hast given us over the common Enemy, be frustrated by a presumptuous confidence in our own might,' and throughout the land bishops, priests and ministers improved on this theme. At the Salter's Hall, the Revd Hugh Worthington unknowingly echoed Nelson's own pre-battle prayer, when he warned: 'let there be no malignity against the enemies with which we contend'. At the Cathedral of St Asaph, in North Wales, the congregation was treated by their Bishop to a learnèd – and extremely long – exposition on the 'watchers and holy ones' mentioned in his text, Daniel Chapter 4, verse 17. It was only in the last few minutes of the sermon that he finally arrived at Nelson and Trafalgar when, echoing the theme of the collect, he contented himself with a simple warning against 'another gross and dangerous perversion of Providence, when we impute any success, with which we may be blessed, to any merit of our own'. Elsewhere the services had a less ponderous touch. At Winchester Cathedral the choir sang a new anthem, 'To celebrate Thy praise O Lord,' composed for the occasion by their organist Dr G.W. Chard, the words of which were based on the metrical version of

Psalm 9. At Aylsham, in Norfolk, there was a procession to the church featuring over twenty banners, each bearing an appropriate legend, including: 'We rejoice for our Country, but mourn for our Friend' and 'Almighty God has blessed His Majesty's arms', the latter a quotation from Nelson's Nile dispatch.

At Portsmouth the Day of Thanksgiving was made particularly poignant by the presence of HMS *Victory*, which had finally arrived at Spithead on 4 December. Originally it had been expected that Nelson's body would be brought home in a fast frigate. His favourite sister, Kitty Matcham, wrote to her son George from Merton in early November: 'We are only anxious to wait here for the last sad scene, when that will happen God only knows, there is no intelligence when the frigate is likely to arrive.'[6] However, all the official plans were thrown out by the ship's company of HMS *Victory* who insisted on their right to bring home their beloved commander. Thus, after being hurriedly patched up at Gibraltar, the damaged flagship limped home, taking almost a month to complete the voyage.

In fact the delay was welcome, since it gave time for all the complicated preparations for the lavish State Funeral which had been decreed. The planning was largely in the hands of the College of Arms, under the control of the senior herald, Garter King of Arms, Sir Isaac Heard. It was to be a full heraldic funeral, one of the last to be mounted in this country. Once it was known that the body had arrived safely, a date was set, advertisements were placed in the newspapers inviting applications for tickets, and the heralds' clerks began to deal with a deluge of letters and personal enquiries. There was a tetchy letter from Lord Hood, Governor of Greenwich Hospital: 'I do not comprehend what you say, that you *apprehend* I shall be one of the Chief Mourners; why not say that I am to be one as the arrangements *solely* rest with you.'[7] On 6 January the new Earl Nelson wrote to deny a rumour that his brother had asked his chaplain, the Revd Alexander Scott, to perform the burial service, adding: 'I think it my duty to give [you] this information in order to satisfy yourself, as well as the Bishop of London, who I am told has not been quite pleased with the other report . . .'.[8] Clearly he had not yet adjusted to his change in status from humble clergyman to peer of the realm.

More practical preparations included the erection of stands for spectators in St Paul's Cathedral, and along the processional route. A prime site was the small churchyard of St Mary-le-Strand, which commanded a view of the Strand down which the cortège was to pass; the enterprising Vestry of the church decided to build a stand at their own expense, under the direction of their parish officers, including the sexton William Gummer.[9]

In the meantime the *Victory* had left Portsmouth on 23 December and made her way round to the Nore. The ship's company were delighted that their persistence had been rewarded and were now looking forward to taking part in the ceremonies. Able Seaman John Brown wrote home to his family in Liverpool on 20 December: 'There is three hundred of us Pickt out to go to Lord Nelson's

Funrall we are to wear blue Jackets white Trowsers and a black scarf round our arms and hats besides gold medal for the battle of trafalgar valued £7 1s round our necks. that I shall take care of until I take it home and Shew it you.' At the Nore the ship was met by the *Chatham*, the yacht of the Commissioner of Chatham Dockyard, which had come to receive the body. By now it had been removed from the leaguer of spirits in which it had been preserved and placed in a plain coffin, made from timbers from the French flagship at the Battle of the Nile, *L'Orient*, and presented to Nelson immediately after the action by Captain Ben Hallowell. This was enclosed in a leaden shell. The *Chatham* brought a magnificent outer casket, designed by the well-known print-makers, the Ackermann brothers, and encrusted with gilt heraldic devices, including Nelson's coat of arms, the stars of his various orders of chivalry, seahorses, and even a crocodile, to represent the Battle of the Nile. This undertaker's confection was placed on the *Chatham*'s deck under a white ensign, while the yacht sailed up the Thames, past the salutes of the great forts at Tilbury and Gravesend, to Greenwich, where the coffin was taken ashore and placed in a private room.

By the end of the year all was ready for one of the most magnificent ceremonies ever to be mounted in Britain. Of a splendour usually reserved for royal occasions, it was a striking demonstration of how completely Nelson had captured the imagination of his contemporaries. It also highlighted the way in which already, within a few weeks of his death, he had achieved significance as a symbol that far exceeded even his unique achievements as a man.

The story of the State Funeral has been retold many times in successive biographies and the full account can be found in a number of contemporary publications, most notably the *Naval Chronicle* which devoted some fifty pages to a precise description of the event. All these re-creations, including the *Chronicle*'s, give an impression of a spectacle that was both smooth-running and enormously impressive – an impression supported by the superb prints produced by Daniel Orme for his biography, published in 1806. But they are all based on the official orders and so describe what *ought* to have happened, rather than what actually occurred on the day; a fact spotted by one of the onlookers in the huge crowd, John Williams, who wrote to his father in Anglesey: 'How can you believe a word in the Papers as to our military operations at a distance when I tell you that they all differ in their accounts of the Regts which passed under their own windows – and all wrong.'[10] Moreover, there were technical hitches and a number of human touches which often went unnoticed in the official accounts but which remained in the memory of those who saw them and, often, seemed more typical of Nelson than all the pomp that surrounded them.

The first problem occurred during the first stage of the ceremonial, the Lying in State at Greenwich, when the authorities underestimated the number of people who would wish to pay their respects. On 4 January the gilded coffin was placed on a catafalque in the Painted Hall, which had been transformed into a mortuary

*Nelson's coffin: the elaborate outer coffin designed by the Ackermann brothers.
The many devices include Nelson's coat of arms, the stars of his orders of chivalry,
seahorses – and even a crocodile to represent the Battle of the Nile.*

chapel; black hangings covered the colourful wall-paintings, and gilded heraldic devices gleamed in the rich glow from hundreds of candles in new wall sconces. The first mourner admitted was the Princess of Wales, who paid a private visit in the afternoon. The following day, a Sunday, the doors were thrown open and a steady stream of people flowed through. But there were so many of them that a large proportion had to be turned away and Lord Hood, the Governor of the Hospital, became so anxious about the size of the crowd that he wrote to the Home Secretary asking for extra troops to help control them.

On Wednesday 8 January came the grand river procession from Greenwich to London, for which a large flotilla of state barges and other boats had been assembled. The weather was fine, but a strong wind was blowing from the south-west, setting up a heavy chop on the river surface and causing the oarsmen to struggle to keep the barges on station. In the prints it all looks splendidly impressive: the stately City barges with their ornate gilded cabins and liveried oarsmen, the black-draped funeral barge with its huge canopy surmounted by tossing plumes, and the minute guns firing from the escorting naval boats. Yet, from the riverbanks, in the dull light of a grey January day, it all looked rather distant and confused and the funeral barge was so small as to be indistinguishable from its escorts.

There was, however, one unscripted moment, so impressive that it remained etched in the memories of all who saw it. As the funeral barge was eased alongside Whitehall Stairs, at the end of its long journey, the sky suddenly darkened. The moment the coffin was landed, a sudden squall of rain and wind erupted, soaking and buffeting the bearers as they struggled to place the coffin on the hearse which was to take it on the short journey to the Admiralty where it was to lie overnight. One of the onlookers, a Miss Berry, then a small girl, recalled the scene for *The Times* in 1865 and commented: 'In ancient Rome . . . such a circumstance would have been recorded as . . . an omen of future bad luck from the instant his last remains quitted that element on which he had so often triumphed.'

The next stage of the ceremonial was, by general consent, the least successful. A vast procession had been assembled to escort the body from the Admiralty to St Paul's for the funeral service, but, in attempting to make the spectacle as impressive as possible, the organizers over-reached themselves. They so packed the procession with soldiers that the blue naval uniforms were almost overwhelmed. The spectators were largely unimpressed by the river of red and reserved their approval for the tiny contingent of Greenwich pensioners and the forty-eight seamen and Royal Marines from HMS *Victory*. They carried with them the battle ensigns of their ship and, as the procession stopped and started in its long progress through London, they opened out the huge flags and proudly displayed the shot-holes to the bystanders. Miss Berry remembered that 'they were repeatedly and almost continually cheered as they passed along'.

In fact the Royal Marines had almost been missed out altogether. Noticing that

Nelson's funeral car: a rough pen and ink sketch drawn from memory by John Williams, at the head of a letter to his father, in which he described the funeral procession. It is remarkably accurate.

there was no mention of them in the first set of official orders, the Adjutant General, Lieutenant-General John Campbell, wrote to William Marsden on 31 December: 'I beg leave to suggest to their Lordships that the Chatham Division from the Artillery Companies and a selection of the Victory's detachment, can furnish a Guard not exceeding 100 men which for discipline and appearance will not discredit any procession.'[11] He got his way.

None the less, there were memories to treasure, especially the moment when the huge, plumed, funeral car went by bearing the gilded coffin high above the heads of the crowd. One eyewitness remembered that there was a noise like the sound of waves on the seashore as the onlookers removed their hats; young Frederick Marryatt, who was in the crowd with his father, remembered later in life: 'As the triumphal car disappeared from my aching eye, I felt that death could have no terrors if followed by such a funeral.'[12]

The cortège had taken so long to pass that it was two o'clock by the time the funeral car eventually arrived at St Paul's. But now, at last, the hitches were over and all accounts agree that the service which followed was both impressive and moving.

Appropriately for a clergyman's son, it had been decided that the burial service would be performed after the Office of Evensong, said or sung daily, then as now, in cathedrals and churches throughout the land. As the familiar Prayer Book words and glorious music flowed over them, the congregation found the sense of solemnity and loss mounting to an almost unbearable pitch. Young George Matcham, who walked with the other male Nelson relatives behind the coffin as it made its slow way up the long aisle, the stark, haunting opening music of William Croft's *Burial Sentences* – 'I am the resurrection and the life saith the Lord' – swirling around him, recalled in his diary: 'It was the most aweful sight I ever saw.'

The choir of some hundred boys and men, drawn from St Paul's, Westminster Abbey and the Chapels Royal, sang music specially assembled and arranged by one of the Minor Canons of St Paul's, the Revd John Pridden. As well as Croft's *Sentences*, it included a setting of 'Thou knowest Lord the secrets of our hearts' composed by Henry Purcell for the funeral of Queen Mary in 1695; the sombre anthem 'Lord let me know mine end' by Maurice Green; and a Grand Dirge which had been composed specially for the occasion by the cathedral organist Thomas Attwood (who had studied under Mozart). But the piece most witnesses remembered, and commented on, came right at the end of the service, just before the coffin was gradually lowered from sight to its final resting place in the crypt. It was Pridden's own adaptation of part of an anthem, 'The ways of Zion do mourn', composed by Handel for the funeral in 1737 of Queen Caroline, wife of George II. 'His body is buried in peace,' sang the assembled choirs in hushed tones, before bursting forth with the splendid, ringing assertion, embroidered with characteristic Handelian flourishes and repetitions, 'But his name liveth evermore!'

The Interment of Lord Nelson, *by W. Bromley: the Bishop of Lincoln (centre)*
reads the final prayers watched by the Prince of Wales (with the light coat,
foreground) and Nelson's friend, the Duke of Clarence (centre foreground).

These last moments were the most personal of all. Among the official dignitaries grouped round the coffin as it lay beneath the dome, brilliantly lit by a huge lantern suspended there specially for the occasion, were people who had known Nelson intimately. There were the male members of the Nelson family: the new earl, the Matchams and the Boltons. There were friends, such as Alexander Davison who was present as the Treasurer of the Household of the Deceased, and who later, with Nelson's solicitor William Hazlewood (Comptroller) and William Marsh (Steward), would break his white staff of office and hand it to Garter to be placed on the coffin. There were professional colleagues, such as Captain Thomas Hardy, carrying the splendid 'Banner of Emblems', and one of Nelson's earliest patrons, Sir Peter Parker, who as the Admiral of the Fleet (there was only one in those days) was acting as Chief Mourner. At eighty-four, he was rather frail and the previous Tuesday Lady Nelson (always seen at her best when thinking of the needs of others) had written to Sir Isaac Heard to ask if Sir Peter's servant, George Roger, could be allowed to stand close to his master, 'near enough to assist him, if he should be overcome or seized with a little giddiness which does happen now and then'.[13] Then, of course, there were the *Victory*'s sailors, still holding the shot-torn flags which they were supposed to fold up reverently and place upon the coffin as Garter read out the titles of the deceased. But, as Sir Isaac reached his ringing peroration, the onlookers noticed that the sailors were tearing off a large portion of flag, which was then subdivided into smaller portions which they kept as mementoes. Mrs Codrington, wife of the captain of HMS *Orion* at Trafalgar, commented: 'That was *Nelson*: the rest was so much the Herald's Office.'

Throughout all the descriptions of these events, from the first moments of dazed reflection as the gunfire slackened off Cape Trafalgar, to the moment when the coffin finally disappeared from sight in St Paul's Cathedral, 'precisely at thirty-three minutes and a half past five o'clock', as *The Naval Chronicle* minutely recorded, one word rings clear like a bass note in a peal of bells – *immortal*. Collingwood used it in his first dispatch, referring to Nelson as 'a hero whose name will be immortal'. It sounds repeatedly in the special verses written for stage and newspaper after the arrival of the news in England and in the sermons preached on the Day of Thanksgiving. And it echoed around the dome of St Paul's at the culmination of the elaborate ceremonial, when Sir Isaac Heard ended the traditional proclamation of the titles of the deceased with the words: 'the hero who, in the moment of victory, fell covered with immortal glory! Let us humbly trust that he is now raised to bliss ineffable and to a glorious immortality!'

The Later Georgians were rather fond of the word 'immortal' and applied it to their great men and women almost as indiscriminately as we use 'star' today. But it is clear that in Nelson's case the word was applied with more precision than usual.

First, it was used in a recognized classical sense: Nelson's shade is frequently pictured, in art as well as in literature, returning to watch over the fate of his country and to inspire his comrades to yet more splendid acts of heroism. Many of the poems of the time, often written by men with a classical education, take up this theme. Possibly the best, and certainly the most moving, was 'Ulm and Trafalgar' by George Canning who, although not one of Nelson's close friends, was Treasurer of the Navy and had accompanied him on his last walk through Portsmouth and dined with him in the *Victory* before she sailed for Cadiz. After highlighting the effect of Nelson's example which, he believes, will 'With living lustre this proud land adorn/And shine and save through ages yet unborn!', Canning goes on to paint a picture of future wars when

> Thou, sacred Shade, in battle hovering near
> Shall win bright Victory from her golden sphere
> To float aloft where England's ensign lies
> With angel wings and palms from paradise!

Seven years later Robert Southey ended his great *Life of Nelson* with two lines of Greek from *Works and Days* by Hesiod, which translate (loosely) as, 'Almighty Zeus in his great wisdom has appointed them deities; and, living still on earth, they guard and inspire poor mortal men.'

Second, amid all the tributes there is a recognizable Christian strand. Nelson is portrayed as the Saviour of his country; a man who had laid down his life for his friends. This is most vividly seen in some of the paintings of his death. On 22 November *The Times* carried an advertisement placed by the print-sellers Boydell and Co., inviting artists to take part in a competition to paint a picture of 'The Death of Nelson'; 'in the manner of the Death of General Wolfe [by Benjamin West]', and offering a very handsome prize of 500 guineas.[14] Among the contestants was Samuel Drummond, who produced a vivid picture which showed Nelson being carried from the quarter-deck in the arms of Sergeant Secker and two sailors. One of his original sketches, now in the Royal Naval Museum, shows only the central group, without the surrounding battle-scenes of the finished versions. Isolated like this, the figures closely resemble a common religious subject: 'The Deposition from the Cross', in which the body of the dead Christ is lowered from the cross into the waiting arms of his mother and the beloved disciple. The similarity is even more striking in *The Immortality of Nelson*, an elaborate allegorical painting produced by the famous historical painter Benjamin West for the frontispiece to volume one of the biography published by Clarke and M'Arthur in 1809 (colour plate 1). Here, the central figure of Nelson, naked and wrapped in a white shroud, is even more Christ-like; while the figures of Neptune and Victory on the left, and of Britannia above, mirror the traditional figures around the cross.

The Death of Nelson *by Samuel Drummond: this preliminary sketch for Drummond's remarkable series of paintings of Nelson's death, shows how closely the central group of figures corresponds to comparable religious subjects, such as* The Deposition from the Cross.

Most poignant of all the death-tributes was Dr William Beatty's book, *A Narrative of the Death of Lord Nelson*, published in 1807. It is so familiar, having been used as the basis of the death scene in almost every biography since, that it is easy to forget just how remarkable it really is: an almost blow-by-blow account of the scene, with every broken phrase and sentence recorded, and pervaded throughout by a mood of sombre reflection, so that it reads almost like a Passion narrative in one of the Gospels. It is sobering to reflect that, were it not for Beatty's precise account – and the lesser-known shorter versions by Burke and Scott – we would be left with only third-hand accounts, most of which were melodramatic and very inaccurate. *The Times* reported that Nelson's last words were, ' I know I am dying. I could have wished to have survived to breathe my last upon British ground, but the will of God be done!' The *Gibraltar Chronicle* was even more imaginative:

during the heat of the action, His Lordship was severely wounded with a grape shot, in the side, and was obliged to be carried below. Immediately on his wound being dressed, he insisted upon being brought upon deck, when, shortly afterwards, he received a shot through his body; he survived, however, until Evening; long enough to be informed of the capture of the French Admiral, and of the extent of the Glorious Victory he had gained – His last words were, 'Thank God! I have outlived this day, and now I die content!'

Perhaps the most striking evidence of the quasi-idolatrous mood of 1805/6 is the extraordinary number of personal relics of Nelson which have survived and which are examined in more detail by John Munday in Chapter Three. Nelson's friends, relatives and professional colleagues were besieged with requests for mementoes. Midshipman Richard Bulkeley, who had carried Hardy's message to the dying Nelson, received a letter from Captain Thomas Bertie asking for some hair and wrote from the *Victory* on 12 December: 'I regret extremely not to be able to send as much hair as I could wish, owing to my having sent away a greater part of it; but I trust you will find sufficient for a ring.'[15] Alexander Davison sent an autograph collector, Thomas Davidson, two letter covers, 'bearing the writing of my ever to be lamented Bosom friend – the Immortal Nelson!'[16]

The association of the word 'immortal' with Nelson is enshrined in the famous toast which is still drunk, immediately after the Loyal Toast, at Trafalgar Night dinners the world over. As with all such customs, its exact origins are hard to trace and it may well have evolved gradually, rather than starting at a precise place and time. According to the *Naval Chronicle*, 'The Memory of Nelson' was drunk at a dinner at the Green Man, Blackheath, on 21 October 1811, but the first recorded use of the correct wording of the toast is in a letter from Emma Hamilton (dated 31 July 1813) to an old friend Thomas Lewis, inviting him to join her on the anniversary of the Battle of the Nile at 12 Temple Place, where she was living 'within the rules' of the King's Bench (in other words, in debtors' prison): 'If you come,' she promises, 'we will drink to his Immortal Memory.' Certainly it was in general use by Trafalgar Day 1846, when Captain Pasco (who had supervised the hoisting of 'England Expects' in 1805 and was now in command of his old ship) presided at a dinner on board the *Victory* at her moorings in Portsmouth Harbour. According to the report in *The Times*, 'The immortal memory of Nelson and those who fell with him' was drunk after the toast to 'Prince Albert and the rest of the Royal Family'.

It is the second phrase of the Nelson toast that is most striking, especially since it no longer forms part of the traditional Trafalgar Night ritual. Yet it is clear that it was common practice. In 1867 John Yule, the son of one of the *Victory*'s lieutenants at Trafalgar, recalled affectionately his father's own private commemoration:

it was observed in the family as an official holiday. I have yet a pleasing &
lively recollection of my Father wearing his Trafalgar shirt, & surrounded by
his seven Sons and four Daughters, proposing after dinner 'The Immortal
Memory of Lord Nelson', and then of those whom 'England expected' (not in
vain) 'that they would do their duty'.[17]

Whoever drank it first, the toast is not unique: Shakespeareans drink to 'The
Immortal Memory' of their hero on 23 April and Burnsians on 25 January.

As the following chapters will show, Pasco's Trafalgar Dinner came at the end of a
rather lean period in the development of the Nelson Legend. Partly, no doubt, this
was due to the publication of Nelson's letters to Emma and the scandal that began
to attach to his name, but it was also a reflection of the mood of the 1830s and
'40s, when political and social reform at home were of more moment than past
glories. This decline in interest was most notably seen in the delay in the
completion of Trafalgar Square, highlighted by Flora Fraser in Chapter Six. It did
not go unnoticed at the time. In the late 1830s a pantomime, *Jack the Giant Killer*,
featured a scene in front of the hoarding surrounding the unfinished monument
with posters heralding 'The Arrival of the Statue'.

However, the 1850s brought a new mood to Britain: a war with Russia,
followed by a series of smaller-scale colonial wars and a long period of rivalry
with France, led to renewed interest in the armed forces and especially in the
Navy. As imperial affairs began increasingly to dominate politics at home, so
Nelson became more and more of a patriotic symbol. For example, when it was
decided that the new Houses of Parliament should be adorned with frescoes
depicting historical and allegorical scenes, the most prestigious sites (two vast
murals covering the walls of the Royal Gallery) were allocated to 'Waterloo: The
Meeting of Wellington and Blucher' and 'Trafalgar: The Death of Nelson'. Rather
than depicting the scene in the cockpit, the artist Daniel Maclise decided to show
Nelson dying on the quarter-deck, surrounded by the debris of battle, all of which
is portrayed exactly, even to words of 'England Expects' chalked on the
signalman's slate beside the dying Admiral. But, for all its meticulous realism, the
over-riding impression of the painting – especially the full-size original – is of
heroism and grandeur. With his eyes raised to heaven, and his face set in a mask of
stern, stiff upper-lipped resignation, Nelson has ceased to be an ordinary human
being. He has become an icon; a symbol of Britain's glorious past and of her hopes
for an equally glorious future.

Other artists painted in the same heroic vein and their works were enormously
popular with all ranks of society. In 1853 T.J. Barker produced his famous picture
of the Battle of St Vincent, *Nelson receiving the swords of the Vanquished Spanish
Officers on the Quarter-deck of the San Josef*, and the *Court Circular* records that

The Death of Nelson *by Daniel Maclise: an engraving of the central panel of Maclise's massive mural in the Royal Gallery of the Palace of Westminster. Note the meticulous detail – even down to the words of 'England Expects' on the signal slate in the foreground.*

he was commanded to take it to Windsor where he 'had the honour to submit it to the inspection of the Queen and His Royal Highness Prince Albert who were graciously pleased to express their approval of both the design and the execution'. Other now-familiar images of Nelson date from this revival period, such as Davidson's splendid recreation of the scene on the *Victory*'s poop as Nelson watches the hoisting of 'England Expects'. The genre continued until the turn of the century when Albert Holden painted a series of reflections on the power of the Nelson Legend, such as *Saluting the Admiral* (colour plate 13), featuring a jovial

Greenwich pensioner saluting a garlanded bust of Nelson; or the moving *Hundred Years Ago* which shows a young sailor gazing raptly at one of the Abbott portraits of Nelson displayed in the Painted Hall.

Nelson's value as a patriotic symbol was enshrined in the creation of the Navy League in 1895 – a pressure group formed explicitly to campaign for a stronger Navy. With branches all over the world (there was even one in Japan, then emerging as a naval power) the League began a custom of celebrating Trafalgar Day with a special service in Trafalgar Square, for which the column and lions were festooned with laurel and flags. This event was in conscious imitation of a longer-established ceremony that had been held on board the *Victory* since early in the century. On one occasion, in 1844, Queen Victoria happened to be in Portsmouth Harbour, *en route* from a stay at Osborne, and she noticed that the old ship was decked with laurel wreaths and flags. On asking the reason, she was reminded that it was Trafalgar Day, and at once went on board. She was conducted over the ship and shown all the important sights, including the plaque

HMS Victory *decorated for Trafalgar Day, c. 1890. Nelson's flagship, moored in Portsmouth Harbour, flies his famous signal on the anniversary of the battle. In fact, the flags were taken from the wrong signal book – a mistake only spotted in 1908!*

on the quarter-deck decorated with a simple wreath. After standing for a moment in silent homage, she plucked a leaf as a memento. The Navy League's more public ceremony has long since ceased, but the older, and more private, commemoration in the *Victory* continues to this day.

Perhaps the most striking surviving evidence of this imperial phase of the Nelson Legend is geographical. There are towns named after him in the Colne Valley, Lancashire, in the Welsh valleys not far from Aberfan, on the South Island of New Zealand, and deep in the Selkirk Mountains of British Columbia, Canada. A Nelson River drains into Hudson Bay and a Cape Nelson overlooks Portland Bay on the south coast of Victoria, Australia. Nelson Roads and Trafalgar Squares crop up in the streetplans of mid-Victorian suburbs all over the old Empire (including some fifty in the Greater London area alone); while his face appears on the signboards of countless pubs – especially in Norfolk, where the name of the pub is often, quite simply, The Hero.

As might be expected, his name has also been given to a number of ships: a 120-gun ship of the line of 1814, a Victorian sail and steam frigate of 1876, and an Edwardian battleship, HMS *Lord Nelson* of 1907. There was also a sailing frigate christened HMS *Horatio* in 1807. Most famous of all was the battleship of 1925, with her odd slipper-like profile, which saw such distinguished service in the Second World War. In peacetime she carried a number of Nelson relics, including one of his uniform coats. When these were sent ashore for safe keeping in September 1939, a lock of his hair was retained and displayed prominently in a small picture frame. Interestingly, at least four figureheads of Nelson have survived, including two in Portsmouth from HMS *Nile* (1839, later the famous training ship *Conway*) and HMS *Trafalgar* (1841). The one from HMS *Horatio* is displayed at Greenwich (with a very obviously blinded eye that makes him look as if he has recently emerged from a boxing match) and the figurehead of the 1814 *Nelson* found its way to Australia, when the ship was handed over to the New South Wales Government. It now occupies pride of place in the Navy section of the splendid new Australian National Maritime Museum in Sydney.

A detrimental effect of this role as a national symbol was that the Hero became even further distanced from the Man. Anything that threatened his heroic role was suppressed or explained away. Most striking was the myth that he said, 'Kismet' (Turkish for 'fate') to Hardy as he lay dying, rather than 'Kiss me'. The suggestion was made that, in all the noise and confusion of the cockpit, Beatty misheard the famous words. Those who invented this ludicrous fiction, and those who perpetuate it today, are presumably unaware that Beatty goes on to record that Hardy in fact kissed Nelson *twice* – once on the cheek and once on the forehead – and that, moreover, Beatty's recollection of the famous request is corroborated by the independent accounts of Chaplain Scott and Purser Burke, both of whom were helping to support Nelson and so were only inches away from him as he spoke. The request for the kiss, and the fact that the normally unemotional and undemonstrative Hardy complied with it, are both key pieces in the complex jigsaw of Nelson's personality and they should be accepted as such and not explained away, or viewed with inappropriate embarrassment.

So, too, with poor Emma Hamilton, another casualty of the Victorians' obsessive desire for pure and blameless heroes. As the damning evidence of the Nelson/Emma letters was gradually revealed in successive publications, the press reacted first with horrified denial of their authenticity and then – when that could no longer be doubted – with condemnation of the unprincipled, scheming woman who had led the innocent, over-trusting, hero astray. Even A.T. Mahan, whose *Life of Nelson* is generally agreed to be one of the great biographies, was unable to avoid an unattractive display of Victorian values: 'it is in entire keeping with the career and self-revelations of the woman that she should instinctively, if not with deliberation, have resolved to parade herself in the glare of his renown. . . . That she ever loved him is doubtful.'[18] Emma, like Nelson, was far from blameless, but to cast doubt so cavalierly on the sincerity of her love was unwarranted and cruel.

The official exaltation of Nelson was reflected in the popular art of the time. He even found his way into those quintessentially Victorian entertainments: the Melodrama and the Music Hall. The most often performed of all the Victorian nautical melodramas was *Black Ey'd Susan*, which concerned the fortunes of an ordinary seaman called William and his beloved Susan and the original play contained no reference to Nelson. However, in a poster advertising one of the many revivals, *Too Lovely Black Eyed Susan* at the Avenue Theatre, Sunderland, in August 1892, William and Susan have been displaced by an extraordinary picture of the dying Nelson surrounded by pantomime chorus girls in short skirts and tights. As for the Music Hall, the song of the two pigeons who live in Trafalgar Square 'with four lions to guard us' and who declare, 'If it's good enough for Nelson/It's quite good enough for us!' is still well known, but it was only one of many featuring the Admiral. The most famous, and the most often sung in the nineteenth century, was 'The Death of Nelson' by John Braham, whom we have already encountered assisting the Theatre Royal Drury Lane in its attempts to outshine the commemorative efforts of Covent Garden in November 1805. The song's first recorded appearance was in Braham and Arnold's comic opera *The Americans*, performed in 1811. Neither the poetry, nor the music, is particularly remarkable and the song has not enjoyed the same popularity in the twentieth century. But it has had one indelible effect upon the Nelson Legend. In order to make 'England Expects' fit the metre, Arnold added the words 'this day' before 'will do his duty', thus creating the most persistent of all misquotations of the famous signal.

The Music Hall tradition continued well into the twentieth century and Nelson songs continued to be popular. Some, like Braham's, were patriotic and stirring, most were comic and irreverent. In 1907 George Arthur Wimperis collaborated

A poster for the play Too Lovely Black Eyed Susan, *1892. As an extra 'draw' for this famous Victorian melodrama, Nelson is shown dying centre-stage surrounded by chorus girls!*

with the composer Harry Ferguson to produce 'Statues on a Spree' in which Nelson gets bored and comes down from his column one night for a 'razzle-dazzle'. Picking up the statues of Charles I, Boadicea, Wellington and Shakespeare, he goes off with them to notorious drinking holes and dance halls. Eventually, rather the worse for wear after a heavy drinking bout and a fight in Covent Garden, the statues stagger home. But, in their inebriated state they get muddled up and so Nelson ends up on Charles' horse and Charles tries to climb the column but falls off and lands in the fountain.

This irreverent song provides an interesting contrast to the more pompous events of 21 October 1905, when the nation and empire celebrated the centenary of Trafalgar. In London there was a service in Trafalgar Square, decorated even more elaborately than usual with garlands and bunting and with a huge pile of wreaths at its base. Among them was one inscribed, 'A tribute to the memory of Nelson from Robert Sayers, Broken Hill, Australia, a British man-of-warsman who cleaned the brass plaque of the flagship HMS *Victory*.'[19] After the ceremony a carriage was seen to pull up bearing the children of the Prince of Wales. Urged by his nanny, the young Prince Edward (later King Edward VIII) stood up and solemnly saluted the column. There followed a Patriotic Music Celebration at the

Royal Horticultural Hall, organized by the women's branch of the Navy League, and the festivities concluded with the Nelson Centenary Banquet at the Criterion Restaurant, Piccadilly Circus. The climax was the drinking of 'The Immortal Memory' followed (as was common at that time) by the singing of Braham's 'Death of Nelson'. In faraway Sydney the mood was the same; the Nelson's figurehead was placed in the entrance of the Royal Exchange in Bridge Street and garlanded with flowers and flags. By evening the city was filled with crowds, and the bands of the New South Wales Naval Brigade and the British cruiser HMS Powerful, played patriotic tunes. It comes as no surprise to learn that the celebrations were organized by the British Empire League.

The message was clear. Nelson had become a political symbol to be exploited to glorify the greatness of Britain and her Empire and to ensure that her armed forces – and especially the Navy – were kept as powerful as possible. His name was regarded almost as a talisman and people simple-mindedly believed that all they had to do in any future war was to find another Nelson and all would be well. The dangers of this simplistic approach were noted by the journalist Fred Jane who, almost alone in this welter of sentimental and patriotic devotion, sounded a note of warning. Claiming that there was 'Too much Nelson', he pointed out that Nelson 'cannot aid us against our future enemies; our own arms alone can do that. Therefore to that future we should give our thoughts, not to hysterical sentiment over the past – ever the hallmark of a declining race.'[20]

Unsurprisingly, Jane's warning went unheeded in the tidal wave of nostalgia. But his words were prophetic; for thanks, at least in part, to 'Too much Nelson', the Royal Navy entered the First World War with a backward glance that almost proved fatal. Sir David Beatty's flag captain remembered how his chief 'longed' for war: 'We had not fought for a century: it was time we repeated the deeds of our forefathers.'[21] This mood was reflected in the popular art of the time: prints, ceramics, paper and silk handkerchiefs and numerous other souvenirs were produced with the head of the British Commander-in-Chief, Sir John Jellicoe, alongside that of Nelson, and with 'England Expects' emblazoned on them. Patriotic cartoons and newspaper articles all invoked the spirit of Nelson. But that 'spirit' was completely misunderstood. The Grand Fleet may have appeared magnificent and powerful, but it was not a band of brothers. Rigidly controlled from the centre, little or no initiative was allowed to the individual captains, and caution, not Nelsonian dash and inventiveness, was the pervading culture. With the benefit of hindsight, it is clear that, because it had become ossified and completely out of touch with the original man, the Nelson Legend was working against Britain: producing, on the one hand, unrealistically high expectations of what the Royal Navy might achieve and, on the other, a fleet that was ill-equipped to meet such expectations. The result, when the long-expected Trafalgar of the North Sea never materialized, was a mood of deep disappointment both within the Service and in the country – a disappointment

A First World War souvenir handkerchief: the Admiral, the Victory *and 'England Expects' adorn a picture of the latest 'super-dreadnought' HMS* Queen Elizabeth, *in an attempt to invoke the spirit of Nelson.*

that even soured the final triumph when the German High Seas Fleet steamed into the Firth of Forth to surrender in November 1918. One eye-witness, Commander Ian Sanderson wrote, 'all of us resented it that Waterloo should precede Trafalgar and that Trafalgar should never happen at all'.[22] In the dazed exhaustion of that unhappy peace, it must have seemed that the Nelson Legend, like so many other dreams, had been shattered in the squalor and bloodshed of the war.

In fact, post-war disillusion strengthened the Legend, rather than finishing it off. For it led, inevitably, to a questioning of the Victorian view of Nelson and this, in turn, led to a rediscovery of the man behind the myth; not just the flawed, irritable adulterer, but the warm-hearted, liberal-minded friend and beloved leader of men. The result was a series of biographies that, for really the first time, began to place the private man alongside the fighting Admiral and to show how each interrelated with the other. And the fascinating tension this dual personality embodied led to another interesting development in the Legend. For the first time, Nelson began to be studied seriously by dramatists.

Nelson had already appeared on stage in various theatrical pieces, but these had been mostly lightweight and ephemeral. Now he became the subject of full-length plays – all of which dealt with the contrast between the lover of Emma Hamilton and the public hero. Most of these plays are very much of their period, with the detailed descriptions of settings and page-long expositions of character made familiar to us by Shaw's works. They have therefore not survived as performing pieces, but they can still be read in handsome hardback editions that crop up occasionally in second-hand bookshops. A good example is *Nelson and the Hamiltons* by Douglas Mann (published in 1934), which, as its title suggests, concentrates on the famous love affair. In the epilogue, set in Calais in 1814, Emma reflects on the way in which England has ignored Nelson's last wishes: 'They gave him a great funeral which, God knows, he richly deserved; but the greatest wish of his heart, and his last wish, they forgot . . . He would have made me his wife – England made me only his mistress.'

In 1969 this aspect of Nelson's life was still more powerfully examined by Terence Rattigan in his very successful play, *Bequest to the Nation*. Beginning life

Happy Days at Merton *by Frank Dadd: in this very romanticized view of the famous relationship, Nelson and a remarkably slim Emma enjoy the company of their daughter Horatia.*

as a television script entitled *Nelson: A Study in Miniature*, screened in 1966, and then expanded into a full-length piece for the West End, this play concentrates almost entirely on the four weeks that Nelson spent in England during August and September 1805. It examines the Nelson/Emma relationship through the eyes of his hero-worshipping nephew George Matcham, and tries to explain the bond that held the extraordinary couple together. The play ends with a scene at Merton, after the arrival of the news of Trafalgar, where Emma, alone, distracted and drunk, is visited by a dignified and tender Lady Nelson. Although apocryphal, the scene is beautifully written, with a genuine understanding of the two women and their widely differing loves for the same man. Indeed, the whole play offers some valuable insights that have eluded more conventional biographers. From his own standpoint as a gay man, Rattigan was always at his best and most sympathetic when exploring unconventional love.

Bequest to the Nation was also made into a film; the latest in a succession of films about Nelson, stretching back to the earliest days of moving pictures. The first on record is *The Death of Nelson*, a re-enactment of the scene in the cockpit dating from 1897 and said to have been produced by the early director Philip Wolff, although this attribution has been questioned. There are also a number of 'actuality' films from the same period, showing Trafalgar Square garlanded for Trafalgar Day, with traffic moving past. There is even one of an old sailor laying a wreath on the plaque on the *Victory*'s quarter-deck, accompanied by two stiff-backed, sailor-suited boys. The first full-length film – a silent one of course – was *Nelson* directed by Maurice Elvey in 1918 and featuring Donald Calthorp as Nelson and an early film star, Malvina Longfellow as Emma. It was so successful that there was a sequel, just a year later, called *The Romance of Lady Hamilton* and once again starring Malvina Longfellow, who is reported to have said that she regarded Emma as her greatest screen achievement. More films followed in the 1920s, all of them concentrating on the Nelson/ Emma relationship: for example, *The Affairs of Lady Hamilton* (1921), a German film, with Conrad Veidt as Nelson looking like 'Nosferatu' in naval uniform; or the British *Nelson* (1920) with Cedric Hardwicke as Nelson, which included an early attempt to film a naval battle using models in a tank.

By far the most popular, and the most influential, Nelson film was *Lady Hamilton* (known in America as *That Hamilton Woman*), released in 1942. Directed by Alexander Korda, it starred Laurence Olivier as Nelson and Vivien Leigh as Emma. Like its predecessors the film highlights their relationship, and the story is told in flashback by a dying Emma, languishing in poverty in Calais. But, as befits a wartime film, it also concentrates on the great battles and on the figure of Nelson himself, and tries to capture something of his spirit. Olivier suffered at the hands of contemporary critics, most of whom preferred Leigh's kittenish, vivacious, and completely unauthentic, Emma. But his performance has stood the test of time rather better and it remains by far the best portrayal of Nelson on celluloid.

Lady Hamilton: one of history's most famous love affairs portrayed by one of the cinema's most famous husband and wife teams. Laurence Olivier and Vivien Leigh pose for a special publicity shot for Alexander Korda's famous wartime film.

Winston Churchill loved the film and once said its effect on morale was equivalent to four army divisions. He kept his own copy which he showed repeatedly, and cried every time. We now know that he was involved in the actual making of the film; Korda's son, in his recent biography of his father, has revealed that Churchill helped in the writing of some of the set-piece speeches, including a climactic passage ending, 'You can't make peace with dictators!', with which Nelson harangues the Board of Admiralty after the signing of the Treaty of Amiens in 1802. With the combination of inspired writing and great acting, Nelson's aggressive spirit is admirably evoked.

In fact, the spirit of the 'real' Nelson – as opposed to the Victorians' wooden superhero – was much more in evidence during the Second World War. It was seen in the remarkable dash and courage in the face of impossible odds, in battles such as the armed merchantman *Jervis Bay*'s lonely and gallant fight with the German heavy cruiser *Hipper*. It shone through in the aggressive spirit of admirals like Andrew Cunningham, confidently leading his fleet into night action at Matapan against the advice of his more cautious staff. It was present in the love which officers and men alike felt for Bruce Fraser. Perhaps most tellingly, it was captured in the extraordinary flow of lighthearted and inspirational signals with which various admirals kept themselves and their subordinates amused. It was almost as if the spirit of Nelson had been unleashed from the shackles of heroism and allowed to wander freely again; an image powerfully evoked in a poem called 'Trafalgar Day 1940' by Clemence Dane. St Paul's is bombed and the blast wakes Nelson's spirit, which slips out of its shroud and wanders through the shattered streets of London, bringing comfort and hope:

> He stands in the wreck of the road
> he sweeps up the broken glass
> he fights with fire and despair.
> He feels for, he fingers your heart
> till it beats in your breast like a drum.
> This is the Nelson touch
> Pass on the news – he's awake!

Since the war the Nelson Legend has continued to grow in strength. Biographies still continue to appear almost every other year; visitors flow in their hundreds of thousands through the two great Nelson centres at Portsmouth and Greenwich. Nelsonia is still produced in enormous quantities – and still sells easily. There are now two societies devoted to his memory, The Nelson Society (founded 1981) and The 1805 Club (founded 1990), both of which regularly publish journals packed with interesting Nelsonian anecdotes. He has appeared in London underground trains advertising a well-known brand of port; in romantic novels (for example, *The Magnificent Courtesan* by Ursula Bloom where, in one particularly torrid love scene – set in the *Victory* of course – he appears, miraculously, to acquire two arms!); in an 'oratorio' (*Hip Hip Horatio*, by Michael Blom and Michael Hurd, in 1975) and in a television mini-series (*I Remember Nelson*, ATV 1982). He has even given his name to a beer (a Norfolk brew, known as 'Nelson's Revenge', with the kick of a double-shotted 32-pounder).

As is only to be expected in this iconoclastic age, there have also been attempts to knock him off his pedestal – sometimes literally, as when the IRA blew up his statue in the centre of Dublin in 1966; sometimes symbolically, as in *The Hero Rises Up*, a play by John Arden and Margaretta D'Arcy. First performed in 1968 (and rarely revived since) it deals, as the punning title suggests, with Nelson's sex life in some detail and includes a song for his servant Tom Allen that echoes Leporello's more famous list of conquests in *Don Giovanni*. In June 1992 he was featured (in his Abbott manifestation) on the front page of the *Sun*, at the height of one of Britain's regular fishing disputes with France, and readers were invited to ring a telephone number to hear how Nelson would 'rout the French pirates'. And, in 1993, he appeared as a toby jug – complete with eyepatch. When it was pointed out at the design stage to the well-known company responsible that Nelson never wore a patch, a representative replied that, as their research suggested that people have a mental image of Nelson with a patch, it had been decided to include one – a notable triumph of market research over historical accuracy!

However, he has survived all these indignities and still manages to inspire his compatriots. So much so, that the years 1995 to 2005 have already been declared the 'Nelson Decade' and, at the time of writing, public opinion appears to be swinging behind a proposal to make Trafalgar Day a national holiday, despite official fears that the French might be offended.

On the starkly beautiful north Norfolk coast the village of his birth, Burnham Thorpe, lies off the main tourist routes. No brown 'Heritage' signs point the visitor in the right direction; there is (thankfully) no 'Nelson Experience' to draw the crowds. And yet, as the well-used visitors' book in the parish church attests, each year pilgrims in their hundreds make their way through winding country lanes to stand where Nelson once stood and see, almost unchanged, the scenery he knew so well. In the 'comments' section of the current book, among the surprised remarks from foreign visitors that so great a hero should be so simply remembered and (a sad sign of the times) the delight of English visitors at finding the church open at all, two brief phrases stand out: a young sailor, on leave from HMS *Fearless* has written, 'Nelson's spirit lives on' and, a few pages later, in a large round schoolboy's hand is the message, 'Thank you Nelson'.

That, in the end, after all analysis is exhausted, is the simple key to the Nelson Legend. In a remarkable way his spirit does indeed live on and people remain thankful for the inspiration that it brings. Nelson still reaches out across two centuries and, in the vivid image of Clemence Dane, 'He feels for, he fingers your heart'.

References

1. Log of Captain Joseph Woollnough, RN, KT, KSW (unpublished, private collection).
2. Sir Nicholas Harris Nicolas, *Dispatches and Letters of Lord Nelson*, Vol. VII, p. 238.
3. Flora Fraser, *Beloved Emma* (1986), p. 326.
4. George Norton to Lord Malmesbury, Malmesbury Papers, Hampshire Records Office, 9n73/190/227.
5. *Sydney Gazette and New South Wales Advertiser*, 13 April 1806.
6. E. Eyre Matcham, *The Nelsons of Burnham Thorpe*, pp. 241–2.
7. Lord Hood to Sir Isaac Heard, undated, RNM240/92 (2).
8. Earl Nelson to Sir Isaac Heard, 6 January 1806, RNM240/92 (1).
9. Ellis Gummer, *Notes on a Branch of the Gummer Family* (privately circulated).
10. John Williams to his father, 11 January 1806, RNM9/56.
11. John Campbell to William Marsden, 31 December 1805, PRO ADM1/3246.
12. Christopher Lloyd, *Captain Marryat and the Old Navy* (London 1939), p. 2.
13. Lady Nelson to Sir Isaac Heard, undated (private collection).

14. I am indebted to Mr Ben Burgess, founder of The Nelson Society, for drawing my attention to this advertisement.
15. *The Naval Chronicle*, Vol. XV, p. 34.
16. Alexander Davison to Thomas Davidson, 14 January 1806, RNM499/88 (14).
17. Unpublished memoirs of John Yule (private collection).
18. A.T. Mahan, *The Life of Nelson* (1897), Vol. I, pp. 385–6.
19. *Navy League Journal*, November 1905, p. 280.
20. Arnold White and E. Hallam Moorhouse, *Nelson and the Twentieth Century* (1905), p. 297.
21. E. Chatfield, *The Navy and Defence* (1942), p. 120.
22. A. Marder, *From Dreadnought to Scapa Flow*, Vol. V, p. 193.

Rear Admiral Sir Horatio Nelson, KB, by Lemuel Abbott. Arguably the most famous of all the likenesses of Nelson, Abbott's portrait was copied many times and many prints were based on it. This is the version painted for Nelson's friend and prize-agent Alexander Davison.

CHAPTER II

The Nelson Portraits
by Richard Walker

'I remember that after the Battle of the Nile, when quite a child, I was walking with a school fellow near Stonehouse, when a little diminutive man with a green shade over his eye, a shabby well-worn cocked hat, and buttoned-up undress coat, approached us . . .'. So said Benjamin Robert Haydon in his autobiography. Nelson smiled at them and the two boys boasted of it for months. One of Nelson's most noticeable physical characteristics seems to have been his diminutive size, observed by many of his contemporaries, though his nephew George Matcham said he was 'not a little man but of medium height and of a frame adapted to activity'.[1] Judging by the effigy in Westminster Abbey, 5 ft 5½ in would seem to be about right. However, though a tall commanding figure may be an advantage in a man's passage through life, his general bearing, his face, voice, colour of eyes, even the shape of his head, all help us to assess his value.

We are singularly fortunate in Nelson's iconography. Apart from Queen Victoria and the Duke of Wellington, both of whom lived to a great age, Nelson's portrait was painted more often than any other of our national heroes. 'That foolish little fellow has sat to every painter in London', were the uncharitable, and indeed inaccurate, words of Lord St Vincent. In fact, there are something like forty-five separate contemporary portraits of him.

Two main themes run through the Nelson portraiture: his ill-health, including his many wounds, and his gradually increasing unhappiness and sense of guilt. Both are clearly reflected in the attempts made by artists of the time to penetrate the inner secrets of this extraordinary man.

Normally kind and tolerant, Nelson frequently admitted to ill-humour and irritability, mostly caused by bouts of illness or pain. As a young man he suffered from 'an ague and fever . . . which has pulled me down most astonishingly'; probably the malaria and scurvy which assaulted him throughout his life.[2] The toll taken by illness, including the loss of his hair, can be seen in the amateurish but revealing drawing by Cuthbert Collingwood. The first of his wounds was to his right eye at Calvi, possibly a retinal lesion. Although Nelson assured his wife that 'the blemish is nothing, not to be perceived unless told', the effects may be seen in the miniature he sent home in 1794, and in many subsequent portraits, particularly in the corner of the eye, at the pterygium.

At Santa Cruz Nelson's right arm was shattered by a musket-ball, and the following amputation, sepsis, and excruciating pain, vividly described by Southey, are visible in the early Abbott portraits. A year later he was wounded again, at the Nile, when a piece of langridge stripped the skin from his forehead. 'I am killed,' he cried, 'remember me to my wife'. It was a flesh wound only, but left a permanent and unsightly scar, apart from, at the time, dizziness, headaches, sickness and loss of concentration. Modern diagnosis suggests concussion, and by the time he returned from the Mediterranean, he was beginning to look like an old man: 'I am so tired, fagged and worn out, that the Nelson you know is gone and but a shadow remains.'[3] In Vienna the British ambassador and his wife, the Mintos, tried to console him; but in Dresden an observer noted his silence and inability to smile – probably scurvy had caused his teeth to decay.

Some of this may be attributable to self-pity, but a major cause of unhappiness, apart from chronic ill-health and disillusion with his own shortcomings in the Mediterranean, was the realization that his infatuation with Emma and cuckoldry of one of his staunchest friends, were bound to lead eventually to doom. Indeed his marriage crashed, he was cruelly snubbed by George III, and only slightly less so by the Duke of Marlborough, and his career as a successful, even idolized, naval commander, appeared to be in serious danger.

The victories of Copenhagen and Trafalgar were, of course, to follow. The 'state portraits' by Beechey and Hoppner show a heroic figure, slightly larger than life. The rugged seaman of Keymer's oil, wooden and stilted though it may be, gives us as good an idea of Nelson's actual appearance as we are likely to expect. And Nelson's own favourite was the little outline by Simon De Koster, jotted down at a City dinner, engraved, '& sold most rapidly'. Not many of these images convey to posterity a true conception of The Hero. To return to Haydon again, 'all who came in contact with him, midshipman, mate, lieutenant or captain, ambassador or admiral, native and foreigner, all loved him, for no one in his presence lost his self-respect'.[4]

The portraits of Nelson as a child, boy and midshipman, are unsupported by any firm evidence. The podgy midshipman, sometimes attributed to his fellow East Anglian, Thomas Gainsborough, is surely neither Gainsborough nor Nelson. Even the stirring incident of the young Horace, clubbing a polar bear, was painted posthumously to illustrate the biographies appearing in 1806 and 1809.

The first authentic portrait (colour plate 2) is the enchanting three-quarter length oil, by John Francis Rigaud, of the young Lieutenant Nelson aged eighteen. This was commissioned by his commanding officer, William Locker, captain of the frigate HMS *Lowestoffe*, and enlightened enough to perceive something unusual in his new second lieutenant. The ship sailed for the West Indies before Rigaud could complete the portrait and it was finished four years later when Nelson returned home in 1780, desperately ill with the Yellow Jack fever. 'It will not be in the least like I am now, that is certain, but you may tell Mr Rigaud to add beauty, and it will be much mended.'[5]

Fortunately Rigaud did not add beauty, only altered the uniform. The air of youthful self-confidence leads us easily to appreciate Prince William's comment, 'the merest boy of a captain I ever beheld'. It hung in Locker's dining-room at Greenwich until 1800 when he bequeathed it to Nelson's brother William, and it remained a treasured family possession until its acquisition by the National Maritime Museum, after the death of the fourth Earl Nelson in 1947.

In September 1784 Nelson, in command of HMS *Boreas*, arrived in the Leeward Islands where an old friend, Cuthbert Collingwood, was captain of the frigate *Mediator*. Nelson had lost his hair, probably from machineel poisoning,

Captain Horatio Nelson by Cuthbert Collingwood. Nelson's close friend (and later his second-in-command at Trafalgar) produced a drawing of him when they were young men serving together in the West Indies. This engraving was based on it.

and wore a grotesque wig. Collingwood made a coloured drawing, and Nelson returned the compliment; neither great works of art but interesting examples of the skill in drawing that most naval officers cultivated, and often used, for making outlines of cliffs and headlands for coastal navigation.

Nelson and the *Boreas* arrived home in 1787, the captain so ill that it was feared he would not live to see England, and a puncheon of rum had been prepared for his body in case he did not survive the voyage. The next five years were spent on the beach, mainly in Norfolk, but in January 1793, much to his relief and delight, he was given command of HMS *Agamemnon* and sailed with Lord Hood for the Mediterranean. Here, during a combined operation in Corsica, his right eye was damaged, '. . . much bruised about the face and eyes by sand from the works struck by a shot'. The *Agamemnon* was refitted at Leghorn that autumn and Nelson took the opportunity to sit to a local artist for a miniature, which both Josiah, his stepson, and Captain Berry said was not in the least like him. However, it became one of Fanny Nelson's treasured possessions, kept in a special casket and frequently admired even after their marriage had broken down.

A small water-colour drawing shows Nelson preparing an attack on a land position, probably Santa Cruz, where he lost his right arm in a disastrous night engagement against a Spanish treasure fleet. The amputation was carried out by the surgeon of the *Theseus* and his French refugee mate, Louis Remonier. The effects were vividly described by Southey: 'his sufferings were long and painful . . . He had scarcely any intermission of pain, day or night, for three months after his return to England.' A drawing by Henry Edridge, commissioned by the collector

Captain Horatio Nelson, by the Leghorn miniaturist. Although Nelson's colleagues did not think this a good likeness, his wife treasured it and kept it in a special casket.

and antiquary Sir Henry Englefield, was probably made in October or November 1797 in Edridge's Bloomsbury studio, well within walking distance of Nelson's lodgings in Old Bond Street. It shows Nelson with his arm still bandaged, the ribbons fastening the slit in the sleeve visible just above the fold. He wears the gold medal for St Vincent, which had arrived on the *Theseus* off Cadiz Bay: 'we have got our medals but no chains', he wrote home to Fanny. He wears the riband of the Bath, given him by George III in September, on which occasion the King had exclaimed: 'You have lost your right arm.' 'But not my right hand, Sir,' he replied, 'as I have the honour of presenting Captain Berry.' Edridge gives him an expression, serious and rather distant, which can easily be imagined to reflect the pain described by Southey. The drawing was sold on Englefield's death in 1823 and bought by a son of Nelson's old companion, Admiral Sir George Home.

Three other artists were lucky enough to get sittings at about this time: Daniel Orme, Henry Singleton and Lemuel Abbott. After the Battle of Cape St Vincent, when the news arrived in London of the destruction of the Spanish fleet, made even more memorable by accounts of Commodore Nelson's daredevil part in the action, Orme conceived the idea of a tableau, *The Surrender of the San Josef*. This was finished in 1798 and shows the Spanish admiral surrendering his sword on his own quarter-deck. Orme's sketch for Nelson's head exists in a private collection. It was reduced in size to an oval stipple engraving, published in February 1798, and suggests the possibility, Orme being primarily a miniaturist, of the existence somewhere of an authentic miniature of Nelson by him. The engraving was a tremendous success. 'Orme must have made a great deal of money', said Lady Nelson, who had been told by the print-dealer that he 'had a load of Admiral Nelsons and sold every one'.

Rear Admiral Sir Horatio Nelson *by Daniel Orme. Nelson as Byronic hero! This romanticized image of him was very popular and appears frequently on the commemorative material produced in his lifetime (see illustrations on pp. 90 and 93).*

Henry Singleton had the same idea as Orme. His picture, *Lord Nelson Boarding the Spanish Ships*, was exhibited at the Royal Academy in 1798. Singleton was also a miniaturist and his modest drawing was worked up into a portrait used for Keating's mezzotint, published after the Battle of the Nile. By this time Nelson had become a national hero and the demand for his portrait was urgent. Rigaud's oil of the young lieutenant had been turned into a scratchy stipple engraving, published in August 1797, but not even showing the missing arm amputated in July. Clearly something more sensational was needed.

Nelson's legendary disobedience of orders at the Battle of Cape St Vincent was followed by the blockade of Cadiz and his detachment from the fleet to capture a Spanish treasure-ship at Teneriffe, where he was forced to retreat during a night action. Between these two engagements lay six months, seminal in the formation of that charisma known throughout the fleet as 'the Nelson touch'. From 'Nelson's Patent Bridge for boarding first-rates' to the grandiloquent war cries, 'Westminster Abbey or Victory' and 'Tomorrow my head will be crowned with either laurel or cypress', the seed was sown that was to blossom into the dazzling flower that Nelson coveted most – Glory. Time and again he wrote home that glory was his real ambition.

The public was becoming aware of this portent stirring in the fleet. The few relatively insignificant engravings by Shipster, Laurie and others, needed to be updated. The many portraits by Lemuel Abbott, perhaps the most widely recognized of the whole Nelson iconography, originate with the desire of his old friend and 'sea-daddy' William Locker, by then Lieutenant-Governor of Greenwich Hospital, to add Nelson to the collection of 'younkers' in his dining-room at Greenwich. The choice of Abbott was reasonable. He had already painted portraits of Locker himself as well as several naval officers of distinction, including Hood and St Vincent. His own self-portrait shows a prosperous-looking artist holding a porte-crayon and a copy of Barnard's immensely popular mezzotint of Nelson. There is no sign of the incompetence and eventual insanity described by Edward Edwards in *The Anecdotes of Painting*.[6]

During the autumn of 1797 Nelson was convalescing at Greenwich, and Abbott was persuaded, without much difficulty, to bring his paints and canvas and have the sittings in the Lieutenant-Governor's house. Lady Spencer, wife of the First Lord, described Nelson's appearance at this time: 'he looked so sickly it was painful to see him'. But Lord Minto, sharing a carriage with him from London, said he looked 'better and fresher than I remember . . . He suffers a good deal of pain and takes opium every night.'

Abbott had two sittings at Greenwich. Of the forty subsequent versions about thirty can be accounted for today, gradually declining in quality as Abbott himself descended into insanity. Probably the first of these, and the original oil, painted at Greenwich and used in the studio as a model on which to base future copies, is known as the 'Kilgraston sketch'. After Abbott's death it was acquired by Francis

Grant, Laird of Kilgraston, Perthshire, who knew Abbott well and coveted the sketch which Abbott always refused to sell. It has an inscription on the back, written by Grant's son, Sir Francis Grant, President of the Royal Academy:

> The original picture for which Lord Nelson gave Abbot [sic] two sittings. My father, the late Francis Grant of Kilgraston, N.B. employed Abbot largely as a portrait painter. Abbot assured Mr Grant that this was the original from which all other pictures of Nelson painted by him were completed. Mr Grant desired to own this picture and requested Abbot to name his price. Abbot's Answer was that no money would induce him to part with the original during his life. After the death of Abbot it was purchased by Mr Grant by private arrangement from his family or executors and the picture has ever since been at Kilgraston.
>
> (signed) Francis Grant P.R.A.[7]

The President knew the sketch well and firmly believed it to be the original study from which all other pictures by Abbott were painted. It was eventually sold at Sotheby's in 1977. By then it had become a wreck, generating a good deal of scepticism. But the President's repeated assurances that this was the original sketch ought not to be lightly discounted.[8]

If the Kilgraston sketch *was* Abbott's preliminary study for his famous portraits of Nelson, the next in sequence was Captain Locker's own portrait, and the prime version of the many copies which formed the main financial prop for the last four or five years of his life. The Locker portrait remained in the family collection till the death of his great-grandson, the poet Frederick Locker-Lampson, in 1872. The picture is in excellent condition and has a note on the back written by Locker-Lampson's father:

> This picture was painted by Abbot [sic] at my grandfather's as a present from Nelson to my grandfather. He afterwards sat to Abbot for a similar-sized picture for Lady Nelson, and though Abbot repeated the picture some forty or more times, Lord Nelson only sat with him twice. I have heard my Aunt Eliza (the little child playing with the dog in the Family Picture) say that this Picture was painted soon after Nelson lost his arm, and she remembers helping N on and off with his uniform coat, in which he sat for the picture before and after the sittings.
>
> F.L. 1872[9]

In spite of some restoration, the portrait probably conveys the best idea of what Nelson looked like during the weeks following his amputation before the wound had healed. The severe unsmiling countenance of a man in great pain, but governed by a spirit that allowed no complaint, bequeaths to posterity an impression that has never been recaptured, even by Beechey or Hoppner. Abbott was not a great artist, sometimes even deplorably bad, but in the Locker portrait he achieved an understanding of Nelson that he was never able to repeat.

Later versions were painted for Lady Nelson (NPG), Alexander Davison (NMM) (see illustration on p. 32), John M'Arthur (NMM), Collingwood (Scottish NPG), and many others. Lady Nelson was delighted with her copy: 'it is my companion, my sincere friend in your absence'. It was acquired by the National Portrait Gallery in 1874, with the tradition of having belonged to her, and Grant himself recommended its purchase, 'for the very reasonable sum of £150 – I think it the best of the many replicas I have seen done by Abbot – from the Original sketch in my nephew's possession . . . a very fair picture . . . But *it is not* the original for which Nelson gave two sittings.'

The subsequent Abbott portraits lose the severe and drawn expression of a man suffering from a hideous wound, and become nearer those of a sweet-tempered country gentleman, not far removed from the breed of Norfolk parson in which Nelson's stock was rooted. But an interesting variant was commissioned by M'Arthur in 1799 to illustrate *The Naval Chronicle*. For this portrait Abbott added a tricorn hat, embellished with the Chelengk awarded by the Sultan of Turkey after the victory of the Nile. No one in England had actually seen the Chelengk, but Abbott managed to paint it in from a drawing and a verbal description (to be seen in Robert's stipple engraving of 1800), later improved when Nelson arrived home himself. Curiously enough the eyes in this version are a greenish-brown instead of the usual grey-blue, the face weather-beaten, and the expression smiling but rescued from prettiness by M'Arthur's dramatic intervention. He had implored Nelson to fit in another sitting, 'as the instant after, I should take the portrait from poor Mr Abbot's presence, that he might not have an opportunity of making a second attempt to adonize it'.

News of the Battle of the Nile was announced by St Vincent on 28 September 1798, as 'the almost incredible stupendous victory'; and a few days later there appeared the first of Gillray's celebrated prints, *Nelson's Victory*, showing disconsolate members of the Opposition receiving the news with disbelief. This was hotly followed by the most magnificent of all Gillray's patriotic and anti-Jacobin satires, *Extirpation of the Plagues of Egypt*, in which Nelson strides through the waves dragging ashore a fleet of crocodiles. The story of his wound had evidently arrived too, though Gillray puts it over the wrong eye.

Nearer the scene of action Nelson's band of brothers, the captains of the Nile squadron, mustered aboard HMS *Orion* and resolved to present him with a sword, its hilt shaped like a crocodile, and, 'as a further proof of their esteem and regard, hoped that he will permit his Portrait to be taken . . . in commemoration of that glorious day'. An 'eminent Italian painter' was invited to breakfast but, to the astonishment and concern of his hosts, refused to begin work: 'There is such a mixture of humility with ambition in Lord Nelson's countenance', he said, 'that I dare not risk the attempt.' The name of the 'eminent Italian' has never been established, but in any case nothing transpired. Perhaps it was just as well. Nelson's appearance at this stage, wounded above the eye, bandaged, racked with headache and pain, and probably concussed – 'my head is splitting, splitting, splitting' – cannot have been prepossessing. The imaginary reconstruction, belonging to Lady Parker and perhaps by Guy Head, is as near as we are likely to approach to his battered countenance after the Nile.

Back at home Sir Horatio Nelson KB was gazetted Baron Nelson of the Nile and of Burnham Thorpe. He received the thanks of Parliament, a pension of £2,000, an award of £10,000 from the East India Company, and, most prized of all, a coffin made from *L'Orient*'s mainmast, given as a wry cautionary tale by Captain Ben Hallowell of the *Swiftsure*. The Nelson Legend was in full swing and several artists seized the opportunity. Lawrence Gahagan, an Irish sculptor specializing in small bronzes, claimed to have had seven sittings at Nelson's 141 Old Bond Street lodgings early in 1798. His marble bust was seen by Lady Nelson at the Royal Academy, and not specially admired: 'the bust is there but too old for you', she reported. It is one of the few portraits to show Nelson with a smile, but was replaced on the Gahagan production lines with a more romanticized type which continued to be turned out by the Gahagan family till Lucius Gahagan's death in 1839.

Wedgwood commissioned several modellers at this time. A black basalt bust by Robert Shout was published on 22 July 1798, but a more heroic figure was needed, provided convincingly by John De Vaer's profile, made to join the Wedgwood series which included Howe, St Vincent and Duncan. The profile was used again and again to adorn the ever-increasing flow of memorabilia which began to gather force after the Battle of the Nile. It answered, to some extent, the popular demand for a portrait of this intrepid, slightly swashbuckling hero, whose consummate seamanship and flair for a broader strategy had led to the frustration of Napoleon's eastern ambitions. It was used as an individual profile in Jasper-ware on various shades of green, blue and lilac dip, and in black basalt applied to vases, urns and jugs. A specially attractive specimen is on the side of a cane-ware jug in the McCarthy Collection in the Royal Naval Museum (see illustration on p. 80).

A combination of the Wedgwood bust and profile was used for Alexander Davison's Nile medal, issued privately 'as a tribute of my respect and admiration': gold for the admiral and captains of the fleet, silver for lieutenants, copper and gilt for warrant officers, and bronzed copper for ratings (see illustration on p. 99). The commission was given to Matthew Boulton of the Soho Mint in Birmingham, the design roughed out by Davison himself and executed by Conrad Küchler. A letter to Boulton, dated 25 October 1798, says, 'you will receive by the night coach a bust of Rear Admiral Lord Nelson, together with a design for a medallion'.[10] The image is rather insignificant, but, although Davison had made a fortune as contractor and ship-owner, his generosity was enormously appreciated,

Bust of Nelson by Lawrence Gahagan. Although Lady Nelson thought the original of this bust 'too old' it was very popular and many copies such as this one were made.

Profile of Nelson by de Vaere: produced for the Wedgwood firm to meet the need for a more 'swashbuckling' likeness of Nelson. It was used on many Wedgwood items and also on a number of medals and other commemorative pieces (see illustration on p. 80).

especially as neither King nor Parliament had considered the Nile to be worthy of a general award, other than the large King's Naval gold medal for Nelson himself and thirteen smaller versions for the captains. Davison's Nile medal never became officially part of uniform, but many of the recipients had their names, and the names of their ships, engraved at their own expense. We are assured by the third earl, that Nelson wore it constantly: ' I believe my great-uncle always wore it, and I have his medal in a red Russian leather case with a gold ring through the top by which it was hung round the neck.' He is shown wearing it on the right breast in the Turkish version of the Guzzardi portrait, and on the left breast in the Palermo miniature and the pastel by Heinrich Schmidt, and elsewhere.

The Hon. Mrs Damer, sculptor and friend of Horace Walpole, was staying in Naples when Nelson arrived from the Nile in September 1798. She is believed to have persuaded him to sit for her in the uniform he had worn during the battle itself. Certainly he gave her the coat, and she offered to execute a portrait, either in bronze or marble, for presentation to the City of London. The original *modello* is lost but echoes of it may be seen in a Wedgwood bust, attributed to Papera, and a bust by William John Coffee, dated 1806 and now at Greenwich. One, together with a bust of Fox, was seen by John Hoppner and his wife at Versailles in 1802, 'both executed by Mrs Damer, not very good likenesses but they might be known'.[11] After some delay the City bust, of marble and slightly larger than life, was exhibited at the Royal Academy in 1804, presented to the City Fathers, and is now in the Nelson Room at the Guildhall, wreathed with laurel and oak every Trafalgar Day. A large engraving of it was published by Daniel Orme a few days before Trafalgar, without acknowledgement to the sculptor – a discourtesy which wounded her deeply, particularly as her work was, in some quarters, looked on as amateurish; and indeed, worse still, it was whispered that she had assistance from 'ghosts'.

Naples was evacuated in December 1798, and the fleet (with the royal party aboard) anchored off Palermo. Here a new chapter in the iconography begins, consisting of the strange portraits by Leonardo Guzzardi.

Guzzardi is a shadowy figure who, apart from the Nelson portraits, appears to be unrecorded though his work may possibly be found buried in Sicilian country houses. He is described in the sub-title of an English mezzotint as 'a Celebrated Artist at Palermo, Court Painter to the King'. His portrait of Nelson originated as a gift in return for the Chelengk and other awards sent by the Sultan, Selim III, for saving the Ottoman Empire from the onslaughts of Napoleon. He may even have had in mind his promise to the captains of the Nile at the meeting on the *Orion*. Certainly many copies were painted, all as rear-admiral wearing full dress uniform, tricorn hat and Chelengk. They may be divided into two types, differing only in the insignia. The first versions, including the largest, in the Admiralty Board Room, show him wearing the Order of the Bath and one King's Naval gold medal (see illustration on p. 187). In later copies, including the reciprocal gift to Turkey, he wears on his right breast the star of the Order of the Crescent together with Davison's gold medal, and round his neck, on the regulation blue and white ribbon, two King's Naval gold medals, one for St Vincent and the newly awarded one for the Nile.

Guzzardi's portrait of Nelson is very far from the popular image of a conquering hero; it shows him lean, emaciated and unnaturally coloured. 'Bizarre' is a word often used to describe this puppet on a provincial Italian stage. But Nelson's battered appearance probably *was* fairly bizarre at this time: he had been much wounded; he was in poor health; his eyes and teeth were already causing trouble; he was barely forty, yet beginning to look old; and, his infatuation with Emma added guilt to this catalogue of woe. Leonardo Guzzardi, minor artist of a remote Mediterranean Court, was clearly aware of his sitter's profound unhappiness.

If there is something sinister about Guzzardi's portraits, Guy Head's fine upstanding gentleman is the opposite, and the sort of unscathed warrior we might expect on the cover of *The Boy's Own Paper*. The scene is fanciful, of course. The battle was fought during the darkness of an August night. The French admiral's sword was brought to Nelson shortly after midnight, not by a midshipman but by the *Vanguard*'s first lieutenant. And Nelson himself had been wounded, was bandaged, bloodstained, haggard and exhausted, and a very long way from the polished officer standing at ease in his best clothes on Head's quarter-deck. The

Sir Horatio Nelson at the Battle of the Nile *by Guy Head. In this highly romanticized painting, an unscathed Nelson receives the sword of the French Admiral. In fact, as another less well-known painting by Head shows, Nelson was dishevelled and bleeding after suffering a severe head wound.*

picture was painted in Naples or Palermo during the winter and spring of 1798/9, and presented by Nelson to Lady Hamilton.

On 7 February 1799 Charles Grignion, a thriving member of the artist colony in Rome, 'had the honour of Lord Nelson's sitting for his portrait at Palermo in Sicily . . . accounted one of the most dignified and expressive likenesses of that brave Admiral'. That the drawing is something of a caricature is not surprising. Grignion, though also a portrait and miniature painter, practised caricature a good deal, and indeed was the author of a book, *Rules for Executing Caricatures*. The drawing of his relaxed sitter, absorbed in his gloomy reflections, was possibly intended to be worked later into an oil portrait, or perhaps even a miniature.

Palermo was also the setting for another drawing, and a group of miniatures, by a local artist. It is difficult to believe they represent Nelson at all. One is inscribed in Emma's flourishing handwriting: *Admiral Lord Nelson Duke of Bronte painted from the Duke of Bronte at Palermo 1799 from Lady Hamilton to her friend Mrs Nelson*. A similar drawing, with hat and a strange variation on the Chelengk, was given by Nelson to Hardy, and still belongs to his descendants. Hardy's nephew John Manfield, while a midshipman aboard the *Ambuscade*, was occasionally invited by his uncle to the *Victory*. On 5 August 1804 he wrote home: 'I dined with Lord Nelson, Admiral Murray and Captain Hardy, and I assure you your picture is not in the least like his Lordship.'[12] It has an italianate cast, echoed in the maxim, 'Inglese Italianato, Diavolo incarnato', though a closer assessment of this ponderous figure is given by a distinguished modern authority: 'the artist in this case has turned Nelson into a complete macaroni'.[13]

Early in 1800 both Nelson and Sir William Hamilton were recalled home, Hamilton after thirty-six years at the Court of His Sicilian Majesty, Nelson after two years service in the Mediterranean, beginning in glory at the Nile and ending in nemesis at Naples. They travelled overland from Leghorn, arriving in Vienna in August. Here both Emma and Nelson sat to Heinrich Füger, whose studio became a popular venue where the Viennese, despondent after Marengo, could meet the Hero of the Nile, the only man in Europe, apparently, able to stand up to the invincible Napoleon with any degree of success. Füger was primarily a miniaturist, but because of failing eyesight had turned to full-scale portraiture. It is revealing to see how his hand, trained in the exacting technique of miniature-painting, had detected in Nelson's expression something that no other artist had hitherto attempted – a ruthlessness, a capacity for concentration, a streak almost of cruelty, all of which were undoubtedly part of his genius. He is dressed informally in a dark blue coat and neckcloth and a light blue jersey, the only portrait we have of him out of uniform. The eyes are a bright grey. In a variant, in the Royal Naval Museum, he wears rear-admiral's full dress uniform, the three Orders of the Bath, St Ferdinand, and the Turkish Crescent, and two King's Naval gold medals (colour

Bust of Nelson by Cardossi. The bust produced by Thaller and Ranson in Vienna in 1800 was copied many times – often without acknowledgement. This version by Cardossi was produced after Nelson's death.

plate 5). As with Guzzardi's portrait, the eyes are a greenish-brown. 'He is a jig from ribands, orders and stars', said Lady Minto, but the famous charm captivated her again: 'he is just the same with us as ever he was'.

The sittings to Füger were not the only ones in Vienna. The sculptors, Thaller and Ranson, produced a marble bust incised: *Franz Thaller et Matthias Ranson / Viennae Aust. MDCCCI*, and now at Greenwich. It was a successful work and copies were made by Turnerelli, Nollekens, Bertolini and others (usually without acknowledgement), and Flaxman's memorial in St Paul's Cathedral is based on it. A version appears in Edridge's drawing of Lady Nelson (RNM). As was often the custom with sculpture, a *modello* for the Thaller & Ranson bust was made in the shape of a life mask. There is evidence for this in the title of a commemorative engraving: 'Lord Nelson, when in Vienna, permitted a cast to be taken from his face. . . .' Further evidence was given by Sir William Beechey who had been called upon to advise on the Trafalgar medal: 'the Bust, tho it was done from a cast from his face, is very deficient; he pursed up his chin and screwed up his features when the Plaister was poured on it . . .'. Until lately this mask, on threadbare evidence, has generally been accepted as a death mask, but most authorities now believe it to be a far more interesting and precious relic – a life mask, and therefore as near to Nelson's true appearance as we are ever likely to find.[14]

After Vienna, Nelson and his companions continued to Prague and then by houseboat on the river to Dresden, where the local Court painter, Johann Heinrich Schmidt, made pastel drawings of both Emma and Nelson, now at Greenwich. A local observer was not impressed by the Hero's physical appearance: 'Nelson is

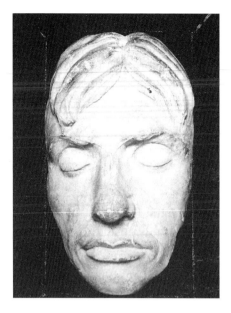

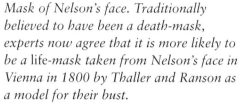

Mask of Nelson's face. Traditionally believed to have been a death-mask, experts now agree that it is more likely to be a life-*mask taken from Nelson's face in Vienna in 1800 by Thaller and Ranson as a model for their bust.*

one of the most insignificant figures I ever saw . . . a more miserable collection of bones and wizened frame cannot be imagined. He speaks little, and then only in English, and he hardly ever smiles . . .'.[15] Schmidt's portrait is by no means the conquering hero. Beneath the thatch of grey straggling hair the pastel shows a melancholy face, depressed and unsmiling, the uninjured eye bold and clear with perhaps too intense a blue, the blinded one darkened and set awkwardly under the brow on which the Nile scar is clearly apparent. The nose is slightly bulbous at the tip. Perhaps we may say it is the face of a man, sick in body and mind, conscious that his precious career is in jeopardy, and conscious too that he is approaching home to a wife to whom he has been blatantly unfaithful, accompanied by a friend whom he has openly cuckolded. The knowledge that Emma was carrying his unborn child cannot have added to his peace of mind. Schmidt's portrait takes some account of this network of constrained emotion and guilt. The only bright aspect of the pastel is the blue of the uniform which is better preserved than in most of the oil portraits. The companion portrait of Emma was one of Nelson's favourites and hung in his cabin near the desk. On the back, in Emma's scrawling handwriting, is a tattered paper: 'He called it his Guardian Angel and thought he could not be victorious if he did not see it in the midst of Battle.'

Nelson's return home, in November 1800, was recorded in Rowlandson's superb satirical water-colour of a giant admiral landing at Yarmouth amid the rapturous welcome of his Norfolk compatriots. Crowds dragged his carriage to the

Lord Nelson by Johann Schmidt. The Court Painter in Dresden captured a haunted and rather melancholy Nelson, rather than the conquering hero. This image matches the verbal descriptions of him at the time.

Wrestlers' Inn where the landlady asked his permission to rename it the Nelson's Arms. 'That would be absurd', said her guest, cracking one of his few recorded jokes, 'for I have but one.' Here the Hamiltons handed over one of the Guzzardi portraits to be copied by a local artist Matthew Keymer. In London the rapture continued. Rear-Admiral Nelson, hero of St Vincent, victor of the Nile, one-armed and partially blind but clearly of considerable virility, sparked off a ray of hope in an atmosphere of depressing Napoleonic victories against the allied armies. The fact that he was flouting the conventions of society added colour to the grey wartime scene. No doubt he also relished the irony of Halliday's medal, struck in honour of his return and engraved: 'Hail Virtuous Hero, Thy Victories we Acknowledge and thy God.'

During his few weeks of leave before sailing for the Baltic campaign Nelson sat to at least seven artists: Beechey for the City of Norwich, Hoppner for the Prince of Wales, Mrs Damer, Catherine Andras, Thomas Bowyer, Simon de Koster, and an unknown sculptor for Mrs Coade's 'gallery of Coade Stone' at Lambeth. The various Abbott portraits had so far supplied the public demand. Now the City of Norwich decided to honour the Norfolk parson's son, and commissioned Beechey, who had married a Norfolk girl and had already painted Nelson's father. The Beechey portrait was begun shortly before Nelson's promotion to Vice Admiral on 1 January 1801, and exhibited at the Royal Academy in May. One of Beechey's preliminary oil sketches was bought in 1985 by the National Portrait Gallery (colour plate 4). It has noticeably brown eyes and the Nile scar over the right eye which is less lustrous than the other. Beechey may have been something of a prosaic artist but in this sketch he achieved an immediacy which gives us one of the most vivid portraits of Nelson we have. It was kept in the studio and eventually inherited by Beechey's son Charles, also a naval officer and one of Nelson's honorary godsons. The final portrait, though run down by the critics in 1801, pleased the City Fathers. It hangs in St Andrew's Hall, Norwich, in a sumptuous frame supported by corinthian columns and festooned with trophies, oak and laurel branches, and Nelson's armorial shield.

Beechey's main rivals in the field of portraiture were Lawrence and Hoppner. There is no record of a Lawrence portrait, which might have been a treasure indeed. Hoppner was commissioned, not surprisingly, by the Prince of Wales, whose Principal Portrait Painter he had become in 1793, to paint a portrait of Nelson to join the array of men of action in Carlton House. One of the preliminary oil sketches, lately acquired by the Royal Naval Museum, shows slight variations from the finished picture (colour plate 3). The eyes are greenish-blue (similar to one of the Guzzardi's and to the Schmidt pastel) and the head is posed four-square on the neck instead of tilted coyly sideways. This suggests a change of mind, either by the artist or by Nelson himself who may have been enduring an arthritic condition due to his wounds or general exposure to foul weather. Hoppner's whole-length portrait, whose delivery at Carlton House was delayed

Lord Nelson by de Koster. Originally sketched quickly at a dinner party, de Koster's likeness was reproduced in a number of different engravings such as this and was very popular. It was Nelson's favourite portrait.

until 1810, mainly because of the need to make copies but also from difficulty in extracting payment, was copied many times, popularized in stipple and mezzotint engravings and finally became the basis for Catherine Andras's effigy in Westminster Abbey.

Nelson's favourite portrait of himself, a drawing by Simon de Koster believed to have been sketched surreptitiously 'while His Lordship sat at a public dinner in London', was engraved by James Stow to be given away frequently as presents. On the back of one of these is a letter from Nelson, dated Merton 2 February 1802: 'there are so many prints of me that it is not in my power to say which is the most like the Original, for no one of these is like the other, but I rather think a little outline of my head, sold at Brydon's Charing +, is the most like me . . .'. Lady Hamilton agreed and produced her own copy when the profile for the Boulton Trafalgar medal was under discussion; and Beechey magnanimously declared it to be 'the most correct likeness he had ever seen', superior even to his own. A black chalk copy by B.R. Haydon is inscribed: 'NELSON a little body with a Mighty Heart'.

Two other artists managed to get sittings of him at this time: the miniaturist Thomas Bowyer, and his adoptive daughter, the wax-modeller Catherine Andras. Bowyer's miniature was one of a series of Admiralty Lords assembled in Smirke's triumphant engravings of the Naval Victors, published by Bowyer himself in 1803. Painted late in 1800 it shows Nelson as rear-admiral, with hair dishevelled and brushed forward to hide the Nile scar. The Andras wax, probably made at the same sitting, has disappeared but was awarded a Royal Society of Arts prize in March 1801 and exhibited at the Royal Academy in May.

Back in Yarmouth Nelson waited impatiently for Hyde Parker to give orders to sail for Copenhagen. But Parker, lately remarried to a girl of eighteen, was in no hurry: as Nelson wrote to Trowbridge, 'Consider how nice it must be laying in bed with a young wife, compared to a damned cold raw wind.' However, the time was well-used by Matthew Keymer, who had earlier copied the Guzzardi portrait and, dissatisfied with his first effort, tried again. The result, a rugged image far-removed from those unconvincing icons the 'state portraits' by Abbott, Beechey and Hoppner, was pronounced at the time as a 'capital likeness'. Nelson was certainly ill and depressed; St Vincent described him as 'very low'; and he wrote to Emma 'my eye is very bad . . . the film is extended so that I only see from the corner furthest from my nose'. He mentioned the green eyeshade for the first time and asked her to make one or two, 'nobody else shall',[16] but characteristically he ends, 'what a fuss about my complaints'. Keymer's unfamiliar and rather wooden image certainly reflects a good deal of this melancholy state of affairs.

Between Copenhagen and Trafalgar very little of significance materialized on the Nelson iconography. Possibly the most uninteresting of all his portraits, an anaemic whole-length oil, was painted by John Rising. An equally feeble chalk drawing by John Downman is idealized beyond recognition. A good drawing by Henry Edridge, his second attempt, was probably made at Merton, where his visit was recorded in Farington's *Diary* for 6 August 1802. Bowyer and Catherine Andras also had a second joint sitting, occasioning another of Nelson's pleasantries: 'I am not used to being attacked starboard and larboard at the same time.' A young marine artist, John Wichelo, had the good luck to visit Merton a few weeks before Trafalgar and produced a pastel drawing which he kept for thirty years and eventually presented to one of Nelson's shipmates, Admiral Sir William Parker. It was later used as the basis for the parian marble bust by Joseph Pitts.

When the great Admiral's body returned home in its leaguer of spirits, Dr Beatty carried out an autopsy and extracted the fatal bullet. His assistant, the painter Arthur William Devis, stayed aboard the flagship making endless drawings of the ship's company and the cockpit itself, to be worked up into his vast picture, *The Death of Nelson*. A spin-off of this was an unassuming little portrait, the only one showing Nelson wearing the green eyeshade. Several copies were made and Beatty used an engraving of it as the frontispiece to his *Authentic Narrative of the Death of Lord Nelson*.

Vice Admiral Lord Nelson, KB, *by Arthur Devis. Devis went on board the* Victory *when she arrived in Portsmouth and did sketches for his famous painting,* The Death of Nelson. *Among them was this portrait of Nelson himself, based on sketches done during the autopsy.*

As for the Battle of the Nile, Trafalgar was only officially recognized with a medal for flag officers and captains, causing resentment among junior officers and other ranks. The injustice was again put straight with a private medal, this time paid for by Matthew Boulton and also designed by Küchler. Emma helped by producing the de Koster drawing and the Andras wax, which she pronounced to be '*the most striking likeness* that has been taken'. Once again the Admiralty refused to sanction the medal as part of uniform.

The wax modeller William Tassie produced a profile at this time. Tassie claimed that 'it is mostly done from De Koster's Print and is thought like', but it also owes a good deal to Catherine Andras. The Tassie profiles were popular with the jewellers for rings and brooches (Lady Nelson had three on cornelian brooches).

Catherine Andras's profile came into its own again, used for a more impressive image – her wax and wood effigy of Nelson commissioned for Westminster Abbey. The Nelson charisma after Trafalgar had attained an intensity beyond anything achieved before or since, even by such national heroes as Marlborough, Wellington or Churchill. So the Westminster Abbey decision was not surprising, and the Andras effigy joined the strange and melancholy company of monarchs and their consorts, among which the only other non-royal figure was that of the great Earl of Chatham. Andras no doubt made good use of her previous sittings, but the figure closely follows Turner's mezzotint of the Hoppner portrait, with the uniform altered to vice admiral's; the cocked hat with eyeshade were produced by the Nelson family. It met with instant public acclaim and Emma herself was in ecstasy: 'the general carriage of the body was exactly his, and altogether the likeness was so great it was impossible for anyone who had known him to doubt about or mistake it.'

The Nelson monuments are discussed by Flora Fraser in Chapter Six. Marble busts continued to be produced long after Trafalgar, mostly by the Gahagan family or by imitators of Thaller and Ranson. Flaxman's busts differ slightly from the monument he produced for St Paul's Cathedral. In the busts Nelson is seen more intimately and at close quarters. The bust by Chantrey was originally commissioned by the architect Daniel Alexander to join those of Duncan, Howe and St Vincent on the new blocks at Greenwich Hospital. In 1833 a larger version was commissioned by William IV for Windsor Castle and is now in the National Portrait Gallery, together with its iron-bound stand made from the foremast of the *Victory*. The most famous monument of all, set on Railton's corinthian column in Trafalgar Square, was E.H. Baily's 17 ft high statue of Granton stone, concocted from a rich amalgam of the Abbott, Beechey and Hoppner portraits, and with a liberal dash of the Andras effigy in Westminster Abbey.

The years following the funeral in St Paul's led to a profusion of memorabilia. The most popular model was the last Abbott portrait, wearing the cocked hat and chelengk. Enamel and miniature copies were turned out by the dozen by Henry Bone, H.P. Bone, Edward Bird, William Essex, George Place and Grimaldi. The Grimaldi catalogue alone lists ten enamel copies. More details of this sort of

Effigy of Nelson in Westminster Abbey by Catherine Andras. Based on Miss Andras' own wax profile and the Hoppner portrait, this effigy was declared, by no less an authority than Emma Hamilton, to be an excellent likeness.

commemorative ware can be found in Chapter Four. The Hoppner and Beechey portraits were also copied, but not in such quantity. Northcote produced a rather striking oil in about 1823, based on the Hoppner portraits; and, in 1853, Charles Lucy a huge and less formal study, also in oils (and now in the Royal Naval Museum) of Nelson in his cabin, the engravings of which were accompanied by a testimonial from some of Nelson's surviving officers declaring that it was an excellent likeness (see illustration on p. 152). Occasional variants made up from the de Koster drawing frequently turn up, and Wichelo's 1805 portrait, itself owing much to de Koster, was used for the polychrome busts by Joseph Pitts. A coloured wax figure by Poole, about 1810, in the Lloyds Collection, is an idealized interpretation deriving from several sources; and Percy's wax high-relief in Brighton is similarly eclectic, probably owing most to Catherine Andras. Davidson's *England's Pride and Glory* shows that the mystique still flourished at the end of the nineteenth century. The 1905 celebrations ensured that the Nelson enthusiasm should not fade, and no doubt in 2005 the Immortal Memory will shine as brightly as ever in the portraits of this remarkable man.

References

1. George Matcham, letter to *The Times*, 6 November 1861.
2. James Kemble, *Idols and Invalids* (1933).
3. Letter to Lord Spencer, 17 April 1799 (*Nicolas*, VII, clxxix).
4. Tom Taylor (ed.), *Autobiography and Memoirs of Benjamin Robert Haydon* (1926), I, pp. 30 and 153.
5. Letter to Locker, 21 February 1781 (*Nicolas*, I, p. 38).
6. Some of Edwards's more colourful mis-statements, perpetuated in the DNB and Thieme-Becker, are corrected in A.C. Sewter's, 'Some New Facts about Lemuel Abbott', *The Connoisseur*, 135 (1955), pp. 178–83.
7. Grant's unequivocal assertion is repeated in letters to the Trustees (NPG Archives).
8. Sotheby's, 23 March 1977 (91a), London. The sketch and the Abbott portraits in general are discussed in more detail in *The Trafalgar Chronicle* (Year Book of The 1805 Club), 1994.
9. Locker's inscription on the back of his grandfather's portrait of Nelson is repeated in F. Locker-Lampson's *My Confidences* (1896), p. 39.
10. Letters in Assay Office, Birmingham, published by J.G. Pollard in *The Numismatic Chronicle*, X (1970), pp. 284–6.
11. Damer: Farington *Diary*, 11 September 1802, and *Diaries of Sylvester Douglas* (ed. Bickley, 1928), I, p. 338.
12. John Manfield's diary in NMM microfilm .
13. Tom Pocock, *The Times*, 26 April 1955, 14c.
14. Masks: see R. Walker, *Mariner's Mirror*, November 1980, pp. 319–27; Michael Nash (ed.), *The Nelson Masks*, Portsmouth Symposium, 1993.
15. Thomas Kosegarten, *Meine Freuden in Sachsen* (1801), cit. Callender in *Illustrated London News*, 20 March 1943.
16. Letter to Lady Hamilton, 28 January 1801 (*Nicolas*, IV, p. 279).

The most famous Nelson relic of all: the Vice Admiral's undress uniform coat he was wearing when he was shot at Trafalgar. The bullet hole can be seen in the left shoulder.

CHAPTER III

The Nelson Relics

by John Munday

Frederick, a grandson of Captain William Locker under whom Nelson served as a lieutenant in HMS *Lowestoffe*, was a founder member of the Burlington Fine Arts Club and wrote his reminiscences. As Frederick Locker-Lampson, he is known to posterity as a poet, noted bibliophile and a collector; his book, *My Confidences* (1896), describes the Nelson-dedicated atmosphere of the Royal Hospital at Greenwich, the naval equivalent of Chelsea Hospital and home to aged and disabled pensioners. There his grandfather was lieutenant-governor from 1793 until his death late in 1800, when Lord Nelson dutifully attended the funeral. The captain's younger son, Edward Hawke Locker (Frederick's father), became a Civil Commissioner of the Royal Hospital from 1824, when he started the Admiralty's great collection of portraits and battle-pieces in the Painted Hall, an idea originally proposed by the captain himself. Frederick's book concludes with an appropriate and charming apologia:

> It is not a misfortune to be born with a feeling for association. I seem nearer to Shakespeare when I have his volume of Sonnets (edition 1609) open before me . . . I am nearer to Titian when I have one of his masterly sketches in my hand . . . Believe me there is an exhilaration in collecting. I would call it a perennial joy if it were not so often pierced by despair.

The 'feeling for association' ran in the family. Captain Locker had J.F. Rigaud RA paint his family and also the portraits of three of his 'younkers', his former lieutenants, Horatio Nelson, Charles Morice Pole and William Peacock, when they each achieved the rank of Captain. These were exhibited in the Royal Academy in 1781 and evidently hung in the lieutenant-governor's quarters. In 1797 he got

Nelson to give sittings to Lemuel Abbott there, after the loss of his arm, and this produced one of the best images of the man (see Chapter Two).

That slightly built figure of Horatio Nelson had of course become a legend quite early in his own lifetime; his no-nonsense attitude had brought him to the attention of authorities at home, abroad his conduct of affairs bore the stamp of an individual, and his exploits in battle were as banners in the breeze to a country hungry for news of victory. This original, daring and not particularly modest character was as acquisitive of honours and fine things as the next man, but he was also generous, in praise and in the giving of presents. He possessed great 'charisma', to use a word currently fashionable; then, they might have said 'great singularity'. As his crusty and usually critical mentor, St Vincent once wrote: 'All agree: there is but one Nelson' and how true that remains.

As a result of his popularity, the objects connected with his name that have survived are many and varied. Men who served with him cherished scraps of his handwriting, that characteristic open scrawl with his left hand, so unlike his earlier conventional, right-handed script. Such odd possessions as he cast aside, or perhaps gave as keepsakes, were likewise treasured. After his death his personal property, ranging from articles of clothing to what can drably be described as 'household effects', was eagerly sought and preserved with a fierce interest, so that his name gave lustre and value to many otherwise humble pieces.

Where such things are sought after, there are all too often those who are ready to supply the demand. Sir Harris Nicolas, who edited Nelson's letters and dispatches, wrote to the newspapers in 1846:

> the manufacture of Nelsonian relics, swords, buckles &c seems so profitable a speculation to certain curiosity dealers, and the folly of persons who can be imposed upon by such things is so glaring, that I should not interfere; but when it is attempted to foist one of these spurious articles on a national institution, it becomes the duty of every Englishman to prevent, if possible, such an imposition.

This was when a reputed Nelson sword, of an unlikely type, was in the market, destined for the growing Nelson collection at Greenwich Hospital. By contrast, as an early example of a personal gift, there is the handsome silver-gilt small-sword with its presentation inscription from Commodore Horatio Nelson to Captain George Cockburn, after the action with a Spanish frigate in 1796, when Nelson had his broad pendant in *La Minerve*, Cockburn's command. Sir George as an Admiral of the Fleet was later painted by Beechey, wearing this sword. Typical of the colourful story of many Nelson relics, it descended to a young naval officer who was killed in a flying accident after the Second World War, having bequeathed it to Greenwich.

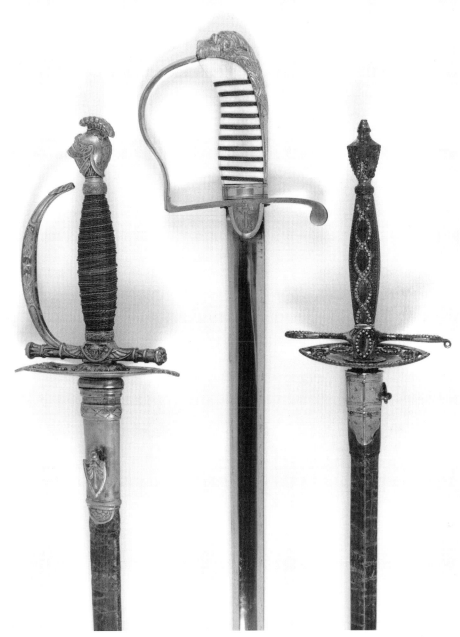

A genuine Nelson sword. The only sword which we can be certain belonged to Nelson, seen here in the centre. On the right is Admiral Villeneuve's sword and on the left the sword of the Spanish Rear Admiral Cisneros – both of which were surrendered at Trafalgar.

The engraving of ownership marks, crests, cyphers and coronets on swords and their scabbards, and on silver, is an easy way of establishing a seemingly good provenance, and time has abated neither the industry of the fakers, nor the gullibility of some collectors. Such enthusiasts, whether private individuals, or public institutions, have to rely on research and a certain amount of luck in order to establish a good line of descent for any supposed relic.

Of considerable interest is a list included in one of the first published biographical notices of Nelson, which appeared in the *Naval Chronicle* monthly magazine Vol. III, April 1800.

Presents to Lord Nelson for his Services in the Mediterranean between October the First 1798 and October the First 1799.

From his King and Country, a peerage of Great Britain and the Gold Medal

From the Parliament of Great Britain for his own life, and two next heirs, per annum £2,000

From the Parliament of Ireland . . . supposed £1,000

From the East India Company £10,000

From the Turkey Company, a piece of plate of great value

From Alexander Davidson [*sic*], a Gold Medal

From the City of London, a sword of great value

From the Grand Signior [of Turkey], a Diamond Aigrette, or Plume of Triumph, valued at £2,000

From the same, a rich pelice [= *pelisse*, a sable cloak], valued at £1,000

From the Grand Signior's Mother, a Rose, set with diamonds, valued at £1,000

From the Emperor of Russia, a Box set with diamonds, and a most elegant letter, value £2,500

From the King of the Two Sicilies, a sword richly ornamented with diamonds and a most elegant and kind letter £5,000

Also the Dukedom of Bronti, with an estate, supposed per annum £3,000

From the King of Sardinia, a Box set with diamonds, and a most elegant letter £1,200

From the Island of Zante a gold-headed Sword and Cane as an acknowledgement that had it not been for the battle of the Nile, they could not have been liberated from French cruelty.

From the City of Palermo, a Gold Box and Chain, brought on a Silver waiter.

Also the Freedom of the City of Palermo which constitutes him a Grandee of Spain.

Nelson's will and its codicils made disposals of his heirlooms to his closest kin and friends. First, in the immediate family, to his reverend brother William, who was created the first Earl Nelson, and to their two sisters, Mrs Susannah Bolton (whose descendants in fact inherited the title), and the younger, Mrs Catherine

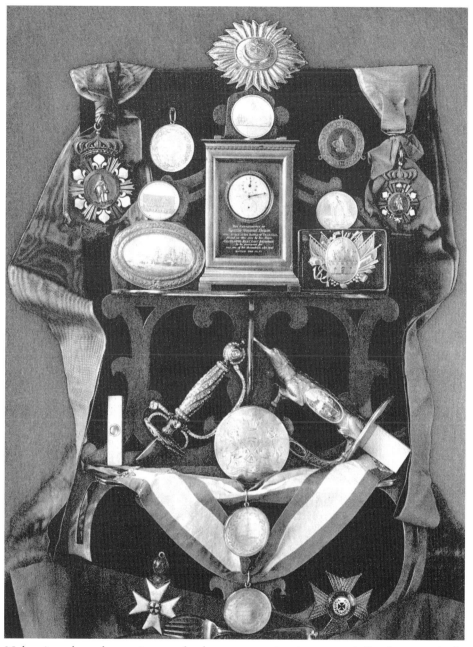

Nelson's orders, decorations and other presentation items specially photographed for General Lord Bridport in the late nineteenth century. They include his gold medals (centre), and the special sword, with a crocodile hilt, given to him by the captains of the Nile (centre right).

Matcham, whose descendants are also still extant. The succession was not, however, exactly straightforward: the male heir to the title – Horatio, Viscount Merton and Trafalgar, the first earl's son – died in 1808 long before his father and the title devolved upon Susannah's son Thomas Bolton who, as second earl, changed his name to Nelson but died in 1835, within months of his uncle. It was Thomas's small son Horatio who became the third earl.

Nelson's Sicilian dukedom of Bronte as well as many relics passed to the first earl's daughter, Lady Charlotte Nelson, who married into the Hood family and became Lady Bridport, Duchess of Bronte. Much of the china services and the silver, as well as the Admiral's orders and decorations, remained in the Bridport family until they were sold at Christie's in 1895. Items that can be traced to this sale (and the catalogue was illustrated) have an impeccable provenance.

In 1904 the third Earl Nelson, now over eighty, wrote an article in *The Windsor Magazine* called significantly, 'Nelson Relics and Relic Hunters', in which he pointed out some of the obvious sources from which, given proof, a genuine relic could emerge. Sitting in the Nelson Room at Trafalgar House, the fine Georgian mansion at Standlynch near Salisbury which had been the grateful nation's gift to the family, surrounded by treasured personal relics, he omitted to mention one interesting point. On the death of the Rt. Hon. and Revd William, the first earl in 1835, and the decease of the second earl in the same year, the entire contents of the mansion had been sold off by Messrs Foster, the London auctioneers, at the Salisbury Assembly Rooms in a four-day sale.

Since the third earl succeeded to the title and an empty mansion at the age of twelve, it was therefore some years before he set about gathering the relics which he quite rightly felt were lacking from his home. He acquired the portrait by J.F. Rigaud when the Locker collection was dispersed in 1849 and it remained at Trafalgar House for a hundred years. Forces which act upon the relic-collecting field are sometimes unexpected; the post-war Labour Government stopped the Nelson family's small annual state pension of £5,000 on the death of the then holder of the title, so forcing the sale of the house and contents, some of which went to Greenwich.

The third earl accepted from well-wishers items which might not have withstood close enquiry into their provenance. An old admiral gave him the couch upon which Nelson supposedly endured the amputation of his arm. On the other hand the Government presented flintlock muskets and pistols with cutlasses, more or less of the pattern in use at Trafalgar. A large octagonal table was made from the wood of HMS *San Josef*, Nelson's Spanish prize at St Vincent which had been taken into the Royal Navy, and presented to the earl when the ship was broken up in 1849.

The third earl also acknowledged the Nelson-Ward family as possessors of true relics, for the Admiral's daughter Horatia, married to the Revd Philip Ward, Vicar

Nelson's pigtail. At his own request his hair was cut off after his death and sent to Lady Hamilton and close friends. Much of it was made into keepsakes – bracelets, rings and lockets – and this is now the only substantial piece remaining.

of Tenterden, had several sons and daughters. Since her mother was Emma, Lady Hamilton, they inherited some closely personal souvenirs. 'Pray let my dear Lady Hamilton have my hair and all other things belonging to me', the dying Nelson said to Captain Hardy in HMS *Victory* towards the end of the battle, and the 'queue', or pigtail, was presented to Greenwich Hospital when Horatia died in 1881 by her children. With each generation, inherited relics become more and more dispersed but any object that is known to have a clear connection with the Nelson-Ward family is likely to be genuine. There are fine groups from that source in both the National Maritime Museum and the Royal Naval Museum. The latter has Horatia's own inscribed silver gilt christening cup, bought by her father at Salter's, the silversmith and cutler in the Strand, during his last weeks in England in 1805.

Then, of course, there was the Admiral's widow Frances, Viscountess Nelson, poor Fanny, who we know kept certain personal items in spite of her unhappy memories of a severed relationship. Certainly she received from the Patriotic Fund at Lloyds one of the taller, silver gilt Trafalgar vases; this now belongs to Her Majesty The Queen and is used as a centre-piece for the dining table on board the Royal Yacht *Britannia*.

The disposals in the will included the 'Chelengk', the 'Grand Signior's' or Sultan of Turkey's, diamond plume, or aigrette, awarded for the Battle of the Nile. This was eventually purchased in 1929 for Greenwich from the Eyre Matcham family with the aid of the National Art Collections Fund, but was stolen in 1951. Forty-three years later a BBC Television programme revealed that one George Chatham,

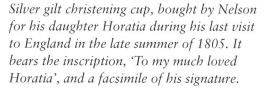

Silver gilt christening cup, bought by Nelson for his daughter Horatia during his last visit to England in the late summer of 1805. It bears the inscription, 'To my much loved Horatia', and a facsimile of his signature.

alias 'Taters' a retired burglar, was the thief, who admitted receiving 'a few thousand' for that priceless piece before it was broken up! The City of London presentation sword, also owned by the Matcham family, is now back in the Guildhall, but the swords from His Sicilian Majesty, and the Nile captains, his 'band of brothers', as well as other items, are presumed to be no longer in existence. It is not, however, a simple story for, by the time the centenary of Trafalgar arrived (and the earl's article was timed for the rising tide of interest and enthusiasm in 1905), all sorts of things had been added to the family collections by gift and purchase.

The will also gave to Alexander Davison, Nelson's agent and man of business, a Turkish scimitar, an elaborate gun and decorated shoulder-slung 'canteen', all Nile presentations. Here is one of those strange transmutations for which an explanation may one day emerge. The scimitar was bequeathed to Greenwich by Davison's son Sir William in 1873 and it is still there. However, it is manifestly made up of oddments. The hilt is a gilt crocodile, perhaps from one of the Nile captains' Egyptian Club celebratory swords (of which there were at least a dozen). The Solingen blade is too small for the ornamental gilt metal scabbard which is engraved with a presentation inscription commemorating Nelson's bequest to Davison, and probably belonged to a foreign cavalry sabre! Were the Davisons robbed of the original Turkish weapon and substituted this oddity? A further puzzling dimension is suggested in the discovery by divers of gold-, enamel- and diamond-studded parts of a scabbard, bearing the star and crescent, on a Surrey river-bed a few years ago. Speculation was renewed but nothing was established.

The 'chelengk', or plume of triumph, presented to Nelson by the Sultan of Turkey and worn by him in his hat. Sadly, it was stolen from the National Maritime Museum in 1951 and the thief has since confessed that it was broken up for its component diamonds.

In trying to map the relic field, so to say, one can look for high points of interest when relics were in demand. In 1805/6, very naturally, even an autograph, let alone a lock of hair, was a prized possession and there were of course commemorative pieces in plenty. These are not to be confused with personal relics, although this is sometimes difficult to judge in view of the fairly indiscriminate use of His Lordship's initials, crest and coat of arms!

The public funeral in January 1806 was probably the greatest spectacle of its sort that London had seen, and printed ephemera, admission tickets to the funeral procession from Whitehall to St Paul's or to the cathedral itself, orders of service, the funeral music, odes 'in memoriam' and so on, were all carefully preserved. Of all the surviving artefacts the figurehead of the funeral car at Greenwich is the prettiest. Ship-shaped, with sable plumes and towering canopy, the car designed by Rudolph Ackerman was kept, until it fell to pieces through woodworm and decay, in the Painted Hall of Greenwich Hospital, where Nelson's body had lain in state. Yarmouth Museum has one of the black velvet festoons, bearing the word 'Trafalgar'. In the Royal Naval Museum is the actual barge used in the waterborne procession from Greenwich, a splendid survival, evidently one of the royal craft.

It was from this date that Greenwich began to emerge as a centre of Nelson pilgrimage, approaching in sanctity the *Victory* herself and his monumental sarcophagus (although made for Cardinal Wolsey) in the crypt of St Paul's.

About the time that the third earl was beginning his new collection, one of the most famous Nelson relics of all came into public ownership – one of the first of the personal relics to do so. The plain, undress uniform of a vice admiral, showing the bullet hole in the left shoulder and the tattered bullion epaulette, came to light in 1845 (see illustration on p. 58). The widow of a city alderman and West India merchant, J.J. Smith, who had known Nelson in Jamaica and had been Lady Hamilton's principal financial helper, possessed certain personal relics, the chief of which were the blood-stained coat and white waistcoat. These had been brought to the distraught Emma Hamilton by Captain Hardy, following Nelson's wishes; a young neighbour at Merton Place, Lionel Goldsmith, recalled later being taken towards the end of 1805 to see her in her bedroom, where the blood-stained coat was lying on the bed beside her.

In view of the carnage on the *Victory*'s deck, and below in the cockpit where the surgeons operated, the blood on the coat was probably not Nelson's, though it most probably was on the waistcoat. The newly created first earl, no admirer of Emma, naturally felt that such a precious relic should be in the possession of the family and a rather unseemly wrangle followed. That a compromise was reached, expressly *lending* the coat to Emma during her life, is indicated by a letter now at Greenwich. Whatever the intended arrangement, in debt she fled to France and probably offered the garment as surety against monies advanced to facilitate her going! A press report said that they 'were transferred under peculiar circumstances' to the alderman. When it became known that such a treasured relic was 'on the market', Sir Harris Nicolas again took a hand; the widow was asking £150, a figure beyond his means and he intended launching a public subscription. However, Albert, the Prince Consort, in a characteristic personal intervention, bought the coat and waistcoat and presented them to the Greenwich Hospital.

The complementary relic, a lead musket-ball, extracted by the *Victory*'s surgeon William Beatty when the body was being examined as the ship arrived at Portsmouth, was enclosed in a crystal locket and presented to him by Captain Hardy. Beatty wore this relic round his neck and bequeathed it to Queen Victoria. It is still in the Royal Collection and is to be loaned to the National Maritime Museum for their new Nelson exhibition in 1995. A fragment of gold wire from the epaulette is still embedded in the softer metal. The surgeon also discovered fragments of the coat, the pad of the epaulette and the yellow silk lining as well as the gold lace and wire from the bullion fringe, and these too were placed in the locket.

There is a third relic associated with the fatal shot: young Midshipman George Augustus Westphal of the *Victory* was in the cockpit with a wound in his head, propped on a convenient bundle, which happened to be the Admiral's coat. When his turn came for treatment it was found that his hair, matted with congealed blood, had become cemented to the bullion of the epaulette which was therefore cut away. He and his family treasured this scrap – he died an admiral in 1875 – and it would be interesting to trace its present whereabouts.

The bullet which killed Nelson. Extracted, together with a piece of epaulette, shirt and uniform coat from Nelson's body during the autopsy, this gruesome relic was worn in a locket by the surgeon, Dr Beatty. He left it to Queen Victoria and it is still in the Royal Collection.

The Crimean War was being fought when the fiftieth anniversary of Trafalgar passed and it was not until 1891 that a major show of naval relics was assembled as part of the great Royal Naval Exhibition, which was held in the Royal Hospital grounds at Chelsea, where the famous Flower Show now takes place. It was a big public-relations exercise, including the latest and most up-to-date technology, achievements of British manufacturing industry, as well as a wide range of historic exhibits. Anybody who had anything of interest seems to have lent it and, as a result, 3,383 maritime relics and *objets d'art* were catalogued. The Queen, the Nobility, the Board of Admiralty, distinguished flag officers, captains and hosts of lesser mortals contributed family treasures, including some which, it must be admitted, had a rather hazy pedigree.

The printed *Official Catalogue* (price one shilling, in paperback), had 536 pages excluding advertisements (which are in fact a most interesting feature). Copies can sometimes be found and are a fascinating and invaluable source of information, not least because the lenders' addresses are given. Paintings, miniatures, letters, snuff-boxes and, above all, relics are listed in all their attributed glory.

Nelson telescopes in formidable array were there, some traceable back to Captain Hardy to whom the Admiral had bequeathed his 'telescopes and sea glasses'. There were others, not perhaps so likely: 'No. 3114 . . . the property of

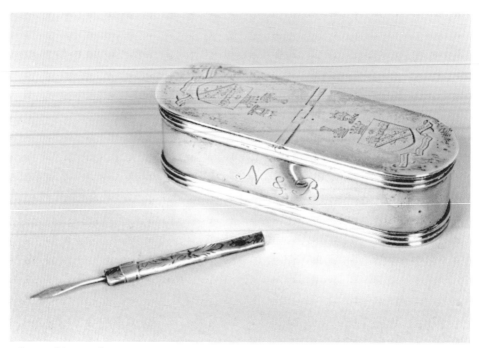

The problems of provenance: two Nelson relics from the Royal Naval Museum's collections. The snuff-box appears genuine – until closer inspection of the coat of arms shows that it belonged to one of the Earls Nelson. The toothpick appears suspicious – until one discovers it was given to the donor's father by one of Nelson's grandsons!

one of the Lieuts of the *Victory* and was lent by him to Lord Nelson as being handy for use by a one-armed man'. Three Nelson desks, one used when a midshipman, were shown, but on what authority was not stated. These were probably the folding writing boxes which appear in some pictures of shipboard life, rather than the fall-front bureau type. The Matcham family exhibited a type of *chaise longue* on which Nelson sometimes slept when at sea; their descendants still have this at their old manor-house, just across from Standlynch. A Mr Arthur Rigg also exhibited a 'Folding Bedstead used by Lord Nelson on board the *Victory*' (No. 3151), together with a large damask dinner napkin embroidered with the Nelson motto '*Palmam Qui Meruit Ferat*', but one suspects that these were available generally over a linen-draper's counter.

Westphal's fragment of gold bullion was there with, from the same owner, a 'Letter weight used by Lord Nelson to steady his paper as he wrote the last codicil to his will, before the Battle.' That item would be interesting to see! 'The pipe said to have been used by . . .', and 'a necklace of 47 intaglios formerly a watch chain belonging to . . .', are bizarre enough to be written off as unlikely, but

'Chronometer worn by Lord Nelson at Trafalgar', lent by General Lord Bridport, has the best of provenances and is now in the National Maritime Museum. But what is one to make of 'No. 3224 A pinchbeck watch which is said to have been used by the late Lord Nelson on more than one occasion but which was not his own'? When the laughter subsides one turns to the catalogue to find that this was lent by Maurice Nelson Girdlestone Esq. and, as the Girdlestones were cousins, it could have a better claim to authenticity than many ('Pray lend me your watch, dear boy, mine has stopped again!'). As late as 1937 a member of the Girdlestone family sold to Greenwich one of Nelson's uniform coats and some of his wine glasses engraved with 'N'. Three left-hand gloves were shown by Lord Bridport and the Nelson-Wards showed the Vice Admiral's rings, seals and a watch he gave his daughter.

For documentary proof of a relic's history, letters, auction and exhibition catalogues and other documents are some help, although descriptions are rarely conclusive unless supported by illustrations. The sale at Trafalgar House in 1835

Muffin dish and egg-cups from one of the splendid china services owned by Nelson. The many pieces from this fine set have long been dispersed in museums and private collections all over the world.

contained only one 'plaister' bust of Nelson, 'a most faithful likeness of that illustrious hero', although there was a lot of fine furniture, including a 'Nelson bed', 11 ft 6 in high and adorned by chintz hangings with glazed linings! Very little of that, if any, would have been known by the Admiral, but the contents of a house in Bond Street 'lately inhabited by Lady Hamilton', passing under the hammer in 1810, included a number of interesting items. She also lived at Richmond and a catalogue of a sale there is said to exist.

Unhappily nothing has been found in print for the disposal of the contents of Merton Place in Surrey, their only real home, 'Paradise Merton' as Nelson named it; although various pieces of furniture are said to have come from thence. There is a contemporary inventory at Greenwich, listing the silver and the different china services, while papers in the British Museum also relate to them. The famous Lloyd's table service, bought by the Admiral with money awarded after the battles of the Nile and Copenhagen, is now scattered world-wide, plates, tureens, sauce-boats and so on (see colour plate 6).

Allowing for confused oral tradition, which over the years often made nonsense out of some perfectly reasonable story, and for the ingenuity which went into the manufacture of some of the more blatant forgeries, it is not really surprising that some very sad little mementoes are to be found. The National Maritime Museum was once offered by an old lady, 'the crown and anchor off Nelson's epaulette', and blood-stained at that! Unhappily, admirals wore only stars on their epaulettes. One wonders, then, whose blood and when?

Piecing together the facts and evidence, against the stories and probabilities connected with a relic, is often difficult but always interesting. Some years ago a walking-stick compendium, an ebony cane which unscrewed to reveal useful accessories such as a spirit-flask, compass &c., was on offer as having belonged to Nelson. It had been in the possession of a British merchant resident in the Balearic island of Minorca, who at the time of the Admiral's activity in the Mediterranean had been helpful in forwarding letters, providing supplies and doubtless on the intelligence front as well. The Admiralty later presented a fine piece of silver in recognition of his services to this Mr Gayner, a Quaker who appears in Nelson's correspondence as 'Friend Gayner', so his part in the story is undoubted. The ebony cane, however, seemed an object of unlikely utility for a one-armed officer and the final opinion was that it had most probably been a gift *from* Nelson to his faithful contact. Whether they kept a stock of useful presents on board the flagship for such eventualities would be interesting to discover, but there was no maker's name or mark on the item to help establish a further history.

To return to the 1891 exhibition we find the Earl of Northesk, whose ancestor was third in command at Trafalgar, showing Nelson's left-handed sword – but it has not proved possible to discover the style of that weapon. However, 'A Green lava Vesuvius snuff-box given by Lord Nelson to Lady Hamilton and by her to the lender's father in Naples' does not seem worth following up and is representative of a considerable section of relicry. 'No. 3098 The Nelson Cenotaph, made of the 84 guineas which were found in Lord Nelson's purse at the time he was mortally wounded. . . . These . . . with other effects, were sent to Alexander Davison, Nelson's intimate friend and agent who had them worked into the design now seen. the handles of the sarcophagus are composed of the stern and prow of the barge . . .', lent by James Griffin Esq. of Southsea, who was a well-known publisher of naval books at Portsea. The later history of this piece is interesting but sad. It was acquired by Lady Llangattock, bequeathed to the Monmouth Museum with her considerable Nelson collection (see below), but stolen some years ago, and predictably not recovered.

The Lords Commissioners of the Admiralty lent, from the Greenwich collections, the embroidered hangings of the Admiral's swinging cot, said to have been worked by Emma and now at Greenwich. The Eyre-Matchams lent a combined knife and fork and also 'No. 3229 Diamond-headed cane presented to Lord Nelson by the inhabitants of the Island of Yauba'. But where on earth is that fabulous island? In fact, it was Zante, so presumably the compositor could not read Mr Matcham's writing! It was one of the Nile gifts, listed above, and the circlet of diamonds is said to have been collected from among the islanders; certainly they are a fine, if mixed, batch.

Many of these relics appeared again in 1905, when a large exhibition in commemoration of Trafalgar was organized for the centenary year at the Royal United Service Institution in Whitehall. In the interim, the Bridports had sold their relics at Christie's in 1895, with HM Government among the purchasers, for the Greenwich collection, but there had been a theft in the Painted Hall in 1900, which sadly cancelled out some items. Nelson's flag-officer's large gold medals, sword hilts and presentation boxes of precious metal disappeared and were never recovered, although the third earl seems to imply that some items had turned up. Mr J.A. Mullens of Battle purchased some of the Nelson silver and presented it to the museum of the Royal United Service Institution, with the gold 'kni-fork' given to the Admiral by Countess Spencer, wife of the First Lord of the Admiralty.

The Admiralty accepted for Greenwich some silver adorned with the appropriate coats of arms, offered by a patriotic and public-spirited gentleman, but it is clear nowadays that its engraving is spurious. A similar group, being then the property of a Mrs F.H.B. Eccles, had been photographed in 1898 for a publication entitled *Nelson and His Times*, the work of Admiral Lord Charles Beresford and the naval writer H.W. Wilson. Stories woven to go with dubious pieces are intriguing, such as the example on page 68: 'The cream jug . . . fell and was trodden on by Nelson "on one occasion when he was worried" on board the *San Josef* (when that ship, captured by him at St Vincent, was serving as his flagship in the Channel fleet); the broken leg was somewhat clumsily mended by

Nelson's sea-going silver chest. Nelson's magnificent silver service, consisting of items ranging from plates and knives and forks to splendid wine coolers (see colour plate 6), was stored in this specially made chest when not in use. The original compartments, with their labels, are still intact.

the ship's armourer, and remains as he left it.' By contrast, a fine silver coffee-pot on a burner, made by Hennell, was part of the Bridport collection; it is now at Greenwich, presented by R. Lionel Foster of the Society for Nautical Research and is undoubtedly the proper thing. Other collectors included Mr Thomas J. Barrett, Chairman of Pears' Soap, who bequeathed a pair of ice-pails from the Copenhagen Lloyd's silver to Greenwich Hospital in 1915 and these are now on display. The Corporation of Lloyd's itself exhibits an impressive Nelson collection, which began with the gift in 1910 by a group of members of some of the Admiral's silver service; this has been augmented over the years and now includes documents and paintings.

Many collections of 'Nelsoniana' have been formed and later dispersed and there still exist others which have unexceptionable relics in them. Descendants of Alexander Davison, now represented by a German noble family, are reputed to have personal items including the shoes he was wearing at the fatal battle.

Enthusiasts meantime have gathered Nelson items, both commemorative and personal, where they could, from auction sales more or less distinguished, from dealers, more or less reputable, and from private individuals whose pieces were more or less authentic! Items from the collection of Miss Pamela Hardy might suggest a link with Captain, afterwards Admiral, Sir Thomas Masterman Hardy, but there was little from that source to inspire confidence. A group of old, but unsubstantiated knick-knacks was purchased and presented to Greenwich by a public-spirited magnate in the later 1930s yet most of this has now joined the ranks of the dubious. A true Hardy connection is of course a sound one, and there are family collections which still contain authentic relics. One of his daughters married Sir John Murray MacGregor of MacGregor, and their family lent very interesting items to Chelsea in 1891.

A Sotheby's auction in November 1923 included Nelson's dressing-table – later the property of the actress Ellen Terry, but this has not been traced. Suitable for the Admiral's dining-cabin, a fine mahogany extending table, of Gillow's patent, with its sideboard and cellarette, was sold at Christie's in June 1931. It had been acquired by Rear-Admiral Henry Warre (a captain of 1790) and passed into the possession of Mr John Hatt Noble of the English factory in Oporto, Portugal, in 1826. The *Victory* limped into Gibraltar after Trafalgar and it is known that the furniture was landed while the flagship was refitted, so its survival on the peninsula is an acceptable provenance and the furniture is now housed in the Royal Naval Museum.

The well-known blue and gold Worcester porcelain service, a large one, each piece decorated by Pennington *en grisaille* with a female figure of Hope, with her 'attribute', an anchor, posed in a variety of bewitching positions, has been exhibited, and also sold, as having been variously presented to Nelson by 'the Women of Britain', bequeathed by him to William IV and later the property of the Earl of Ferrol. For the design of this service moreover, it is said that Lady Hamilton was the model; she was after all celebrated for her classical poses. It was in fact ordered from the Worcester factory during a visit by the King (when Duke of Clarence), and pieces of it are scattered world-wide, although there was no Nelson connection.

Lady Llangattock, Georgiana Shelley Rolls, mother of Charles who in partnership with Henry Royce produced that automobile of assured immortality, was a formidable Nelson enthusiast. Her collection was bequeathed to the town of Monmouth which was near her husband's family seat and which already boasted a Nelson connection from the Admiral's visit with the Hamiltons in 1802. The Monmouth collection has letters, silver, china, all of first-class authenticity, but also naval swords engraved with 'HN' and crests, of a pattern not introduced until a quarter of a century after Trafalgar! However, the museum has a genuine Nelson sword, the only one to which it is possible to give credence, and of a type favoured by naval officers in the years before the Admiralty's first regulation pattern, which incidentally was introduced in the summer of 1805. Somewhat shorter than usual, suitable for left-handed draw, it is thought to have come from the same source as the Trafalgar coat. That the Admiral possessed one of these swords, with the so-called 'oval side-ring hilt', is substantiated by an annotated sketch on the back of a surviving invoice from his gold lacemakers Barrett, Corney & Corney, who also supplied him with the stars for his four orders of knighthood in September 1805.

Nelson's glass eye is also at Monmouth, enclosed in a sort of egg-cup! As everyone knows, he lost the sight of his right eye, but not the optic itself.

However, that particular curiosity turns out to be an important anatomical model of the human eye, of great interest in its own right, which has been exhibited at international optical conventions.

Furthermore, the black patch that Nelson never wore – at least, not when sitting for his portrait – is another popular misconception perhaps, but there is at Greenwich, among the relics obtained from Lord Bridport, a single black silk patch lined with green silk. So one cannot be absolutely sure that Nelson was never seen to wear one! In fact a letter exists from Horatio to Emma in January 1801 about the trouble he was having with his eyes, and saying that his doctor had prescribed green *shades*, and asking her to be so kind as to make him one or two. We know from the A.W. Devis portrait of 1805 that he did wear such a shade and indeed one has survived, sewn into the lining of the cocked hat supplied to His Lordship by the old firm of Locks, hatters of St James's Street. This is on view with the life-sized effigy of him by Catherine Andras, wax-modeller to the Crown, in the Undercroft Museum at Westminster Abbey. The figure is clothed in items of uniform which may be the Admiral's own garments, but the uniform coat itself is an incomplete dummy.

Among the many who have been fired with admiration for the immortal naval hero was Sir Henry Sutcliffe-Smith, a wealthy master-dyer, who had a very varied assemblage which was deposited on loan at Greenwich but later dispersed. It included porcelain and a lot of rather distant commemorative pieces, ranging from long-case clocks with *The Death of Nelson* on the dial, to enamel patch-boxes inscribed with pathetic mottoes and mourning scenes. There were medals too, mainly commemorative, such as the Nelson Testimonial medal mentioned in Chapter Four. Mr J.H. Walter of Drayton Manor, Norwich, of the family who owned *The Times* also made a very interesting Nelson collection which included books, many of them uncommon, and this was also lent to Greenwich in 1937, and purchased from his heirs some twenty-five years later.

While these private collections also encompassed rare commemorative material, including things of an ephemeral nature, each contained authentic pieces of personal interest. However, almost all the keen and acquisitive enthusiasts seem to have fallen victim to their own wishful thinking or credulity, or occasionally to unsubstantiated claims or skilful faking!

The restoration of HMS *Victory*, which must be the largest of all the Nelson relics, was an expensive business even in the inter-war years. It was aided by the Council of the Society for Nautical Research, the Honorary Secretary of which was Geoffrey Callender MA, teacher of History at the naval cadet colleges of Osborne and Dartmouth, and then Professor at the Royal Naval College, Greenwich. Author of not only a life of Nelson but also a history of the *Victory*, Callender was, like so many, a somewhat complaisant Nelson enthusiast, although he was just the man to arrange an exhibition of relics to raise money for the 'Save the Victory Fund'. This was the big public appeal to help finance the restoration of the ship in her permanent dry-dock. The catalogue of the show, which was held in 1928 at Spink & Sons in King Street, St James's, includes much material from the Nelson-Ward collection, some of which was later given to the National Maritime Museum, of which Callender, sixty years ago, became the first director. In passing, it is significant that some of this material was facsimile; Horatia's descendants vied with each other over relics and if one branch had the original material, another branch would have it copied so as not to be left out of the picture!

The Greenwich Hospital Collection, paintings, Nelson relics and all, had become the nucleus of the new museum in 1934. With the 'Save the Victory Fund', one has to say that behind its successful story (it still functions) is the mighty generosity of the Scottish shipowner Sir James Caird, Bt., of Glenfarquhar, who was a benefactor dedicated to the permanent illustration of Britain's sea history, naval and mercantile, in a truly national collection. A founder Trustee of the National Maritime Museum, he was fortunately at hand when the Nelson family had to sell Trafalgar House with most of the collection and was able to secure for Greenwich some immensely important material, including family portraits. This

Personal relics. The Royal Naval Museum's collections include some of the most intimate Nelson relics of all. They include his watch and the locket of Emma – containing a lock of her lovely auburn hair – which he habitually wore.

was put on view in 1948 with a small illustrated catalogue giving some details of the third earl's acquisitions.

In more recent times devoted tribute must of course be paid to Mrs John McCarthy – Lily Lambert McCarthy, Commander of the Most Excellent Order of the British Empire, an American citizen and Nelson collector extraordinary. Her benefactions have certainly enriched Greenwich, but it is in the Royal Naval Museum at Portsmouth that an extensive gallery containing many marvellous items of commemorative ware gathered by her over many years is named in her honour. Here, too, is displayed the museum's own excellent collection of Nelson relics. At its core is a large group of Nelson-Ward material featuring some of the most personal and intimate relics in existence, such as the locket, containing Emma's portrait and hair, that Nelson wore round his neck and the one she had made after his death to house a lock of his hair and inscribed with the words from the last codicil to his will, so resolutely ignored by his country. Over the years the museum has been able to add items to its collection from time to time, such as the prayer-book given to Nelson by Captain William Locker and later presented by him to Emma Hamilton.

A final note on a similar theme is provided by *The Naval Magazine or Maritime Miscellany* (Volume I, 1799) under the heading, 'Lord Nelson's Cabin Companion – An authentic anecdote':

> . . . the noble Admiral, accompanied by his Lady, went to the shop of Messrs Rivingtons in St Paul's Church-yard to purchase a handsome Family Bible. As he was a stranger to the booksellers and presented a bill in payment, one of the Messrs Rivingtons requested the signature of his name, but on being informed that it was Nelson instantly apologised . . . and could not refrain from expressions of his happiness in seeing such a religious tendency in our great naval commanders. 'Mr Rivington,' replied the good and gallant Admiral, laying his hand on the Bible, 'I never sail without having this as my Companion in my Cabin'.

Sources

1. Books and Articles
Lord Charles Beresford and H.W. Wilson, *Nelson and His Times* (1898).
Warren Dawson, *The Nelson Collection at Lloyd's* (1932).
Edward Fraser, *Greenwich Hospital and the RUS Museum* (1911).
John Knox Laughton, *The Nelson Memorial* (1896).
W.E. May and P.G.W. Annis, *Swords for Sea Service* (1970).
Horatio, Earl Nelson, 'Nelson Relics and Relic Hunters', *The Windsor Magazine* (1904).

2. Catalogues
British Museum, *Guide to the Manuscripts, Printed Books, Prints and Medals Exhibited on the occasion of The Nelson Centenary 1905.*

Christie Manson and Woods, *Relics of Lord Nelson, the property of General Lord Bridport, London 12 July 1895*.

National Maritime Museum, *Exhibition of Nelson Relics from Trafalgar House, 1948*.

Royal Naval Exhibition, 1891, *Official Catalogue and Guide*.

Royal United Service Institution, *Catalogue of the Exhibition of Nelson Relics In Commemoration of the Centenary of the Battle of Trafalgar, 1905*.

Spink & Sons, *Exhibition of Nelson Relics in aid of the 'Save the Victory Fund'* (with a foreword by Sir Geoffrey Callender).

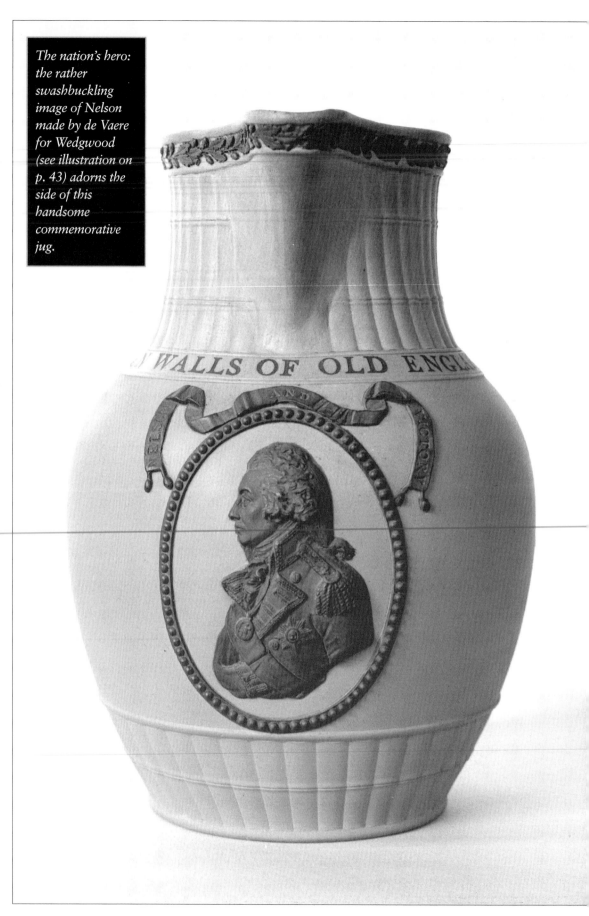

The nation's hero: the rather swashbuckling image of Nelson made by de Vaere for Wedgwood (see illustration on p. 43) adorns the side of this handsome commemorative jug.

CHAPTER IV

Nelson Commemorated
by John May

Second only to Queen Victoria, and perhaps not in the final count even second to her, Nelson was the most commemorated person in history. And this in a career that, for commemorative purposes, was concentrated into just seven years: 1798 to 1805.

He had caught the public attention a year before of course, as a result of his exploits at the Battle of St Vincent. But, so far as is currently known (a caveat most necessary when dealing with commemoratives) there was nothing made to mark his part in that battle. Admiral Sir John Jervis, or Lord St Vincent as he became, did not escape the attention of the commemorators. His victory was celebrated both by the potters and by the makers of enamel boxes. But for the newly promoted, and knighted, Rear-Admiral Sir Horatio Nelson, the commemorative moment had not yet come.

He did not, however, have long to wait. His astonishing and overwhelming success at the Nile unleashed a flood of porcelain, pottery, enamels, glass-pictures, fans and favours; so numerous and so varied that it would be impossible to list every sort and kind of item that was dreamed up to celebrate his victory. He was clearly the nation's hero.

From the Nile he went on to Naples and Emma (no mention of her in the Nelson commemorative saga); to his activities in coastal defence (no mention of these either); to the Peace of Amiens in 1801, that brief and unsatisfactory pause in the war, where he does figure as Nelson the Peacemaker; to the resumption of the war and so, of course, to 1805, to Trafalgar and to the great deluge of celebratory mourning items that lauded the great victory and so regretted his death.

What of Copenhagen? A considerable victory, certainly, but not a popular one, either with the government or with the people. After it, Nelson was forced to write bitterly to the Lord Mayor of London complaining about the City's failure to recognize the victory and the King, never, admittedly, much of a Nelson fan after his liaison with Emma became known, refused to have an official medal struck to mark the occasion. There was a similar dearth of commemoratives. There are records of a watch and just one glass-picture and that, it would seem, is all.

Naturally the adulation, and its Sancho Panza, the commemorative, did not stop with Nelson's death, and here he certainly scores over Victoria. As Colin White explains in Chapter One, his fame, and the public enthusiasm for him and his great deeds, surged and ebbed through the rest of the nineteenth century and on through the twentieth. And, in each case, the commemorative material surged and ebbed in sympathy.

There was a small surge in 1814 when, as everyone supposed, the great war had ended – until Napoleon returned to prove them wrong. A long ebb followed during the time of political riots and rapture leading up to the Catholic Emancipation Bill and the great Franchise Reforms of 1832 and the Abolition of the Corn Laws in 1845. Then the surge began again in the middle of the century with the pride in Britain and the British engendered by the Great Exhibition, the final completion of Trafalgar Square and by the benign influence of Prince Albert, who personally bought Nelson's blood-stained Trafalgar coat and presented it to the nation for display in Greenwich Hospital (on show today in the National Maritime Museum). Another ebb followed in the gloom following Albert's death and then began a long, sustained surge through the closing years of the nineteenth century, spurred on by the activities of the Navy League, and reaching a pinnacle of enthusiasm in the 1905 centennial. Two world wars brought other heroes: how many small boys wore their caps at that rakish Beatty angle; how many Churchillian V fingers were raised to salute Hitler in 1939 to 1945.

Wartime austerity and restriction limited the commemorative trade severely, although there were Victory V lozenges, each one bearing stamped on it a fine impression of the great ship. Since 1945, however, where we have seen Britain decline and surge again ahead; where we have suffered the regrets of nostalgia and the resurgence of pride in our greatness, the little Admiral has grown and grown in public knowledge and public acclaim. And, aided by mass production and vastly improved communications, the commemorators have redoubled their efforts. So much so that the gift shops in the National Maritime Museum and the Royal Naval Museum probably sell, in one year, more items connected with Nelson than were made to celebrate his achievements in his entire lifetime.

The scope of commemoratives was, and is, wide and ingenious. The simplest way through the maze of collecting possibilities is, perhaps, to examine the various forms, one by one.

Without doubt the most popular, for Nelson as for all other heroes (and villains), was the ceramic. And of all the Nelson ceramics, the grandest and most spectacular was a porcelain mug made to mark his victory at the Nile. It was

Modern Nelsonia: Nelson is still a best-seller – even when he is produced as an extremely inaccurate glass painting or fridge magnet!

manufactured at the Derby Porcelain Works and decorated after the style of Alexander Davison's Nile medallion. Production of these mugs must have been limited. They are, today, rare. But there was also a plethora of cheaper pottery to mark the Nile, the bulk of which was cream-coloured earthenware, or 'creamware', printed with various designs, almost all including a portrait of the hero and many including plans of the battle and a variety of patriotic verses, ranging from the bravura to the banal. All, with one exception, refer to the Admiral as Lord Nelson, in recognition of the peerage he had been granted as a reward for his victory. There is just one print, of which there is only one known example, which refers to him as Sir Horatio. It is tempting to postulate that this might have been a piece commemorating St Vincent, but this would probably be stretching an overlong commemorative bow. News travelled slowly in those days; rumour often presaged news. Perhaps some potter, striving to be first off the mark to honour the hero, did not wait long enough to hear he had been ennobled – a supposition that is supported by the fact that other pieces of pot, bearing an identical print, are captioned 'Lord Nelson'.

Printing was not the only way the potters decorated their wares. They also produced a number of excellent moulded jugs, many decorated in Pratt colours. Prattware, as it is usually called, employed a limited number of high temperature underglaze colours, as opposed to the overglaze enamelling that was becoming

An eighteenth-century 'joke': as the contents of this Nelson commemorative mug are drained, a frog appears to surprise the drinker.

more and more popular. It is very distinctive and very decorative but does not permit of any great reality. Many of these jugs have Nelson on one side and Captain Berry, who commanded his flagship HMS *Vanguard* at the Nile, on the other. Some are of the period. Many are not but were made, as were similar jugs and mugs combining Nelson and Hardy, late into the Victorian years.

A considerable amount, indeed the bulk, of this sort of ceramic ware was made in Staffordshire, but some creamware can be found that originates from the factories fringing the Tyne, in Newcastle and Sunderland. These, if mugs, often have frogs inside them: a very unamusing eighteenth-century joker who was meant to surprise the drinker as his head rose slowly through the murky ale. More likely, it produced the sort of inner or outward groan accorded to notably poor jokes today.

Perhaps the ultimate accolade of ceramic fame came when Josiah Wedgwood commissioned John de Vaere to model the Admiral in wax; from which likeness his firm then produced an extremely handsome jasperware portrait medallion. But once again a warning: Wedgwood continued to produce Nelson portraits well into the nineteenth and indeed the twentieth centuries, so by no means all the examples available today are contemporary.

For Copenhagen the potters were, in common with almost all of the other commemorators, notable for their total lack of production. On the other hand the Peace of Amiens did produce one interesting Nelson ceramic: a printed transfer on

A rare and unusual 'Portobello' jug commemorating Trafalgar. It bears a yellow transfer portrait of Nelson on a dark brown background.

creamware where, paired with Lord Cornwallis, he is hailed as our 'old friend' together with the invocation, 'success to the peacemakers'. Even here, as so often with the commemorators, it was a case of employing not just an old friend but an old transfer as well, for the print of Nelson that hails the peace had done prior duty in hailing him as 'The Hero of the Nile' in 1798.

Then, of course, there came Trafalgar. A tidal wave of mourning swept the country and was commemorated in an immense diversity of pottery. Worth singling out for comment are, perhaps, the pieces made in the north-east which, interestingly, often mirror the glass-picture prints in their content (see below). Then there are the pieces made in Staffordshire which look, at first glance, handpainted but which were, in fact, made by a careful and clever use of guide prints decorated with overglaze. Finally, there is the strange so-called Portobello ware with its yellow transfer on a brown background glaze, which is particularly notable for being the only print to show Nelson wearing an eyepatch over his supposedly missing blind eye. This, as Richard Walker has highlighted in Chapter Two, he never did, contenting himself instead with the sort of shade sported by early Hollywood newspaper editors as they shouted instructions to 'hold the front page!'

Trafalgar Prattware pieces were produced in considerable number. Some feature Nelson and Hardy (buyer beware!), others show HMS *Victory* and many are decorated with a symbol of the hero's various victories, involving a pyramid, a castle, guns and flags and the word 'Trafalgar'. The number of variants of transfer that mark the great event has never been accurately recorded. There must be at

Death of Nelson

A typical Staffordshire group showing Nelson dying in the arms of two of his officers – resplendent in pink breeches!

least fifty that have survived and, such was the intensity of the funereal trade in 1805/6, probably twice that number were actually produced.

Once Nelson was dead, of course, attention switched to more lively heroes. But the Peace of Paris in 1814 inspired a number of linked Nelson/Wellington pieces, notably some extremely fine bisque figures. And the invention of 'parian', the Victorian potters' solution to the problem of how to make marble on a mass-produced basis, gave birth to a number of extremely well-modelled busts of the Admiral. The best, undoubtedly, was made in 1853 by the firm of J. Pitts and Son, modelled under the direction of Admiral Sir William Parker KCB and based on the painting by Wichelo, which he had in his possession. This same era also produced the Staffordshire figure. In his book *Naval Ceramics*, the late Rear-Admiral Pugh listed fifteen variants showing Nelson or the death of Nelson. All are, to my eye, hideous. But commemoratives are, as are most things, a matter of taste. No collector should let a dealer dictate on so personal a matter.

The 1905 centenary brought some excellent ware by Royal Doulton and a most beautifully decorated 'Loving Cup' by Copeland. Since then, there have been some horrors. Look in any gift shop and even, sad to say, in some museum shops and you will find some truly monstrous images of the hero. To misquote Captain Suckling: 'What has poor Horace done that he above all the rest should be sent to rough it out?' What indeed? But that is the price of fame. And it is also a perhaps regrettable, but none the less very real, part of the Nelson Legend.

After ceramics, glass-pictures are probably the most prolific forms of commemorative. In the most complete and well-documented collection of these

Copeland 'Loving Cup' produced to commemorate the Centenary of Trafalgar in 1905. It is beautifully decorated with enamelled pictures, including a portrait of Nelson and the flags of his famous signal.

items, in private hands, there are thirty-five variants of the death of Nelson and no less than four different versions of the funeral car and three of the barge. There are also, and these are exceptionally rare, representations of the battles of Trafalgar – and of Copenhagen.

Glass-pictures are a unique and most decorative art form. To produce them, a mezzotint was pulled up on particularly soluble paper, soaked in water and then applied to the back of a sheet of crown glass, using as an adherent a mastic varnish-cum-adhesive called Venice Turpentine. The paper was then rubbed away, which left the black lines of the print, like a transfer on the glass. The colours were then painted in, last colour first, with a coat of varnish for each colour. The result is a picture that positively glows (see colour plate 7).

These glass-pictures or, as they are more properly called, 'transfer engravings on glass', were, if contemporary instruction books are to be believed, originally intended to be made by talented amateurs. Early in the eighteenth century, however, the technique was taken over by the professional print-makers and so successfully that by the middle of the century they had become a separate art form in their own right. At the time of Trafalgar the firms most famous for their production were Messrs Walker of Fox & Knott Court, Messrs Stampa, Messrs Baraschina, Messrs Patriarcha and Messrs Hinton. They made their glass-pictures in two regular sizes: the larger approximately 10 in by 14 in and the smaller about half that size. All of these firms were London print-makers and print-sellers; all operating within the purlieus of St Paul's and Fleet Street. Judging by the large number that have survived, these glass-pictures must have been immensely popular at the time. They must have also been, limited as they were by their fragility, an almost exclusively Metropolitan fancy. They can, and do, form an entirely separate and wholly attractive Nelson commemorative collection. (Occasionally, the original mezzotints can be found untransformed. They are usually coloured but this was almost certainly done well post-Trafalgar.)

Second to ceramics, one of the biggest decorative industries in Britain in the late eighteenth and early nineteenth centuries were the trades of japanning and enamelling. There are a number of variants of small japanned boxes made to mark Nelson's victories and death, but far and away the greatest production from this manufacturing area – the towns of Birmingham, Wolverhampton and Bilston (the last giving its name to the entire art form) – was enamelling. And far and away the greatest part of this was enamelling on so-called snuff- or patch-boxes. In truth, it is doubtful that these were ever used for snuff or for patches. They would have been too impractical compared to other materials. Most were probably bought as 'toys' and displayed, as many are today, in vitrines and cabinets in withdrawing rooms and salons. The boxes, very broadly, come in two sizes. Their body colours vary widely, although navy blue was not unnaturally a favourite, particularly for naval boxes. Their tops were most often white and decorated either with freestyle painting, or with transfers embellished with colours, and featured scenes and verses and allegoric devices marking the careers and achievements of Britain's admirals and generals.

Since the vogue for them came into force in the 1780s, the first naval commemorative boxes feature Admirals Rodney and Hood (for their victory in 1782 over the French fleet at the Battle of the Saintes). By the time warfare was resumed against the revolting French in 1793, commemorative enamel boxes had clearly, judging again by the number that have survived, become extremely popular. One finds His Royal Highness the Duke of York (he of the ten thousand men), Sir Arthur Wellesley (a.k.a. the Duke of Wellington), and, of course, the naval heroes: first Howe and his Glorious First of June, then St Vincent, then Duncan, then Nelson.

There are at least five variants marking the Battle of the Nile, the best of which show, in most graphic form, the luckless French flagship *L'Orient* blowing up; there are nineteen directly marking the Battle of Trafalgar and at least twenty-eight more featuring Nelson and/or the *Victory*, all, presumably, made at this sad time. Their designs are varied, ingenious, patriotic, and totally charming. They range from the outright sentimental to the slightly macabre (witness a one-legged sailor with the rhyme: 'A Leg & Arm his Loss would have wained/If Nelson's life had been retained'); to the humorously diverting (a rather more entire sailor roistering with glass in hand); to portrayals of the famous signal (this last in a number of variants showing the British fleet splitting the French and Spanish line, while the caption reminds us that 'England Expects') (see colour plate 8).

Like glass-pictures, these boxes can either be part of a general Nelson commemorative collection or be collected on their own. For this latter purpose they are, perhaps, the ideal collectible: small, not too expensive, very varied in design and colour, capable of an absolute collecting discipline. There are excellent collections in both the leading museums, but the very best collection is in private hands in London. It has taken its owner some fifteen years to assemble and it speaks much for his dedication that he should, in times not always ideal for collecting, have mustered such a comprehensive selection.

Boxes, however, were not the end of the enamellers' art. They also produced most decorative roundels to be set as 'cloak' or 'sword' knobs. There are two Nelsonic variants of these, one featuring The Hero, the other his flagship at the Nile. These roundels, by the way, are all too often catalogued as curtain ties or door handles. They are neither. They were fitted with a screw attachment and were, demonstrably, screwed into the walls of suitable rooms for visitors to use as cloak, coat, or sword hangers. No contemporary print has yet been found that shows them in a military or naval setting. But in addition to featuring the aggressive heroes of their day, such roundels were also decorated with actors and actresses. And there are prints of late eighteenth-century theatre 'green-rooms' in which these pegs are clearly shown being used for the purpose for which they were intended.

The enamellers also produced watch faces. Judging by the number of contemporary watch faces that remain, featuring events like naval battles, balloon ascents etc., it may well have been the habit of the fashionable to change their watch face to suit the latest fad, whether this was a peaceful ascent or a great and bloody victory. Certainly, not every face is contemporary to the watch it adorns, since many of the silver cases were hallmarked years before the event shown on the dial. Unsurprisingly, Nelson features on watches marking both the Nile and Trafalgar. There was even a watch featuring Copenhagen, but only a single example of it is known.

Just as these products of the enamellers' art often have a jewel-like quality, so there was an interesting amount of actual commemorative jewellery made to mark Nelson's life and career (see colour plate 9). Notable among these designs are gold anchors, about 2 in long, shaped like the typical naval 'fouled' anchor and engraved on the shank with the details of Trafalgar. Similar anchors can be found

*Enamelled roundels and watch. The roundels commemorate the Battle of the Nile,
with a picture of Nelson's flagship HMS* Vanguard *and his portrait based on the
engraving by Daniel Orme (see illustration on p. 37).*

marking the first naval battle of the Anglo/French war, the Glorious First of June. It is tempting to think that, in all probability, some fashionable London jeweller or goldsmith fabricated them for all the five great naval actions of the era. These anchors, usually worn today as pendants, were originally intended to be worn on the coat, attached to, and the central feature of, a patriotic 'favour'.

However, the most available precious commemorative is certainly a ring. Nelson rings fall into two broad categories: mourning and commemorative. The best made and best recorded mourning rings were the family rings issued by Nelson's executors after his death. Fifty-eight of these were made by John Salter, a silversmith in the Strand much patronized by Nelson and from whom he bought a number of personal items, including Horatia's silver gilt christening cup now displayed in the Royal Naval Museum.

A few of the rings, a very few, went to the late Admiral's famous contemporaries, notably to Captain Hardy who carried the Banner of Emblems at the State Funeral and who, presumably, wore the ring to that sad event. But the majority were genuine 'family' rings and were distributed to a variety of relations in the Matcham and Girdlestone families. In 1915 an excellent article was published dealing with the making of these rings and listing their recipients, and I have in the past decade attempted to track down their current locations, but with little success. So far I have managed to identify only fourteen of the fifty-eight. And I am not at all sure that one at least of these fourteen may not be the same one surfacing twice! However, Dr Goulby, in a most interesting contribution to the *Genealogists' Magazine* in June 1990, lists not only the eleven now in museum collections, but also has done better than I in identifying thirteen in private hands.

Strictly speaking, these rings are not commemoratives at all, since they were not made for general sale and were available only to a selected band of owners. They fall, perhaps, into the category of personal memorabilia, a rather more couth and cultured equivalent of a film star's revealing blouse or a rock star's battered guitar.

Of real commemorative rings there are a number of designs in gold and enamel. One of these, a coronet on a pale blue background, was sold at Christie's in 1985, when the famous Bullock collection of Nelson memorabilia came under the hammer. Interestingly, some years later another exactly similar example was found which had been mounted as a brooch. At first blush it looked like a later adaptation. But closer scrutiny, and the highly skilled views of the relevant department of the British Museum, suggested that it was still in its original form. It is unlikely to be unique. It would seem, therefore, that commemorative jewellery may well have been produced and marketed in more than one form. A surprising omission, however, are any rings holding miniatures of Nelson. Admittedly, miniatures as ring bezels had very much gone out of favour by the end of the eighteenth century, having been replaced by the typical enamelled bezel and/or the enamelled inscribed hoop; but it is extraordinary that at least one example has not survived with a design throwback to the earlier days of the eighteenth century.

In addition to rings, brooches, *et al*, there are also many Nelson seals. These again range from personal relics of the Admiral (for details of the variety of devices he used see Chapter Seven), to the more popular seals that were readily available from the jewellers of London. Some have stones cut with an impression of The Hero himself, some carry his most famous message. The stones range from the rather mundane bloodstone to, perhaps most decorative of all, a brilliant topaz. Most of these seals are of the 'fob' variety, worn on watchchains. Some, however, are for desks or escritoires. All are infuriatingly hard to find. Most seals, in most shops, stalls, and auction sales, are displayed standing on their sealing faces. One either has to have immense patience and laudable diligence, or be the beneficiary of unusually efficient cataloguing, to spot a Nelson seal in the welter of less important examples.

There is a further category of Nelson jewellery which can also be a miniature collecting field on its own: portrait medallions made by the famous firm of James & William Tassie. James Tassie was a Scot who came south to London to seek fame and fortune. He set up a workshop in Leicester Square for the production of glass-paste imitation jewels. At first he concentrated on the production of 'jewels in the antique style', but in the last quarter of the eighteenth century he began to manufacture, in his unique Tassie Paste, exquisite miniatures of the famous. These were set into a variety of pieces of jewellery and varied from elaborate (and presumably extremely expensive) to comparatively simple settings. Some are signed, usually 'Tassie F.', all are magnificent. Most, if not all, of the Nelson profiles must date from the era of James's nephew William Tassie, since James died in 1799. Not that either Tassie necessarily modelled the original wax himself. Both James and William employed the leading modellers of their day and James modelled not only for himself but also for Wedgwood.

From jewellery, it is a natural jump to silver and to gold. Of the latter, there are few, if any, 'popular' Nelson items. Gold was the material used for presentation pieces, such as the exquisite enamelled Freedom Boxes, the tributes presented by Lloyd's of London, or other generous civic bodies, the swords, the medals and the decorations. These all fall into the category of personal memorabilia.

Silver is another story. Here, too, there are a number of presentation pieces among the personal memorabilia, including some engraved pieces, the most famous of which are, of course, the two services bought by Nelson from Rundell Bridge and Rundell with the monies voted to him by the Lloyd's Patriotic Fund after the battles of the Nile and Copenhagen. Some engraving, however, is less authentic and must be regarded with judicious suspicion. Avoid particularly any piece that incorporates with Nelson's armorials a fouled anchor. Several highly suspect items of silver and plate carrying this motif surfaced in the early 1990s.

There are also a number of silver commemoratives. There is silver jewellery probably originally made, like the gold anchors, to be the central feature of favours. There are also a variety of most beautiful Nelson 'vinaigrettes'.

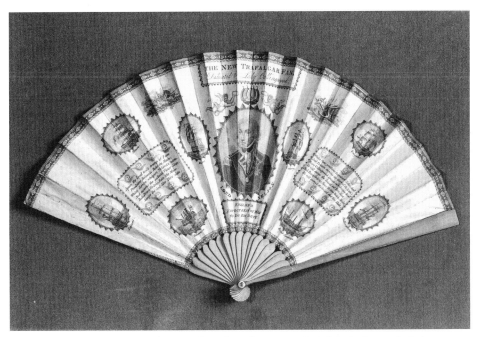

The Funeral Fan: a paper fan produced at the time of Nelson's funeral. It bears views of some of the Trafalgar ships, some specially composed verses for 'Rule Britannia' and a portrait of Nelson based on Orme's engraving (see illustration on p. 37)

Whether these were ever used for their ostensible purpose of guarding the nose against the foulness of the city streets, and much of the city's population, is doubtful. It is fairly certain that, like the enamel boxes, they were more usually displayed as 'toys' in the homes of the rich and commemoratively cultured. Perhaps the most common of these (although in this context 'common' is a singularly inappropriate word) are vinaigrettes made by Matthew Linwood and hallmarked London 1806. They show the hero on the front and have as their grill a representation of his most famous ship. But Linwood himself made two other designs and there are at least two other manufacturers who are known to have produced them.

Turning to a completely different medium, there is a whole range of exquisite Nelson fans. Most of these are paper leafed, printed, and show scenes of his battles, portraits of himself, lists of his ships. There are a variety for the Battle of the Nile and a further selection for Trafalgar. Again, none is known marking Copenhagen. Fans are, of course, not unique to Nelson. Like so many other facets of the Nelson industry, they are part of the much wider commemorative scene of the eighteenth and early nineteenth centuries. There are commemorative fans for many battles and many heroes. There are fans for kings and queens and, like poor unlovely Queen Caroline, for queens who were hardly done by and hardly there. There were fans for trials, such as the scandalous and long-drawn-out ordeal of Warren Hastings, and fans for balloon ascents, actors and actresses, achievements and scandals. Many, incidentally, have beautifully pierced ivory sticks. Most were printed in London and, presumably, were sold in those prints shops around St Paul's churchyard that we have already encountered when dealing with the glass-pictures.

There were also printed textiles. Most of these were curtain hangings with repeat printed patterns. These were plate printed and most often produced in red and black in a variety of designs, the most dramatic of which shows scenes from Nelson's funeral. Some of them were large snuff handkerchiefs bearing complete scenes of battles and pictures of the hero.

There were embroidered pictures. One bought the background 'canvas', often already printed with the face and hands of the subject, and then stitched over the rest of the design to make a firescreen, or a cushion, or possibly even a picture for the wall of a boudoir. Embroidery was a popular pastime for the fashionable and fairly fashionable ladies of the period as Miss Austen often reminds us. Nelson, of course, featured in quite a few of these designs but all are limited to his death, rather than his battles. He also appears on samplers, another form of popular stitching, though probably for the rather younger seamstress. There are various Nelson samplers and again, most are dated 1806 and regret his death, although some are known dating from as long after the event as 1810.

A home-made 'sampler' commemorating Nelson's death with a simple tomb underneath a willow branch (a sign of mourning).

One of the most beautiful of all commemorative pieces: an exquisite Nautilus shell intricately engraved with pictures of Britannia, St George, Victory and the Royal Coat of Arms – all in honour of Nelson and his victories.

Another form of 'home industry' much offered in the sale-rooms and elsewhere nowadays are scrimshaws; those supposed products of the sailor in his leisure hours. I may well be wrong but I have never seen a Nelson scrimshaw which I believed to be 'period'. Undoubtedly there are some perfectly genuine ones that were made in the mid-nineteenth century (though even these were most likely made in small factories ashore, rather than in the crowded and boisterous confines of a mess at sea), but far and away the greater proportion of them were made in this century. Unless you are yourself an expert, the only sensible advice one can give about buying scrimshaws is: don't. What certainly are genuine are the magnificent nautilus shells engraved 'with a common penknife' (and, if you believe that, as the Great Duke said. . . .) by Charles Wood, in or about 1851, with supremely complicated designs recalling the Admiral's exploits and death.

While on the subject of doubts and pitfalls, a particular warning must be given about innumerable small moulded waxes of Nelson that can be found in all too many 'antiques' arcades. Again, sometime, somewhere, some of these must have been genuine, but they are among the most copied, and the most dubious, 'antiques' you will ever meet. Again, when in doubt, don't.

This advice, incidentally, should have been engraved on the heart of Georgiana, Lady Llangattock, that fervent and indiscriminate collector of the late nineteenth and early twentieth century. In her great collection at the Nelson Museum in Monmouth are some quite simply marvellous items and some (quite a lot in fact) of the most blatant and disgraceful fakes ever foisted off on to a collector by traders who may have been mistaken but who were, far more likely, simply

A Nelson fake: a large loving cup, said to have been presented to Nelson during his visit to Monmouth in 1802. In fact, the coat of arms includes the word 'Trafalgar' which means it must have been produced after his death – probably for his brother, the first earl.

dishonest. My favourite, possibly everybody's favourite, is a vast silver centre-piece loving cup, said to have been presented to Nelson on the occasion of his well-documented visit to Monmouth in 1802 during his tour of the west with the Hamiltons. The inscription is detailed and highly believable, the decoration rich, ornate and extravagant. It is, in every way, a perfect cup to present to a hero. It has only one small error in its authenticity. As part of his Lordship's armorials is the word 'Trafalgar'.

What other materials were there? Glass, curiously, plays little part in the Nelson commemorative story. There are tumblers, presumably made at the time of the Peace of Amiens, featuring the famous admirals of the time, including Nelson of course. There are large 'rummers' (the name derived from the German word for

A glass 'rummer' commemorating Nelson's funeral. The sides of the glass bear a superb engraving of the magnificent funeral car used to carry Nelson's body through London to St Paul's Cathedral (see illustration on p. 11).

this type of large glass and not from the expected contents) engraved with the funeral car. A very few of these may be early nineteenth century, many more are mid-century. There are sulphide paperweights: very decorative, but a product of the 1830s rather than the 1810s. And, again there are a considerable number of fakes. Engraved glass is, after all, one of the easiest materials to fake. All you need is an engraving tool, some skill, and very little scruple.

What else was there? There is record of one, and only one, contemporary Nelson jigsaw. I personally have seen only two of the impressive anchor charms showing a fouled anchor surmounted by a medallion bearing Nelson's profile (you will find an excellent reference for these in *Nelson and His Times* by Lord Charles Beresford, a book of dubious text but multitudinously marvellous illustrations). There are innumerable copies of *The Times* containing reports of all three of the battles in very, very few of which anyone should have much faith (*The Times* itself has printed innumerable facsimiles of the original edition of 7 November 1805 to mark the various anniversaries of Trafalgar). You will find numerous early nineteenth-century stamped boxes, many of excellent quality, which clearly were originally sold packed with snuff, and many many more heavy brass boxes which certainly date from rather later on and are probably entirely innocent of all connection with snuff.

Every day I expect to see many of the old pretenders and, very occasionally, I see something new and exciting. For that is the charm of commemorative collecting, particularly as applied to the Admiral. Not only can you build your own collection with items dating from the days of Nelson to the present, but you can also, because of the wide variety of items (trays – did I mention japanned trays?), never cease to hope to find something new.

Where, finally, can you see the items I have mentioned and where should you go to buy your own collection? There are two great treasure-house museums. There is the National Maritime Museum at Greenwich where, as well as perhaps the most poignant of all souvenirs, the coat he wore at Trafalgar, you can see a fine collection of commemoratives, now splendidly re-displayed in a brand new exhibition. There is the Royal Naval Museum, in the very shadow of the *Victory* at Portsmouth, where, as you might expect, there is an outstanding collection both of personal relics and of commemoratives. The latter is a special inspiration to collectors, since at the heart of it is the Lily McCarthy Collection, built up with great and diligent care over the last forty years by a remarkable American lady who has enjoyed a love affair with Nelson since her early childhood. Finally, there is the Nelson Museum at Monmouth, the home of the Llangattock Collection: a bit indiscriminate, but not to be missed.

As for buying, there are the auction houses of course. Occasionally they are able to offer you a wealth of possibilities, as happened with both the Bullock and the Wolfe collections in the last two decades. More often, individual pieces of Nelsonia appear in the more general sales: a fine pottery mug in a sale of important English ceramics; a vinaigrette in a silver sale; a ring in a jewellery sale; a glass in a sale of maritime objects. There are, in addition, specialist shops and specialist dealers. There are fellow collectors to meet and trade with, perhaps most happily through membership of the Nelson Society and/or The 1805 Club.

But, above all, there has to be your own enthusiasm. To find, in whatever way is most appropriate, the treasures of the past to make the collection of today. It can be hard work but worth it. He was, and he is, a remarkable man.

THE NELSON MEDALLIONS *BY TIMOTHY MILLETT*

The story of the development of the medals commemorating Nelson follows a very similar pattern to other commemoratives.

The first, and nowadays one of the best known, was the medal produced in 1798 to celebrate the Battle of the Nile by Nelson's prize agent Alexander Davison, who amassed a huge fortune during employment as a Government contractor. The obverse shows Hope standing on a rocky outcrop, holding a large medallion of Nelson; on the reverse is a depiction of the opening stages of the battle with the British fleet attacking the French ships moored in Aboukir Bay. The work of Conrad Heinrich Küchler, the chief medal engraver at Matthew Boulton's Soho manufactory, the medal was awarded in gold (admirals and captains), silver (officers), bronze gilt (petty officers) and bronze (others).

Boulton's particular forte was the time and trouble he spent over designs. By

The Davison Nile medal. Produced, at his own expense, by Nelson's prize-agent and presented to every officer and man who had fought at the Nile. The reverse (right) bears a splendidly executed view of the opening stage of the battle.

bringing together the best techniques of the period (in particular the new steam presses), while at the same time thoroughly researching the designs for his medals, he was able to produce items of real quality, although they were not necessarily cost effective. While other makers were interested in quick profit, Boulton was more interested in advertising his mint. The recipients of Davison's medal were obviously proud of them and many of them have survived. Although issued unnamed, some recipients had their name and ship engraved in the 'field'.

In all, there were seven other medals produced for the Nile but none were so attractive as Davison's and they are now quite scarce.

In 1799 two more medals were produced for Boulton by the distinctive Küchler to commemorate the assistance given by Nelson in the restoration of Ferdinand IV as King of Naples and, in 1800, a medal was produced by Peter Kempson for Nelson's return to England. A year later two medals were issued to mark the Battle of Copenhagen, one of which celebrates the triumph of 'Maritime Justice and British Valour', with Justice proudly displaying the profiles of Nelson and Hyde Parker.

However, as in other areas of collecting, it was the Battle of Trafalgar and the death of Nelson which produced a veritable avalanche of commemorative pieces, by no fewer than eight separate makers. Once again, however, it is Boulton's medal, to a design by Küchler, which has proved most durable. A full description of the remarkable care Boulton took to obtain a good likeness of Nelson for the obverse can be found in Chapter Two.

Throughout the nineteenth century a number of other Nelson commemorative medals were issued, often to mark notable events such as the unveiling of the Birmingham monument in 1809. Among the most striking was one (known as The Nelson Testimonial Medal) produced to commemorate the completion of the Trafalgar Square Nelson monument, a view of which was shown on the obverse. The intention had been to present copies to veterans of Nelson's battles at a ceremony in the Square, but, when the completion was delayed, the presentation was made at Greenwich Hospital instead.

In 1897 a medal was produced commemorating Nelson and one of his flagships, HMS *Foudroyant*, which includes the legend, 'Medal struck from copper of vessel after breaking up.' The ship, which had been wrecked off Blackpool the previous year, produced enough metal for the Birmingham Mint to make somewhere in the region of 25,000 medals between 1897 and 1905. The

The Orme Naval Victories Box: a delightful commemorative item, based on two of the Trafalgar medals, and containing miniature coloured engravings of the great naval victories of the Napoleonic period.

Centenary of Trafalgar was marked by the issue of a commemorative medal for the British and Foreign Sailors Society, depicting a standing figure of Nelson on the obverse, with a broadside view of HMS *Victory* on the reverse. Fifty years later another very handsome medal was issued for the 150th anniversary, and there will, no doubt, be many more to mark 2005.

One of the most interesting and attractive items of the whole Nelson period is a boxed medal, published by Edward Orme around 1820. It contains twelve circular coloured prints, each commemorating a naval action from the period 1782 to 1816, including Nelson's four great battles. Although not strictly a numismatic piece, the lid of the box, a profile of Nelson, is taken from one of the 1805 commemorative medals – thus neatly demonstrating the links that often exist between various areas of collecting.

Sources

Details of the books consulted in the preparation of this chapter may be found in the bibliography.

The greatest of all the Nelson sites: his flagship HMS Victory *now magnificently restored in Portsmouth Historic Dockyard and open to visitors, while still flying the white ensign as a fully commissioned ship in the Royal Navy.*

CHAPTER V

In Nelson's Footprints

by Tom Pocock

There can be few, if any, great historical figures whose travels can be plotted with more accuracy than those of Horatio Nelson. Although most of his travelling was of course at sea, his ships carried log-books recording exact positions at exact times, and most of these have been preserved. Therefore it is easier to follow accurately in his wake than in his footsteps on land, although these have been well-recorded in his letters.

Every historical biographer tries to get as close to his, or her, subject as the laws of time and mortality will allow. The primary means must always be letters and diaries but another is the attempt to see the same sights and experience some of the same sensations. For example, our first view of Gibraltar from the sea will be exactly the same as Nelson's. His experience in a ship's boat of the ebb-tide surging through the narrow entrance to Portsmouth harbour was for him in a cutter as it is for us in a sailing dinghy.

So, as a biographer of Nelson and a journalist – first a foreign correspondent and then a travel writer – I took, or made, opportunities to visit as many Nelsonion sites as I could; indeed, there are now none of importance that I have not visited.

The following survey of such places takes them in geographical, rather than chronological, sequence for the convenience of the reader who may be travelling within reach of some. Where relevant, buildings open to the public are noted; seasons and times of opening are advertised locally. This is not a wholly comprehensive list; Nelson is too mercurial and elusive a character to be pinned down and fully and finally dissected by any biographer, so it is proper that there should be a touch of mystery about his path through the world.

GREAT BRITAIN – NORFOLK

Horatio Nelson was born in the village of Burnham Thorpe in Norfolk on 29 September 1758, as commemorated in his baronial title. Less certain is the actual site of his birth. He himself wrote that he had been born 'in the Parsonage House', but there remain persistent traditions in the village that he was, in fact, born either at a former farm known as the Shooting Box, where his family was living while the Parsonage was being redecorated, or at Ivy Farm, when his mother went into labour prematurely while visiting the church, half a mile from her home.

The Parsonage he knew, an old L-shaped building with a steep-pitched roof, stood close to the road but was demolished in 1803, when his father Edmund Nelson died, and replaced by the present double-bow-fronted house on higher ground, which he himself never saw. His garden, of course, remains and it is said that the pond near the road was dug by Nelson and his gardener, when he diverted the stream while unemployed in the later 1780s; another theory is that the actual pond is in the field opposite on the far side of the little River Burn. One of the

Nelson's birthplace: a contemporary oil painting of the Old Parsonage at Burnham Thorpe, Norfolk. The clerical figure in the foreground is probably Nelson's father, Edmund, and tradition has it that one of the small boys playing with him is Nelson himself.

The Burnham Thorpe village pub. Known in Nelson's day as The Plough, it has now been renamed The Lord Nelson.

most telling views is from the top of the public bridleway that runs from the village up Gravelpit Hill, behind the house. From the crest, where Nelson must often have walked, is the one vantage point on his father's glebe land from which he could see the sea: a short line of horizon between the shoulders of shallow chalk downs, then often flecked with sails.

He obviously knew the church of All Saints well, but it looked different at that time, being much dilapidated. The ancient roof had collapsed and had been replaced by a flat wooden ceiling, while the south aisle had fallen into dereliction and been demolished. There were box pews and, probably, a double- or triple-decked pulpit. The larger houses, which he knew as 'homesteads by the stream', and the little inn (then probably called The Plough but, since his time, The Lord Nelson), still stand. It was at the latter that he entertained his neighbours on being recalled to duty in February 1793. In the yard in front, a village lad from the High family earned the nickname (and a future family Christian name) 'Valiant', which was accorded him by Nelson for the fight he put up when teased by his friends for not being invited to the adults' party.

Nelson knew Burnham Market well and it has changed remarkably little since his time. When Captain and Mrs Nelson took up residence at the Parsonage House at Burnham Thorpe, his kindly old father stayed near the church of

Burnham Ulph, also named All Saints (still standing but much restored). Old Edmund Nelson had taken a house now named Church House, describing it as, 'My town residence . . . warm and in the vicinity of what is useful in food, clothing and physic and, most likely, by and by, a little social chat may take place'. His third church was St Margaret's, Burnham Norton, a round-towered building, originally thought to be Anglo-Saxon, on the crest of the chalk down between Burnham Market and Burnham Norton.

When an unemployed captain, Nelson would also have visited Westgate Hall and Burnham House, then occupied by Sir Mordaunt Martin. He also frequented Burnham Overy Staithe, which was then a busy little seaport and he later boasted that the '*Agamemnon* is as well known through Europe as one of Mr Harwood's ships is at Overy.' The author traced a strange memory of him in this village, when, around 1960, the village postmaster Mr James Riches, then an old man, told him that, when young, he heard that 'On Saturdays Captain Nelson would take his work down to the bank.' This has been interpreted, after much deliberation, as meaning that on Saturday afternoons, when the *Norfolk Chronicle* reached Burnham Market in the coach from Norwich, he would buy a copy and ride over the embankment – 'Overy Bank' – along the east side of the tidal creek to find a sheltered spot to read undisturbed the latest news of international affairs.

At Holkham Hall there is a 'Nelson Room', in which Nelson is reputed to have slept, but in fact the only recorded visit was to have his official papers for drawing half-pay while unemployed signed by Thomas Coke, the future Earl of Leicester, who was a magistrate; presumably this was done in Coke's ground-floor study. Coke was, however, a Whig and Nelson a Tory at that time – although later he was virtually apolitical – and he refused Coke's invitation to the annual sheep-shearing festivities at Holkham.

Nelson was related through his mother to the powerful political and landowning Walpole family. However, he was never invited to their principal seat, Houghton Hall, although he and his wife did, during his five years 'on the beach', enjoy annual visits to the Walpoles' second mansion, Wolterton Hall near Aylsham.

The young Horatio spent childhood holidays at Hilborough, where his father had been rector before moving to Burnham Thorpe; indeed, every rector between 1734 and 1806 was a Nelson except one, and he was married to a Nelson; the last being his brother William. The rectory is an old house, now known as The Nunnery, and the church, another All Saints, one of the most beautiful in the Perpendicular style in the county, stands on the edge of the park of Hilborough Hall. It was here that, as a boy, he was said to have been looking for birds' nests, became lost in the woods on the far bank of the little River Wissey and, on his return, made the famous remark when asked if he had felt fear: 'I never saw fear. What is it?'

Nelson's school: the Paston School, North Walsham, Norfolk, which Nelson attended from early 1768 until he went to sea with his uncle Captain Maurice Suckling in March 1771.

Nelson was said to have been to school at Downham Market but there is no documentary evidence of this and it is probable that he was confused with another boy of his name. He first went to Norwich School, next to the cathedral, and then to the Paston School at North Walsham, both of which remain in use; at the latter, his schoolroom is shown to visitors.

He called at other Norfolk houses when visiting his brothers and sisters, including his younger brother Suckling, who failed to make a living as a draper at a shop in North Elmham, which still stands, named Nelson House, in the village on the B1110 road. His sister Susannah married into the Bolton family of Wells-next-the-Sea and he visited her there, also joining the Wells Club, which played cards in rooms hired at various taverns in the town; the Boltons later moved to a farmhouse at Cranwich, which survives on the north side of the A134 road between Mundford and Northwold. Kate, his favourite sister, married the well-to-do George Matcham, and for a time they lived at Barton Hall, a fine Georgian house still standing near Barton Turf.

After leaving Burnham Thorpe for the last time in 1793, he returned to Norfolk three times, always to Great Yarmouth. The first occasion was when he arrived in England with Sir William and Lady Hamilton in 1800 and stayed at the Wrestler's Inn, which survives, although much rebuilt after bombing in the Second World

Barton Hall, home of Nelson's favourite sister Catherine ('Kitty') who married the well-to-do East India Company merchant George Matcham in 1787.

War. The second occasion was when he embarked for the expedition to the Baltic as second-in-command to Admiral Hyde Parker; finally, after the Battle of Copenhagen, he visited wounded in the Naval Hospital which had been opened there (this was rebuilt between 1809 and 1811 and still stands), remarking to one seaman who had lost his right arm: 'Well, Jack, you and I are spoiled as fishermen.'

On arriving with the Hamiltons in 1800, he drove over the border into Suffolk to meet his wife at Roundwood, the house she had bought him at Ipswich (demolished by Ipswich Borough Council in 1961, when St John's School was built on the site), but, not finding her there, continued to London.

GREAT BRITAIN – LONDON

Other than Norwich, London was the first city that Nelson saw when, as a boy of twelve, he passed through on his way to join his first ship at Chatham. He and his father stayed, however, in a northern suburb with his uncle William Suckling, a Commissioner in the Excise Office who lived in Kentish Town – local historians are currently researching the claims of two possible addresses, one of them in Kentish Town Road – among the beer-gardens, villas and wayside taverns.

1. The Immortality of Nelson *by Benjamin West. In a painting laden with allegory, Nelson's body is raised by Neptune (bottom left) and Victory into the arms of mourning Britannia while the French and Spanish swirl away in dark confusion (bottom right).*

2. Captain Horatio Nelson *by J.F. Rigaud. Begun while Nelson was still a lieutenant and completed on his return from the West Indies in 1780, this fine painting includes a view of Fort San Juan in Nicaragua, which the young captain had helped to capture (see illustration on p. 126).*

3. Vice Admiral Lord Nelson, KB, *by John Hoppner. Discovered only recently, this raw, unfinished preliminary sketch has not been 'prettified' like many of the completed portraits, and so is now generally agreed to be one of the best available likenesses of the mature Nelson.*

4. Vice Admiral Lord Nelson, KB, *by William Beechey. A preliminary sketch for the huge formal portrait commissioned by the City of Norwich.*

5. Rear Admiral Lord Nelson, KB *by Heinrich Füger. A fine study by the court painter of Austria, who managed to capture something of Nelson's ruthlessness and capacity for concentration.*

6. Nelson relics: his mahogany dining table from HMS Victory *is set with silver and glass from the services that Nelson took to sea with him. All the silver items are engraved with his distinctive coat of arms.*

7. Nelson commemoratives: *glass-paintings produced in 1805/6 depict his death, the Lying in State at Greenwich Hospital, the funeral barge and the funeral car.*

8. Nelson commemoratives: enamel boxes produced to commemorate the battles of the Nile and Trafalgar and Nelson's death. Note especially the wooden-legged, one-armed sailor, mentioned in Chapter Four.

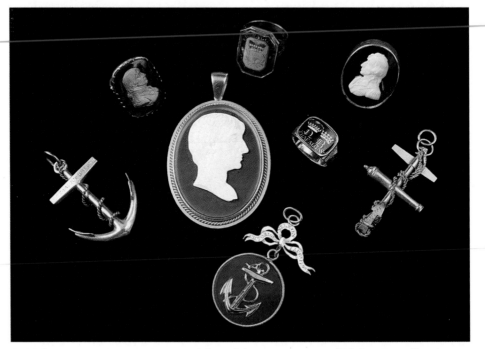

9. Nelson commemoratives: examples of the many types of Nelson jewellery mentioned in Chapter Four. The large central pendant includes a portrait medallion by Tassie.

10. Nelson and the polar bear. *A famous incident in Nelson's life that was very popular with artists. This is the first depiction of it, by Edward Orme, for his illustrated biography of 1806.*

11. *The frontispiece of* The Nelson Memorial *by Sir John Knox Laughton showing the flags that were used throughout the Victorian period for 'England Expects' – until it was discovered that they had been taken from the wrong code-book!*

12. *The Nelson Tower at Forres in Morayshire. A Trafalgar Club used to meet for riotous Trafalgar Night dinners in a room in the tower.*

13. Saluting the Admiral *by Alfred Holden. This typical turn-of-the-century popular print depicts a Greenwich pensioner saluting a laurel-garlanded bust of Nelson in the Painted Hall at Greenwich, presumably on Trafalgar Day.*

A year later, Midshipman Nelson was commanding a ship's boat plying between the Nore and the Pool of London, then crowded with shipping unloading into lighters. He would particularly have noted at Greenwich the Royal Hospital for naval pensioners (now the Royal Naval College) designed by Wren, Hawksmoor and Vanbrugh (*open*) and the naval dockyard at Deptford. However, the buildings of the Admiralty's Victualling Yard, some of which survive by the river, date from the 1780s so he would not have seen them until later visits.

Subsequent visits to London took him to the Navy Office, the administrative department housed in the west wing of Somerset House, which still, of course, stands. He also regularly visited the Admiralty, Thomas Ripley's familiar porticoed building in Whitehall. There he will have known the Board Room, now much restored after war damage, but still displaying the indicator of the wind vane on the roof, set amid carvings in wood by Grinling Gibbons. On the ground floor is a small room to the south of the entrance, overlooking the courtyard. Then known as the Captains' Room it is now known as the Nelson Room because it was there, candle-lit, the walls hung with black crêpe, that his body rested on the night before his funeral on 9 January 1806. The Board Room and the Nelson Room both still belong to the Navy, which has otherwise been moved out of its historical

The Admiralty building, Whitehall, London. This contemporary view shows the famous main entrance through which Nelson passed many times during his career: first as a lowly captain seeking employment, later as a distinguished admiral offering advice.

home. (*Both rooms are occasionally shown to special interest groups such as, for example, the Georgian Group.*) In the adjoining Admiralty House, then the official residence of the First Lord of the Admiralty, he twice dined with Lord and Lady Spencer: on the first occasion, he was clearly much attached to his wife Fanny; on the second, after his return from Naples, he was irritated by her. Admiralty House is now used for Government entertaining and ministers' flats. An alternative setting for these dinner parties might have been the Spencer House overlooking Green Park.

As a young officer he would take lodgings to be near both the Navy Office and the Admiralty at 3 Salisbury Street, south of The Strand, and 3 Lancaster Court, close to St Martins-in-the-Fields; both have long gone but the type of houses they probably were can be seen in 33 and 34 Surrey Street, running from the eastern end of The Strand towards the river. It was at this period, when a young captain, that he would visit his friend, and future prize agent, Alexander Davison at his rooms in Lincoln's Inn and, shedding his 'iron-bound' uniform coat, sit for hours in one of his host's silk dressing-gowns talking politics. (The archives of Lincoln's Inn might reveal which Davison's chambers were and whether they have survived).

Other London streets Nelson knew as a young man were Park Street at the Hyde Park side of Mayfair, where his uncle, Captain Maurice Suckling, had a house, which may well survive, and Wimpole Street, where Lord Hood occupied a smart new house. After his marriage to Fanny Nisbet in 1787, he and his bride stayed with her uncle John Herbert at his grand rented house, 5 Cavendish Square; this *might* be the present house of that number, which is Georgian, but the row has possibly been renumbered during the rebuilding of some and, if so, Herbert's house may have been on the site of what is now number four. The Nelsons also lodged at 10 Great Marlborough Street (now much rebuilt, although a four-storey Georgian pub, the Coach and Horses, still stands on the nearby corner of Poland Street) and 6 Princes Street, in which all but two of the Georgian houses have been rebuilt.

Later, when he returned wounded from Tenerife, the Nelsons took two lodgings in Bond Street: first, in September 1797, number 141, just to the north of Bruton Street; then, early the following year, number 96 – now numbered 103 New Bond Street, and which bears the plaque recording his stay. Nearby, stands the church of St George's, Hanover Square, where Nelson left the note reading, 'An officer desires to return thanks to Almighty God for his perfect recovery from a severe wound . . .' (*open*). This area Nelson liked but, when writing to Fanny from Naples in 1798, he asked her to rent 'neat house in London near Hyde Park, but on no account on the other side of Portman Square. I detest Baker Street.'

Nelson visited St James's Palace for the King's levees and, in 1797, the Guildhall, where he was presented with the Freedom of the City of London, and the College of Arms to decide upon the form of the heraldic recognition of his achievements. The public areas of the last two are both open to visitors.

Merton Place, Surrey: 'Paradise Merton', the home which Nelson shared with the Hamiltons. In the foreground is an ornamental canal, which was nicknamed 'The Nile'.

On his return from Naples with the Hamiltons, the fateful meeting with his wife took place at Nerot's Hotel on the south side of King Street, St James's, where the St James's Theatre later stood before it was replaced by successive office blocks. Then the Nelsons moved to 17 Dover Street (rebuilt, but neighbouring Georgian houses survive), while the Hamiltons stayed at 22 Grosvenor Square, also long gone. During the next three years the Hamiltons' London house was 23 Piccadilly, on the north side, just east of Air Street and close to what is today Piccadilly Circus; now, of course, long gone. After Sir William's death in 1803, Nelson took lodgings over a saddler's shop at 19 Piccadilly. He bought his hats from Lock, which still sells hats at 6 St James's Street.

In September 1801 Nelson became the owner of Merton Place, in Surrey then, now in Greater London. The charming Georgian house survived until 1846, when it was demolished and the site and grounds have since been built upon twice. Now there is nothing to see but blocks of flats, although the River Wandle nearby, where Sir William Hamilton used to fish, still flows between grassy banks. The church of St Mary the Virgin, however, remains and within is preserved the bench from the box pew in which Nelson and the Hamiltons sat. On the walls are the hatchments of Nelson and Sir William Hamilton, placed there at Lady Hamilton's expense.

Nor far from Merton, in Wimbledon, Southside House survives and it was there that the 'Trio Juncta in Uno' from Merton would spend convivial evenings with the owner John Pennington (*open*). In the music room the low dais on which Emma Hamilton performed her 'Attitudes' is shown to visitors, as is a portrait of her by Romney, which once hung at Merton Place, and the table at which the party played cards. Another house nearby known to Nelson and the Hamiltons is Morden Hall (*now council offices; the park, owned by the National Trust, is open*), where they were entertained by the Jewish financier Abraham Goldsmid, who 'beamed with genial kindness' but whose taste in interior decoration they found too gaudy.

For medical consultations Nelson called on his old friend from Jamaica, Dr Benjamin Moseley, who was now the senior physician at the Royal Hospital in Chelsea (*open*), near to Whitelands School (Whitelands House flats stand on the site), where his niece Charlotte was at school and where he would ask the headmistress that a half-holiday should mark his visits.

The rooms Nelson knew at the House of Lords were, of course, destroyed in the fire of 1834. But the room where he had the famous, unexpected encounter with Major-General Sir Arthur Wellesley in 1805 is still in use as an office on the ground floor of 12 Downing Street. During his final twenty-five days in England before embarking to take command of the fleet off Cadiz, Nelson stayed at Merton and at Gordon's Hotel, 44 Albemarle Street (rebuilt and now a post office; No. 50 nearby survives as a house of the period), and also frequented Emma Hamilton's house at 11 Clarges Street (demolished around 1960).

The final places in London associated with Nelson are, of course, those where his body lay on its return after Trafalgar; the Painted Hall at Greenwich, where it lay in state (*open*); the Nelson Room at the Admiralty, where it rested overnight before the great funeral procession and service; finally the crypt of St Paul's Cathedral, where it still lies (*open*).

GREAT BRITAIN – THE PROVINCES

The naval ports of Portsmouth, Plymouth and Chatham were, of course, familiar to Nelson. At Chatham, where he joined his first ship, the naval base covering the Thames and London is now preserved as Chatham Historic Dockyard (*open*) and several buildings he would have known as a boy still stand: notably the Main Gate, the Admiral's House, the Officer's Terrace, the Sail Loft and the Mast House. Plymouth he seldom visited and no buildings there, or in Devonport Dockyard, survive that are directly associated with Nelson. The bombing of 1941 destroyed most architectural coherence in both areas, but in Devonport Dockyard he would recognize the Pay Office (built 1780), which is now the Naval Base Museum, the three surviving senior officers' houses of The Terrace, the Roperies, the Hemphouse, the Armourer's Shop and the Powder Magazine. In nearby Stonehouse, the Royal Hospital (1758–62) and the Royal Marines Barracks (1779–85) remain.

Portsmouth is another matter, for this was always the core of British maritime power. In the Naval Base, as the dockyard is now named, the buildings he knew all cluster round the dock where his flagship, the *Victory*, found her final berth; she, of course, is the greatest Nelson memorial of all, although most of her timbers of 1805 have since been replaced – with the notable exceptions of the lower gun deck and the orlop deck, where he died. The buildings standing before 1805 would have included the storehouses, now housing the Royal Naval Museum, the Ropery opposite, the former Royal Naval Academy (now the Staff Officers' Mess), and the Long Row and Short Row terraces of officers' houses.

Bombing in the 1940s destroyed much of Old Portsmouth and Portsea, the district near the dockyard. The Portsmouth of 1805 would have been recognizable

The Great Storehouses, Portsmouth Dockyard. Built between 1776 and 1783 as part of the great expansion of the dockyard, these buildings were designed to hold the ready use stores for the Nelsonian fleet. They now house the Royal Naval Museum.

until 1941 but now only a few dozen Georgian houses remain of the densely packed town within the fortifications. The landward defences were removed in the 1870s and 1880s but the Landport Gate – built in 1760 and said to have been designed by Nicholas Hawksmoor – through which Nelson would have entered the town by coach, survives on its original site although this is now a playing field. The Dolphin Hotel remains but almost all the other taverns of Portsmouth and Portsea have gone, several of them demolished in the past quarter-century; one survivor, the two-storey Royal Standard, in Edinburgh Road near the Royal Naval Barracks in Portsea, still gives an idea of what a sailors' pub was like: now decorated with ships' crests and cap-tallies instead of prints and curiosities. Nelson ordered his uniforms from the tailor Meredith at 72 High Street, Old Portsmouth, which was bought by Gieves, the famous naval outfitters, in 1852. Gieves dresses naval officers to this day in Portsmouth and London.

The George Hotel, where he stopped on his final journey to the sea and Trafalgar, was bombed; a charming old building with the shallow bow windows characteristic of eighteenth-century Portsmouth, it had survived to become a Trust House. His path from the back door, along Penny Street and Pembroke Road to the boat waiting in the surf, can be followed. Perhaps, however, the George was not his final call. There is a tradition that his favourite sister, Kate Matcham, was staying at a house nearby in Pembroke Road and he is said to have briefly visited her on his way to the beach and it may have been there, and not in Merton or London, that he spoke to her of the fortune-teller's warning that she could see ahead no farther than his fortieth birthday: 'Ah, Katty! Katty, that gipsy!'

Sadly the house, which stood near the surviving Royal Naval Club and was, after Nelson's death, renamed Trafalgar House, disappeared in the bombing. A photograph of it shows a three-storey, double-fronted, stone-faced house with a miniature cannon and two large cannon-balls mounted on top of its pillared porch. From there he would have walked through the fortifications, via a vaulted tunnel under the main earthwork and across a wide moat by a wooden footbridge to the shingle beach beside the Spur Redoubt. The tunnel and bridge have recently been opened to the public and can give the visitor a *frisson* that seems to endorse the authenticity of the scene the crowds watched there on 14 September 1805.

Deal – or, rather, the Downs anchorage between the shore and the sheltering sandbank – was Nelson's base when he was given command of counter-invasion forces in 1801. The Three Kings pub – now named the Royal Hotel – on the beach was where the Hamiltons lodged, when they visited him there. In Middle Street, the little house, where his young friend and protégé Captain Edward Parker died of wounds received in the abortive attack on Boulogne, still stands, although there is debate as to which it is. Parker was buried in the churchyard of St George's which survives (its lofty gallery with a separate entrance was for smelly fishermen), but his gravestone has been moved and the tree against which the weeping Nelson is said to have leaned, was recently felled.

*Pierrepont Street, Bath. Here Nelson stayed
with his father in early 1781 while he was
recovering from the malaria and dysentery he
had contracted while serving in Nicaragua.
He was so haggard that he visited the famous
baths in the evenings so as to avoid being
seen.*

After Portsmouth, the provincial town he knew best in adult life was
undoubtedly Bath. There he stayed in 1781 to recuperate from the malaria and
dysentery he had suffered in Nicaragua. He lodged at 2 Pierrepont Street, which
bears a plaque commemorating the fact. This was near the Pump Room and the
theatre in Orchard Street where Mrs Siddons was performing. It was also near the
medicinal baths, where he was treated, and the consulting room of Dr Woodward
in Gay Street. It was also to Bath that he returned in 1797 after losing his right
arm in the attack on Tenerife. Fanny had taken rooms at 17 New King Street,
which stands, little changed, in the south-west of the city, while his father stayed
nearby in Upper Charles Street. Bath was, indeed, the old man's second home and
that, together with his son's two visits, makes the whole of the Georgian centre a
Nelsonian site.

In March 1781 he visited his friend Captain (later Admiral Sir) Robert
Kingsmill at Sydmonton Court, south-east of Newbury in Berkshire. In late April
and May 1788 he and Fanny stayed at Exmouth and it was this happy holiday
that was to prompt her to settle there in 1807 at 6 The Beacon, which survives in
a terrace overlooking the sea, until 1829 and then at a house in Louisa Place
nearby. She died in London – at 26 Baker Street; ironically, the street that Nelson
detested – on 6 May 1831; she was buried near her son Josiah in the churchyard
of Littleham parish church, near Exmouth (the tomb has recently been restored by
The 1805 Club).

A spectacular social occasion in Nelson's life, to compare with the Bourbons'
fêtes for him in Naples and Palermo, was the party, lasting three days and nights,

given by the eccentric William Beckford at Fonthill Abbey in 1800. The gigantic folly with its Gothic tower 278 ft high was the scene of an extraordinary banquet-cum-masque, which left guests feeling 'as if waking from a dream, or just freed from the influence of some magic spell'. The tower collapsed in 1825, but a few fragments of the bizarre building survive in the Wiltshire woods. However, the four-poster bed in which Nelson slept on his visit to the abbey is on display at Charlcote Park, the mansion near Stratford-upon-Avon in Warwickshire, which is owned by the National Trust.

In 1802 Nelson went on a provincial tour with the Hamiltons to visit Sir William's estate in Pembrokeshire. A resounding success, it set the seal on his acclaim as the nation's hero and many of the places in which they stayed, and which they visited, still survive. A detailed account, together with particulars of all the surviving buildings, is given in *Nelson and the Hamiltons on Tour* by Edward Gill (Alan Sutton Publishing and the Nelson Museum, Monmouth, 1987).

Of all the roads Nelson travelled it was, of course, the Portsmouth road from London that he knew best. Of the coaching inns, where he breakfasted, or dined, while the horses were changed, the most magnificent survivor is the red-brick Talbot Hotel at Ripley in Surrey, with its great arch and doorways opening on to the stable yard and its cosy, heavily beamed parlour. It makes much of its Nelson connection but perhaps the inn is more redolent of Mr Pickwick.

EUROPE

Nelson's first excursion into the mainland of Europe was his visit to St Omer in 1783 to learn French. Some of the substantial, stone-built houses of the time survive and, perhaps, the lodging house of Madame La Mourie, where he fell in love with the English clergyman's daughter, might be traced in the municipal archives.

But his only major experience of mainland travel was during his tour with the Hamiltons on their protracted return journey from Naples in 1800. Crossing Italy, they embarked at Ancona for Trieste and from there made their way via Laibach (now Ljubljana) in Slovenia, into Austria to halt at Klagenfurt and Graz before reaching Vienna, where they were received at the royal palaces; then on to Prague and Dresden. Continuing through the German states, they were entertained at the palaces of Wittenberg and Taugermunde and Prince Franz von Anhalt-Dessau named a conical mound in his park at Dessau, the 'Nelsonberg'. The party entered Prussia at Magdeburg and continued to Hamburg, where they embarked for Great Yarmouth, Nelson's baggage including the coffin made from the mast of *L'Orient* after the Battle of the Nile. Most of the German cities Nelson visited were devastated in the Second World War, but the route from Trieste to Hamburg would make an unusual motoring tour. Nelson is said to have visited Germany again briefly after the Battle of Copenhagen, landing at Rostock and visiting the orientalist Professor Tyschsen, whom he called 'Dixon', and giving him one of the Nile medals struck by Alexander Davison.

There was also his descent upon Copenhagen in 1801: first to destroy the Danish fleet and batteries and then to talk terms. The site of the Battle of Copenhagen, fought close inshore against moored ships, floating and shore batteries, has been changed out of recognition by the expansion of the harbour, dockyard and the waterfront promenades. However, the Trekroner (Three Crowns) island-battery remains off the park at Langelinje. After the battle Nelson went ashore in the city to negotiate an armistice and many of the buildings he saw survive. He walked along the wide Amaliegade to the Amelienborg Palace to meet the Crown Prince of Denmark and it was there, while conducting his carrot-and-stick diplomacy, that, ascending a great wooden staircase to dine, he remarked in a stage whisper to a British officer, 'Though I have only one eye, I can see all this will burn very well.'

It was of course the Mediterranean that he knew best. Apart from the brief spell in the Baltic and North Sea in 1801 and the chase to the West Indies in 1805, he served there, or in the Atlantic waters off Spain, continuously between 1793 and 1805.

Soon after his return to sea in 1793, Nelson took his new command, the *Agamemnon*, into Cadiz – Spain was not then at war with Britain, of course – and enjoyed a 'run ashore'. He was to return there to blockade it and fight in a hand-to-hand boat action close inshore. The long, low town on its spit, with its churches and sea wall, has changed little in essentials but here, as at Portsmouth, it is the great harbour that has changed least and is more redolent of those times.

Nelson's disastrous attack on the port of Santa Cruz on the island of Tenerife in 1797 is best remembered as the action in which he lost his right arm while leaping ashore at the head of the assault. Below the jagged silhouette of the volcanic crags, the town has expanded greatly and the harbour is infinitely larger than it was then. But there are a number of buildings and fortifications that recall the abortive British attack and two are of particular note: the church of Nuestra Senora de la Concepcion, where captured British flags are stored in a glass case, the name of the frigate *Emerald* visible, painted across one of the Union flags; and the semi-circular battery of the Castillo de Paso Alto, where a cannon named *El Tigre* is said to be the gun which fired the grape-shot that smashed Nelson's arm.

The site of the Battle of Trafalgar is the heaving ocean 20 miles west off the cape of that name. Stand on the low, jagged cliffs, look out to sea and the imagination's eye may conjure up the great mushroom of gunsmoke on the horizon that watchers there remembered seeing on 21 October 1805. Gibraltar, to which the shattered *Victory* steered after the battle, is rich in Nelsonian memories for almost all the fortifications and many of the houses he knew still stand among the high-rise concrete blocks and shopping streets. In

Rosia Bay, where the flagship anchored after Trafalgar, there is a tradition that Nelson's body was taken ashore to one of the Georgian houses still standing, but in fact there is no evidence that it left the ship.

Into the Mediterranean his first port of call, Toulon, rewards students of battlefields, although Nelson himself was soon sent away on a mission to Naples. His next, and far more important, involvement was in Corsica, where he played a leading part in the sieges of Bastia on the west coast and Calvi on the east. At Bastia Nelson landed his guns on the beach by the Genoese tower at Miomo, now a small seaside resort about 3 miles to the north. From there, he supervised the dragging of the naval guns cross-country to the city walls and the building of the batteries.

At Calvi the diligent explorer with a large-scale map can easily find the little inlet of Porto Agro, where he decided to form the beach-head for the siege. His route can be followed across rough country, over a ridge 900 ft above sea level to the sites of the batteries. The huge rock, near where he was standing when a cannon-ball threw gravel into his face, damaging his right eye, is marked with a plaque; but a few years ago a bungalow was built upon it. Close to the city walls the forts of Mozzello and Monteciesco can be identified and the huge Genoese citadel sheltering the narrow streets of the Haute-Ville (*open*) is little changed but for the needs of tourism. Sadly the monument to his friend Lieutenant James Moutray of the *Victory*, the only son of his friend from English Harbour, in the church at San Fiorenzo (Saint Florent) has now disappeared, although much of the old town is as it was. Here, as elsewhere in Corsica, the scenery is little changed and most of the fortifications – including that at Mortella, which inspired the 'Martello' towers on the English coast – can be found.

Taken in sequence, the famous sites of his activities in 1798 and 1799 are Aboukir Bay in Egypt, Naples and Palermo. The bay where the Battle of the Nile was fought on 1 August 1798 is almost exactly as it was: even the underwater sandbanks are little changed. Seen from the scruffy town of Aboukir, there is just the sweep of the bay below low sandy shores, the fort on the point of Aboukir and the surf curling white over Culloden Reef, where the English ship of that name ran aground during the approach to battle. A few relics salvaged from the French flagship *L'Orient* can be seen in the meagre maritime museum in the castle of Qait Bey, built in 1840 from the stones of the ancient lighthouse, the Pharos (*open*). Here among nails, bottles and broken navigational instruments is the most telling of relics: a sheet of copper sheathing from the ship's bottom, crumpled like tinfoil by the explosion of her magazine.

After the battle Nelson took his flagship, the *Vanguard*, to Naples for repairs. Most of the city he knew survives, embedded in the teeming commercial and industrial sprawl. The Palazzo Reale, where he was received so often by King Ferdinand and Queen Maria Carolina, dominates the harbour but within its red walls much has changed, notably the marble staircase installed by Marshal Murat,

Porto Agro, Corsica. Here, in June 1794, Captain Nelson of HMS Agamemnon
*landed guns and supplies to construct batteries for the siege of the fortified town
of Calvi, where, later, he was wounded in the eye.*

whom Napoleon made King of Naples (*open*). But some of the *saloni*, with their red damask walls hung with dark, golden-framed paintings, and coffered ceilings alive with frolicsome frescoes, must be much as he saw them. The secret passages through which he led the royal family at Christmas 1798, to rescue from the Revolution by his ships' boats which were waiting in the harbour below, must still be there.

The Palazzo Sessa, Hamilton's embassy, broods above the Piazza dei Martiri with its memorial to the radicals executed after Nelson had retaken the city for the King. Externally, it is shabby; internally, it is in multi-occupation and so is never open to the public. However, it can be seen from the street below as can the tall window of Nelson's room; its entrance and *porte-cochère* can be approached from the other side by the road sloping uphill past new concrete buildings to the courtyard, which must have been familiar to the visiting admiral. The Villa Emma, the Hamiltons' little seaside villa, still stands on the low cliffs above the beach at Posillipo, much altered, its back sliced away by the corniche. Towards Vesuvius, where Hamilton studied volcanology, he rented a house at Portici, then a country resort of the nobility known as the Villa Angelica and said to have been renamed the Villa Salvatore, but there is no evidence that Nelson ever visited it. Out at the royal palace of Caserta, near which Hamilton occupied a villa on occasion, the English garden he and Emma so enjoyed still flourishes (*open*).

In Palermo, to which Nelson escorted the fugitive royal family, much of the centre (near the docks), where the Hamiltons lodged, was destroyed by bombing in the Second World War. Yet out in the royal hunting park of La Favorita, a marvellous survival is the Palazzina Cinese, where on the walls on one charming oriental room hang English prints given by Nelson to the King and Queen (*open*).

His own house, the Castello di Maniace, which went with the gift of the Dukedom of Bronte, can be seen on the lower, western slopes of Etna (*occasionally open*). Although he fantasized about life there with Emma, and sent gardening tools to await his arrival, he never visited it. However, it descended through his niece Charlotte and her husband Samuel Hood, Lord Bridport, and remained in that family until recent years when it was sold to the municipality of Bronte. Most of the original furniture and pictures remain there, as Italian law considered them part of the Sicilian national heritage and Lord Bridport was forbidden to take them to England. The future of the house has been under discussion for years and at the time of writing is undecided.

Nelson visited Genoa in 1794 – 'This city is, without exception, the most magnificent I ever beheld, superior in many respects to Naples,' he wrote to his wife – and was received by the Doge, presumably in the Palazzo Ducale in the Piazza Matteotti, which was largely rebuilt in 1806. He was a regular visitor to Leghorn and there, before his infatuation with Emma Hamilton, conducted an affair with an opera singer. He called at Port Mahon, Minorca, but his brief association with the port hardly warrants the claims made by the municipality for

The Palazzo Sessa, Naples. The British Embassy in Naples, where Nelson first met Sir William and Lady Hamilton in September 1793 and where he stayed with them, in autumn 1798, while recovering from the wound he received at the Battle of the Nile.

Castello di Maniace, Bronte Estate, Sicily. Nelson's castle, presented to him in 1799 by King Ferdinand of Naples when he was created Duke of Bronte. Nelson always dreamed of retiring there with Emma but, in fact, he never saw it.

the benefit of tourists. Finally, the Maddalena Islands, north of Sardinia, which provided an anchorage for Nelson's fleet during the final blockade of Toulon between 1803 and 1805; here, Nelson is said to have presented silver candlesticks to the church. Other Mediterranean islands and ports of call include Malta, Majorca, Tunis and Siracuse in Sicily.

THE AMERICAS

As a young captain Nelson knew the North American seaboard well, particularly New York and Quebec. At the former, he doubtless went ashore into the town with its tall, Dutch-style houses, but it was the roadsteads – spreading some 15 miles from the Battery to Sandy Hook, where they opened to the Atlantic – that saw most of him. The principal anchorages, where his ship would lie, were Sandy Hook Bay, just inside the sand-bar; Rariton Bay, Staten Island, where there was a good supply of fresh water; and finally, close to the town, the East River. The North River, now known as the Hudson, divided the British-held town from rebel-held territory during the American War and was not, therefore, safe for mooring.

Quebec, taken from the French in 1759 by General Wolfe and Admiral Saunders in a brilliant campaign, which the older officers of Nelson's time could remember, became the principal British base in Canada. Captain Nelson arrived here in 1782, having sailed up the St Lawrence past wooded hills blazing with autumn colours. It was here that he fell vainly in love with the sixteen-year-old Mary Simpson, daughter of the garrison's provost-marshal, and here that his friend, Alexander Davison, dissuaded him from abandoning his naval career to continue his courtship. Colonel Simpson's stone house is thought to survive among those near the St Louis Gate in Old Quebec. There were compensations for his disappointment in love: 'Health, that greatest of blessings, is what I never truly enjoyed till I saw Fair Canada', he wrote.

Nelson once called the Caribbean, 'The Grand Theatre of Actions', and although that was not to be the case for him, it was where he passed his formative years and where he married. It can be assumed that he called at, or at least saw, almost all the islands of the West Indies and much of the coastline of Central America, so only the sites most directly associated with him need be considered.

The jewel in the West Indian crown was, for the British, Jamaica and its sugar-cane. In Spanish Town, the old capital, the remains of the Governor's residence, the King's House, mostly destroyed in a fire, still stand as does a splendid commemorative shrine to Admiral Rodney. The present capital is Kingston, its vast anchorage shielded by the sandy spit culminating in the old buccaneers' town of Port Royal, and it was there, during the French invasion threat of 1779, that Nelson commanded the Fort Charles battery (*open*). This remains, although farther from the sea than it was then, as two tiers of guns behind thick brick embrasures, commanding the harbour mouth. 'I was both Admiral and General,' he wrote, 'As this place was the key to the whole naval force, the town of Kingston and Spanish Town, the defence of it was the most important post in the whole island.' The wooden deck of the upper tier is still known as Nelson's Quarterdeck and, near his quarters, a metal plaque bears the words, 'In this place dwelt Horatio Nelson. You who tread his footprints, remember his glory.'

A similar plaque adorns Admiral's Mountain, a stone-built house facing the harbour mouth on Cooper's Hill in the suburbs of Kingston, one of two houses used by Nelson's patron, Rear-Admiral Sir Peter Parker. It has been restored and named Cooper's Hill House; the other house, Admiral's Pen, stood in the town itself. Admiral's Mountain was where Nelson recovered from malaria and dysentery after the disastrous expedition into Nicaragua in 1780 and from which he wrote, 'Lady P. not here, and the servants letting me lie as if a log and take no notice.'

When serving further south on the Leeward Islands station, Nelson frequented Barbados, where old plantation houses, which he may have visited, survive. More importantly, he spent much time – notably the summer hurricane season of 1784 – at English Harbour, the naval dockyard deep in the sheltered 'hurricane hole' of the island of Antigua. Here he suffered from 'mosquitoes and melancholies' before forming a romantic friendship with an older woman, Mary Moutray, wife of the local Commissioner of the Navy. This has been preserved as a tourist attraction and is now known as 'Nelson's Dockyard', which it was, although most of the buildings, including the Admiral's house where he is said to have stayed, date from after his time (*open*).

Here two houses are of note: one still remains in perfect condition; the other has now vanished. Across the harbour from the dockyard stands Clarence House, built for Nelson's friend Prince William Henry (later the Duke of Clarence and King William IV), when he was commanding a frigate in these waters in 1787; a perfect example of the type of house built by the eighteenth-century British, it is now a summer residence of the Governor-General of Antigua (*open*). The vanished house, named 'Windsor', stood on the now scrub-covered knoll above the dockyard and was the residence of Captain Moutray and his charming and sophisticated wife, with whom both Nelson and his fellow captain, Cuthbert Collingwood, conducted close and emotional friendships. One of the most telling relics of Nelson's time is the water-catchment outside the dockyard where sailors scratched the names of their ships on the low walls and these can still be read.

The Admiral's House, Antigua. English Harbour, Antigua, was Nelson's base when he was in command of HMS Boreas *in the West Indies between 1784 and 1787. It was during this period that he met his future wife Frances Nisbet.*

The gates of Montpelier House, Nevis. Fanny and Horatio Nelson were married on 11 March 1787 at the house of Fanny's uncle, the President of Nevis, John Herbert. The house has long since disappeared but its gates survive.

While Nelson was here, Governor Shirley was fortifying what came to be known as Shirley Heights above the harbour; the Monk's Hill fortifications already existed.

It was on the island of Nevis that Nelson met and married Frances Nisbet. Then it was the most fashionable of the sugar islands and some of the great plantation houses and their factories survive, several as hotels. The Nisbet plantation – now a hotel – lies by the sea, while the factory at Montpelier, near the plantation house where Fanny lived with her uncle, has also been converted into a hotel; the house itself has gone, only the stone gate-posts remaining and a great silk-cotton tree beneath which the wedding guests gathered. Fig Tree Church, where the marriage was entered in the register, is much as it was and Nelson would recognize many of the buildings in the capital, Charlestown. One of these, the Bath Hotel, had been built in 1778 to accommodate fifty guests, who were taking hot thermal baths in the spring over which it had been built. On the shore, Fort Charles overlooks the anchorage which its guns commanded.

The most inaccessible Nelsonian site around the Caribbean – or anywhere, perhaps – is the Castle of San Juan (called the Spanish, El Castillo de la Inmaculada Concepcion) on one of the upper reaches of the Rio San Juan in Nicaragua. Far from any road, it can only be visited by light aircraft from Managua, landing on an airstrip at a ranch close to a tributary of the river and completing the journey by canoe. The river, as wide as the Thames at Richmond, is overhung by the trees of the rainforest, standing to 200 ft tall. The island of Bartola below the rapids, which the castle commanded, cannot now be identified

Fort San Juan, Nicaragua. In 1780 the young Captain Nelson took part in an expedition to capture this lonely outpost of the Spanish Empire – and nearly lost his life in the process. Photograph taken by the author when he visited in 1978, arriving there by canoe!

with certainty, but there is such an island with the thick red mud in which Captain Nelson lost his shoes when he led the storming of the Spanish battery. The castle itself, exactly identifiable from a drawing of 1780 (now in the library of Brown University, Providence, Rhode Island, USA), stands on its little conical hill above the rapids. Now derelict, its massive walls, painted white two centuries ago, are now black with age and damp. On a hillock close to the gateway of the castle, above the village graveyard, traces of a small earthwork can be seen and assumed to be all that remains of what was marked on a contemporary sketch-map as Captain Nelson's Battery. Even more evocative than the castle is the surrounding forest, the torrential rain that can blot out the view of one bank of the river from the other, and afterwards, the rainforest steaming in the sun. A full account of the campaign in Nicaragua can be read in the present writer's book, *The Young Nelson in the Americas* (London, 1980).

Where can one get closest to Nelson? A muddy lane and a sandy creek in Norfolk? A river through the rainforest of Nicaragua? The surf curling over Culloden Reef off Aboukir? The narrow, dark, sulphurous streets of Old Naples? The entrance hall of the Admiralty in Whitehall? The admiral's cabin of the *Victory*?

Casting my mind back, I am reminded of words written by one who was far better qualified than I to write about the great naval officer: Edward Young. A submarine captain in the Second World War, he wrote in his own memoirs, *One of Our Submarines*, that once, when about to enter the Mediterranean, his boat remained on the surface at dawn and he looked out across the sea from her conning-tower:

There Gibraltar surprisingly was, grand and grey in the dimmest north-east distance . . . For the past two nights we had been smelling the land-breezes of Portugal, the previous afternoon we had had Cape St Vincent in view through the periscope (for we travelled dived by day), and all night Cadiz Bay had been invisible but somehow palpable on our port hand. Now . . . at daybreak we had Cape Trafalgar and the Spanish coast in sight to the north of us, and to starboard the mountains of Africa thrusting away southward behind Cape Spartel. All these names were an incantation to raise the immortal past, and the spirit of Nelson moved about the ruffled face of the water.

Sources

Most of the research material used in the preparation of this piece comes from the author's own notes, made during his visits to the sites mentioned.
For details of the main books consulted, see the bibliography at the end of the book.

The most famous memorial. A contemporary engraving of the original design for Nelson's Column in Trafalgar Square. In fact it was not completed until almost thirty years after this engraving was published in 1839.

CHAPTER VI

If You Seek His Monument

by Flora Fraser

In one of his most bizarre utterances, Adolf Hitler declared in 1940 that, once Operation Sealion (the invasion of England) had been successfully accomplished, he would remove Nelson's Column from Trafalgar Square and place this object of fetish in Berlin. For, he said, 'ever since the Battle of Trafalgar, the Nelson column represents for England a symbol of British naval might and world dominion. It would be an impressive way of underlining the German victory if the Nelson Column were to be transferred to Berlin.'[1]

Although Hitler's assumption about the date of the column's erection in Trafalgar Square was incorrect, he had a point. The column, based on Trajan's Column in Rome, became a popular London landmark – even totem – following its installation in Trafalgar Square some forty years after Nelson's death. The Navy League used to decorate it with bosky garlands, suspended from the lions' jaws and attached to the fluted shaft every 21 October. And Trafalgar Square itself, ever since it was laid out, has been a focal point in the capital for demonstration of public feeling – be it celebratory, in the fountains on New Year's Eve, or political. The removal of the column to stand abjectly in Berlin alongside statues of Frederick the Great and other German heroes might well have aroused, contrary to Hitler's intentions, a patriotic wrath in Britain which the removal of other British monuments would not have occasioned.

Nelson nearly didn't get his monument, Trafalgar Square was nearly called King William Square, and a statue of William IV, the Sailor King, was designated for the site of the present column. The change of name was made when an Admiralty architect, George Ledwell Taylor, approached the King. Taylor's first tenant,

Mr Barton, had leased a flat in the new building overlooking the as yet nameless square, and Barton was 'very pressing to know how to have his cards printed'. Taylor had audience with King William and suggested the name Trafalgar Square (Waterloo Place had been recently laid out). 'Trafalgar Square. William Rex', the King wrote on Taylor's plan, and sent him off with it to the Office of Woods and Forests.[2]

Poor William. After this act of generosity, as soon as he was dead – in 1837 – the committee of taste, who superintended public statuary and monuments, decided that there was no longer any need to honour him with a statue in Trafalgar Square. A statue of the new eighteen-year-old girl Queen also seemed to them, never guessing how many monuments Queen Victoria would later inspire, inappropriate. The choice fell on Nelson for the very good – if astonishing – reason that at that time no public monument to the Admiral existed in all the streets, squares and open spaces of London.

William Wilkins, architect of the National Gallery, proposed that the square below should be levelled, and a terrace erected, to give the Gallery greater elevation. In 1838 the southernmost space created was given to a committee of Nelson Monument subscribers and they approved William Railton as architect of a corinthian column, to be surmounted by a statue of Nelson sculpted by Edward Hodges Baily. A banquet was held atop the column before Baily's statue was put in place in November 1843. The progress of the bas-reliefs on the base of the column was dilatory. The Nile, Copenhagen, St Vincent and Trafalgar (by W.F. Woodington, J. Ternouth, M.L. Watson and J.E. Carew respectively) were not all in place until 1854 – and there were still to come the guardian lions, to designs by Landseer. These were eventually executed in bronze by Baron Marochetti and installed in 1867.

But this is to leap far ahead of all the earlier monuments that Nelson's name generated. Even before his death, his victory at the Battle of the Nile in 1798, and the string of naval successes that preceded it, had generated a public competition, organized by William, Duke of Clarence, and inviting sculptors to submit designs for a 'naval pillar or monument' in 1799. Among the entrants were several designs for a 'rostral column', a form of column surmounted by the 'beaks of captured enemy galleys' and used in antiquity to celebrate naval success. John Flaxman, later the first Professor of Sculpture at the Royal Academy, produced, instead, a design for a figure of Britannia, 200 ft high, based on descriptions of another classical form – the lost colossal statue of Athena in her temple of the Parthenon. He proposed that his Britannia, flanked by colossal lions couchant, should stand on Greenwich Hill. Sadly this bizarre effigy was never erected. The funds raised were insufficient for a monument of any size, and the monies were returned to the subscribers.[3]

In the same year, while Nelson was aiding the King of Naples to effect summary justice on the offenders in the late Revolution there, one monument was erected in

A Nile memorial. Erected in 1799 this pyramid was the brainchild of Captain Charles Herbert, Earl Manvers. The surrounding trees are arranged in clumps named after naval captains and ships.

England to honour the Nile victory – a pyramid, with a base 28 ft square and with a Georgian porch, in the grounds of Thoresby Hall, near Mansfield in Nottinghamshire. It bears an appropriate inscription, based on the account in the Bible (the Book of Exodus) of the defeat of Pharaoh's host and chariots. The author of this was a naval captain, Charles Herbert, Earl Manvers, who in 1798 had himself enjoyed a victory. On 8 January, as captain of the *Kingfisher*, a brig sloop, he gave chase to a French privateer, *La Betsy*, and forced her to surrender. Called home in 1801 to inherit his elder brother's titles and estate, he not only commissioned the pyramid but also surrounded it with a Union Plantation, where each of the original clumps of trees was given the name of a naval captain or ship. Whether word of this reached Nelson is not known. His thirst for recognition – be it an endearing failing or the driving force in his career – was anyway amply met by Lady Hamilton's caresses, and by the makeshift triumphal arches and tableaux that she devised. 'On my birthday night', he wrote to his wife from Naples in 1798, '80 people dined at Sir William [Hamilton]'s, 1,740 came to a ball . . . A rostral column is erected under a magnificent canopy, never, Lady Hamilton says, to come down while they remain in Naples.'[4]

When Nelson and Emma, with her husband Sir William, set up house in 1802 at 'Paradise Merton' near London, visitors exclaimed in disgust at the interior, which Emma had made a shrine to the Admiral – and to herself: 'the whole house, staircase and all, are covered with nothing but pictures of her and him, of all sizes and sorts, and representations of his naval actions, coats of arms, pieces of plate in his honour, the flagstaff of *L'Orient* etc.', wrote Lord Minto.[5] From the moment Nelson stepped on shore at Naples in September 1798, wounded and frail following the Battle of the Nile, Emma had promoted his fame, dashing about Naples in a bandeau marked 'Nelson and Victory', wearing a dress embroidered 'Nelson and Bronte' (the hem of which can still be seen in the Royal Naval Museum) and sporting miniature anchors in her ears. Her life from that moment till his death was, as she described her dress, all 'alla Nelson'.[6]

Although King George III, who did not condone adultery, might turn his back on Viscount Nelson at Court, the Admiral's admirers continued to agitate for a public monument, especially after his victory at Copenhagen in 1801. Major Cartwright expounded in 1802 an ambitious plan for a 'Hieronauticon', or naval temple, designed by J.M. Gandy the architect, which was to contain banqueting halls, a gymnasium and a central statue of Nelson among other splendours.[7]

When Nelson was mobbed in the streets of London and Portsmouth in 1805 shortly before sailing, ultimately for Trafalgar, he was a contented man. The fame which he had sought was comfortable in his grasp. 'I had their huzzas before,' he remarked of the people crowding him, 'I have their hearts now.'[8] This feeling of affection for Nelson found expression in, among other monuments, two which

An instant memorial. When the news of Trafalgar reached Scotland, this ancient stone was erected above Taynuilt, near Loch Etive, by ironworkers from the local iron smelting centre.

were apparently raised in November 1805, the very month the news of his death reached Britain. In County Cork, Captain Joshua Rowley Watson and his Sea Fencibles raised the memorial arch already mentioned in Chapter One. In Argyllshire, an ancient stone was stood on end as a crude memorial by ironworkers at Taynuilt. Taynuilt, by Loch Etive, was an important iron smelting centre; for all its remote location, the area was heavily wooded with oak and beech and attracted a great many Englishmen, especially natives of Lancashire. Evidently it was these Englishmen who dragged a 12 ft high granite stone on rollers from the loch side at Airds Bay to the grassy mound where it still stands. However, there is another tradition that the Taynuilt furnace provided the cannon-balls used by Nelson's fleet, and so the Scottish ironworkers felt moved by his death to make this gesture. The inscription of the slate slab, now in the local museum, gives no clue.

In 1813, Robert Southey wrote in his famous *Life of Nelson*:

The most triumphant death is that of the martyr; the most awful, that of the martyred patriot; the most splendid that of the hero in the hour of victory: and if the chariot and horses of fire had been vouchsafed for Nelson's translation, he could scarcely have departed in a brighter blaze of glory. He has left us, not indeed his mantle of inspiration, but a name and an example which are at this hour inspiring thousands of the youth of England.[9]

As the war against Napoleon continued, various public monuments to Nelson's memory, financed by local subscription and with the artist chosen by open competition, were planned in Glasgow, Dublin, Birmingham, Liverpool and later Edinburgh. However, an attempt to raise by national subscription a public monument to Nelson failed. The money accumulated had to be returned to the subscribers, and, as we have seen, no public monument to Nelson existed in London until 1843.

While HMS *Victory* was limping back to England with Nelson's body on board, Prime Minister Pitt and the Tory Cabinet were consulting with King George III about where the Admiral should lie. Westminster Abbey, originally the British Valhalla, was crammed full with tombs. Besides, there had been a plan afoot for ten years, ever since the war began, to make of St Paul's Cathedral a pantheon of heroes in the mould of the Parisian Panthéon, originally the Church of St Geneviève. So, with the idea that a monument to Nelson should be raised in the body of the cathedral, it was decided to bury him directly beneath the crossing. Nelson himself, incidentally, despite crying on occasion, 'Westminster Abbey or Glorious Victory!', had voiced a preference for St Paul's: 'I heard an old tradition when I was a boy that Westminster Abbey is built on a spot where once existed a deep morass, and I think it likely that the lapse of time will reduce the ground on which it now stands to its primitive state of a swamp, without leaving a trace of the Abbey.' When the *Victory* arrived in England, Nelson was laid in his coffin made of wood from the mainmast of *L'Orient*, the French flagship which exploded at the Nile. The climax of his state funeral on 9 January 1806 was the deposition of this coffin in a Italian porphyry tomb, originally destined for Cardinal Wolsey and donated by George, Prince of Wales, in the crypt of St Paul's. The trapdoor through which the coffin was lowered can still be seen in the ceiling of the crypt. A viscount's coronet, the Admiral's name and dates were the only additions made to the tomb.

The matter of placing a monument to Nelson in the body of the cathedral was more vexed. A committee of taste had been appointed in 1802 to commission memorial statues and monuments to the fallen or the victorious in the war against France. On the death of Nelson they allotted £6,300 of their fund to be paid to a sculptor, and declared open to members of the Royal Academy, and later to non-members, a competition inviting them to submit designs. As the designs flooded in, monuments in St Paul's to Cornwallis (Commander-in-Chief of the British Army in India), to Captain James Cook and to William Pitt – who died in January 1806 – were also contemplated.

John Flaxman won the commission, although it was a Pyrrhic victory because he was instructed to use his rival Richard Westmacott's design. Flaxman told a friend privately that the figures on the monument would be his own and in the finished work in St Paul's one can distinguish Flaxman's designs. The group of Britannia pointing out Nelson on his pedestal as their exemplar to two sailor boys repeats a configuration that he used at St George's, Kabul. These figures and other subordinate ones in the Nelson monument are classically 'pure', or idealized. In the figure of Nelson – whether following Westmacott or not – Flaxman breaks with the neoclassical tradition of this period, where the man memorialized is idealized both in features and figure, and draped in classical dress. Flaxman's Nelson, however, is a portrait statue, in which Nelson's blind eye and hollow cheeks are apparent. He is also in modern dress, and the only nod to the older convention is the way in which the pelisse, given by the Grand Signor, falls over Nelson's right shoulder, so that what Nelson called his 'fin', or stump of his amputated arm, does not appear.[10]

Beset by other commissions, Flaxman did not finish the monument for twelve years. From the date of the commission, however, the public grumbled that the monument was to be placed in St Paul's, where there was an admission fee of 2*d*. A print entitled *The Sailor's Monument* illustrates the complaint: Jolly Jack Tar stands sulkily in his backyard beside a crude memorial to Nelson of his own making.

Yet another competition exercised the wits of Rossi, Flaxman and Westmacott in the year following Nelson's death. At an emotional Lord Mayor's Banquet in November 1805, where Mrs Damer's idealized bust of Nelson was placed on the table, the Common Council vowed to erect a monument to Nelson in the

A public memorial. The official monument in St Paul's Cathedral by John Flaxman.

Guildhall. Mrs Damer offered to make it free of charge. This was refused and, in order to advertise her skills, she felt obliged to make mention instead of the fact that she had sent a bust of Nelson to the Emperor Napoleon. A Dubliner, Samuels, offered to carry out the work for £4,000.

When the time came to choose the winner of the open competition, however, the Council and the number of architects helping it adjudicate were divided. Rossi, who had entered once more, was told that he was sure of the prize. When the votes were cast, a number of aldermen, hostile to their fellow alderman Boydell who supported Rossi, formed a majority to select a virtually unknown sculptor called James Smith. The Council was then so wary of its selection that it sent a body of judges, including Boydell, two aldermen, the Town Clerk and the Common Sergeant to survey Smith's handiwork on Flaxman's monument to Lord Mansfield in Westminster Abbey. The distinguished group then called on Flaxman to ask his opinion of his former assistant. Flaxman refused to look at Smith's design for the Guildhall, as he himself was engaged in drawing a design for a Nelson monument for a Liverpool competition. However, he assured them that 'they had his authority for the ability of Smith in case of failure in their expectations'.

Smith's monument, in which they all had so little faith, can still be seen at the Guildhall, in a niche to the right of the steps below the clock. It is rather ponderously symbolic. The City of London, in allegorical female form 'murally crowned', turns away from a recumbent Neptune with trident and a grieving Britannia seated on a lion, to inscribe Nelson's victory on an obelisk. Beneath, between two sailor boys in niches, the Battle of Trafalgar is depicted in low relief. It is more interesting as an example of office politics than inspiring as a monument.[11]

Where calls for national subscription had failed, local civic pride dictated that in provincial towns both the wealthy and the impoverished gave willingly when a proposal for a monument to Nelson was mooted. We have seen that Flaxman was making a design for a Liverpool contest. The stages of completing this monument took several years; on the other hand the making of the Nelson monument in Birmingham, a more modest affair for what was then a more modest town, was a more efficient process. The choice of London sculptor Richard Westmacott again reflected civic aspirations and a wish to escape the narrow bounds of provincialism. Westmacott's statue was exactly calculated to realize most of the Birmingham fund, leaving a large profit margin for himself. Favouring naturalism, he produced a faultless statue of The Hero in contemporary dress. Part of a flag is draped over his amputated arm, and the prow of a ship gives depth and mass to the slim figure of Nelson. His good arm rests on an anchor. The rest of the piece is more allegorical, in keeping with contemporary taste. On the base, for example, 'the town, Birmingham, is represented in a dejected attitude, murally crowned, mourning her loss; she being accompanied by groups of genii, or children, in

*A provincial memorial. A contemporary engraving showing the
design for the Nelson monument in Birmingham.*

allusion to the rising generation, who offer consolation to her, by producing the trident and the rudder'.[12]

The modest appearance of the monument was not an indication of the amounts available. It reflected the fervent wish of the Quaker subscribers, who formed a powerful constituency in the town, that the monument should not glorify warfare, or exult over the vanquished enemy. Indeed, they would much have preferred the building of a dispensary with the funds, in place of a massive stone statue. So much in earnest were these dissenters that a design for a dispensary was proposed with a concessionary bust of Nelson for the front of the building. There were also cries that the local sculptors like William Hollins should be commissioned in place of London sculptors, but in vain. A civic monument was what was wanted to dignify the town. It would be the first public monument in Birmingham, and it was placed, when Westmacott completed it in 1809, in the Bull-ring, where the old Shambles had been cleared in 1800 to make way for a market 'for the inspection of rawhides'. The monument was inaugurated on 25 October, the anniversary of King George III's accession, and auctioneer Joseph Farrar left instructions in his will that 6d should be paid once a week to someone to clean it. The statue remained in its original position until 1959, when it was removed while the new Bull-ring complex was built. It was replaced near, but not on, its original site, where a flyover was now constructed.

Westmacott's statue was so successful that he was commissioned by subscribers in Bridgetown, Barbados, where there was a large British garrison, to sculpt another monument. Nelson had been to the island as recently as the summer of 1805, when he was chasing Villeneuve. The statue which Westmacott sent to Barbados was very like the Birmingham monument, and presumably the sum

A colonial memorial. A late nineteenth-century postcard showing the Nelson monument in Barbados.

raised by subscription was roughly equal that of the Birmingham venture. Despite some changes of position, even a change of base, the statue has survived sea-changes in government and still stands in Fountain Gardens. On neighbouring Antigua, in English Harbour, Nelson's Dockyard memorializes the young and older Nelson's visits to that island.

Closer to home in Dublin there had been a public meeting in early November 1805. A competition was proposed for a monument to Nelson, and, unlike in Birmingham, a local man named Kirk was entrusted with the commission. However, he was to work from the design of the London architect William Wilkins, which was a 103 ft fluted pillar with a 30 ft base and crowned by a statue of Nelson. It was erected in Sackville Street, now O'Connell Street and one of the widest streets in Europe, with many of the garrison soldiers from all over Ireland giving a day's pay towards its cost. It survived until 8 March 1966, the fiftieth anniversary of the Easter Rising, when members of the Irish Republican Army blew up the column and statue as a protest against British imperialism. The remains of the pedestal were then pulled down and today a fountain plays where Nelson was once raised on high above Dubliners shopping beneath.

The Liverpool monument, of which mention has already been made, was not erected in the Mansion House quadrangle where it now stands until 1813. Again Westmacott was chosen, in preference to Flaxman as well as local Liverpool artists, although the winning design was actually by Matthew Cotes Wyatt, greatly

An allegorical memorial. A contemporary engraving of the monument in Liverpool. Death reaches out to claim the hero while Victory adds another crown to his trophies.

junior in experience to Westmacott. Nelson, in a classical-style nude pose, is laid across the lap of Britannia. Meanwhile an 'enraged seaman' gestures at the sky, and Death as a skeleton hides under cover of a flag, reaching out to touch the Admiral with a bony finger. Above, Victory lauds Nelson with four crowns, symbolizing his great battles. Sadly, however, two of the crowns are missing today.

The choice of a London sculptor was not popular. One local man, George Bullock, enjoyed the patronage of William Roscoe among other members of the Liverpool committee. His design was remarkably similar to Wyatt's. Both feature enchained figures and a large group. Bullock was so incensed at being overlooked in favour of a London sculptor that he said he would make his design and erect it in a different part of town. Liverpool merchant Mr Downward was another malcontent. He had offered an obelisk to the city and Corporation, but they had thought it only a 'half-Nelson'. He therefore erected it on his estate outside the city at Knotty Ash, and had a very mercantile inscription affixed remembering the man 'to whose skill and valour Britons are indebted for domestic security and the tranquil enjoyment of industry'.

There were a number of other monuments raised by private individuals. Alexander Davison, Nelson's agent, built an obelisk in the grounds of Swarland Hall, Northumberland, a house with a fine neoclassical façade set among fir trees. The inscription was touching: 'Not to commemorate the public virtues . . . of Nelson . . . but to the memory of private friendship'. In Wales the story of Paxton's Tower, locally known as Paxton's Folly which stands above Llanarthne in Dyfed, is rather more eccentric. Sir William Paxton, a London banker brought down by the Whig party in 1802 to contest the County Carmarthen election, promised to build a bridge over the River Towy if he was elected. Further, he lavished enormous sums on the victualling and vinous demands of the electorate: 11,070 breakfasts, 36,901 dinners, 25,275 gallons of ale and 11,068 bottles of whisky were among the items, which cost in sum over £15,000. Despite all this electoral blandishment, the voters repulsed him and, having appealed and lost, Paxton built his tower to provide a constant reproach. There was more to come. When, in 1809, Clarke and M'Arthur published their *Life of Admiral Lord Nelson*, Paxton had illustrations from that book copied to provide stained glass windows in his tower celebrating Nelson's achievements. The tower was damaged by lightning and the windows are now in the Carmarthen Museum, but the tower with its wide-ranging views of the Towy Valley has been restored. The Landmark Trust offers a splendid weekend in the cottage below.

Paxton's Folly was not complete until long after his failure at the 1802 hustings, but in that year Nelson and the Hamiltons admired a 'naval temple' on the Kymin, above Monmouth, during their tour of Wales. Some congenial spirits in the locality were used to picnic on the hill, and after the Nile victory in 1798 they collected enough money to build the structure in commemoration of the great naval victories of the war. Nelson's words on the Kymin were reported by the local newspaper: 'This temple is the only monument of the kind erected to the English Navy in the whole range of the Kingdom.' After referring to the national subscription scheme of 1798 to 1799 for a Nile monument which had failed, he added: 'This at the Kymin is enough, for which the admirals whose successes are here recorded, are very much obliged to you.'

Another Welsh monument to Nelson was erected in the 1850s on a rock overlooking the Menai Straits. Admiral Lord Clarence Paget (eldest son of the Marquis of Anglesey who lost his leg at Waterloo) was Commander-in-Chief in the Mediterranean in the 1850s and modelled this statue of Nelson himself during his retirement at nearby Plas Llanfair. There are other lesser-known figures of The Hero to be found in secluded parts of the British Isles. In the grounds of Corby Castle, near Carlisle, a steep descent to the river gives access to a bridge by whose side a coadstone figure tinged pale green of Nelson, lifesize, stands solemnly. There is no known provenance for this statue and no rhyme or reason for its chosen site, although with water cascading down from a loggia on the steep hill above it is very picturesque. The statue may be a copy made by Elinor Coade of Lambeth's manufactory. It resembles the statue from that workshop which was sent to Montreal and is today that city's oldest monument. Another lifesize figure of The Hero stands by a sheet of water in Williams-Ellis's model village, Portmeirion. So brightly painted is the statue that Nelson looks disconcertingly like a toy soldier.

The coadstone statue, dispatched in the Canadian packet-boat to Montreal in May 1808, was commissioned by a committee of that town, which formed three years earlier soon after a waiter interrupted the first assembly of the season with a New York paper carrying Collingwood's dispatch which announced 'the ever to be lamented death of Vice Admiral Lord Viscount Nelson . . . in the hour of the victory'. A sum of £1,300 was raised, and a London architect, Robert Mitchell, was approved to make the pillar and base. There were fears whether the artificial stone would survive in the arctic temperatures of Montreal, but the monument survives to this day and looks remarkably unweathered.

Returning to private monuments, Charles, Lord Feversham at Duncombe Park near Helmsley in North Yorkshire, hit on a novel means whereby to commemorate The Hero of England. He had two wrought-iron gates set within a classical frame at Sproxton on his estate. 'Lamented Hero!', runs the inscription, 'Oh price his conquering country grieved to pay! Oh dear bought glories of Trafalgar's day!'

Most touching of all the private monuments to Nelson is that which the officers and men of Trafalgar erected on Portsdown Hill overlooking Portsmouth. All of them gave two days' pay towards the granite obelisk, 150 ft high, with a niche at the top for a bust of Nelson, whose foundation stone was laid on 4 July 1807. It still stands today, clear on the skyline, and commands a spectacular view of Portsmouth Harbour, Spithead and the Isle of Wight. Alongside is the squat

A private memorial. Special commemorative gates erected at Duncombe Park by Lord Feversham.

outline of Fort Nelson, one of the great chain of Victorian forts encircling Portsmouth. Another Nelson monument at Portsmouth had a less happy fate. Lord Frederick Fitzclarence bestowed on the mayor and Corporation a statue of Nelson, and one of Wellington, which were erected on the site of Clarence Pier and unveiled on 18 June 1860. The craftsmanship was thought very poor, and the figures were soon subject to pronounced wear and tear. When they were in a very bad way, a joker added tar to their faces, and a few days later they both disappeared. The pedestals were pulled from their roots and consigned by a party of seamen to the deep.

One other Nelson monument at Portsmouth, or properly at Southsea, has since been erected. In 1951 a Dr H. Aldous gave to the town a very swashbuckling portrait statue of Nelson in bronze on a square pedestal. F. Brook Hitch, who designed the Royal Navy Submarine Service War Memorial on Victoria Embankment in London, was the artist employed. On the west side a plaque gives Nelson's prayer before Trafalgar; another, on the east, records Nelson's brief stay, during his last morning on English soil, at the George Hotel in the High Street. The George was destroyed during an air raid on 10 January 1941 in which the *Victory* also suffered.

At Birchin Edge on the Derbyshire moors stands a simple obelisk of gritstone with a surmounting ball, 12 ft high, overlooking the Derwent Valley. A Mr John Brightman commissioned it in 1810. Enthusiasts went further and carved the names, 'Victory, Defiance and Royal Soverin', on three nearby slabs of stone. The 1805 Club, among whose aims is the restoration of Nelson monuments, and the

A modern memorial. The maquette for the statue by F. Brook Hitch on Southsea Common, Portsmouth, erected in 1951.

Peak National Park authorities replaced the missing ball in 1992. A testimony to the worthy activities of Edwardians is preserved. 'This bottle is to be buried near Nelson's monument on October 21 1905', the paper reads. Teachers and schoolchildren and 'many inhabitants' ascended from Baslow to Birchin Edge on the centenary of Trafalgar. 'Mrs Wrench placed a wreath on the monolith and Mr Wrench addressed the children on the subject of Nelson's famous signal "England expects that every man will do his duty".'

It is not now generally known that the column surmounted by an urn and trophy on Castle Green in Hereford honours Nelson. However, it does so with his bust in relief on the south side and with an inscription commemorating Trafalgar, 'which nearly annihilated the marine of France and Spain and confirmed in the eyes of Europe and the world the naval superiority of Great Britain'. The subscription committee had originally thought of a statue of Lord Nelson, but, on discovering it would cost 100 guineas, and an urn only 39, plumped for the latter. The first stone was laid as early as 31 March 1806 by the representative of the Palladian, Royal Edward and Mercian Lodges of Masons. A dinner followed for 150 at the City Arms Hotel, where 'A number of soups enlivened the festive board . . . the company did not break up till a very late hour'.

One of the most elaborate ventures by a small community was the Forres Tower on Cluny Hill in Morayshire. Its sophisticated Gothic and octagonal design was supplied 'gratuitously' by Charles Stuart (see colour plate 12). It was a happy choice. As 'architect at Darnaway', home of the Earl of Moray, Stuart was streets ahead of other local builders. As the 70 ft tower rose, gentlemen of the town founded a Trafalgar Club and, first at Mrs Maclean's Inn, then in the tower itself, celebrated Trafalgar Night in riotous fashion. One of the club's possessions, bequeathed to the Town Council in 1851 when the last of its members was dead, was a china chamber-pot with Napoleon's head stuck to the base.

The painter Joseph Farington visited Nelson's birthplace, Burnham Thorpe, shortly after his death and was surprised to find no memento of The Hero. The parsonage where he was brought up had been pulled down, and the incumbent rector showed no enthusiasm for a memorial to the village's most famous son. He thought people might then visit, which would disrupt the rural peace.[13] A fine memorial to Nelson, a village sign, was presented by the Navy to Burnham Thorpe in 1975, at the suggestion of Lord Zuckerman, a resident of the village. The plaque, which shows Nelson between flags below a view of the old rectory, is set in a deep oak frame within a wrought-iron bracket on top of an oak post. It was made in HMS *Sultan*, the Royal Navy's Marine Engineering School.

There is another curious monument in 'Nelson country' which was erected following the Peace of Paris in 1814. A Mr John Drosière built, 'in commemoration of peace' (and featuring a small medallion honouring Nelson), an obelisk in 'gault brick . . . with the angles, cap and surbase in stone'. It stands in what was an avenue in the grounds of Curds Hall, near Fransham in Norfolk. There is a strong possibility that there was a family connection. Drosière is said to have married Nelson's aunt, the daughter of the Revd William Nelson of Hillingdon.

A plan by a larger community – the whole county of Norfolk – to raise a Norfolk Pillar to The Hero was beset by difficulties, not least because there was a

A peace memorial. An obelisk erected in the grounds of Curds Hall, Norfolk, by John Drosière. Although it was intended mainly to commemorate the Peace of Paris in 1814, it includes a medallion honouring Nelson.

difference of opinion about where to put it. By March 1806 over £800 had been collected, as was disclosed at a meeting at the Shire Hall in Norwich. However, no agreement was reached where to site the monument. The matter lay in abeyance until August 1814, when, following the Peace of Paris, there was a new upsurge of enthusiasm for a victory monument. By January 1815 they had selected Great Yarmouth as an appropriate coastal site and agreed that the monument should take the form of a column, which would serve as a seamark and would be situated on the South Denes.

Sir Francis Chantrey submitted designs for a colossal statue of The Norfolk Hero, 130 ft high on a pier jutting out to sea which was to be illuminated. Colossal statues of antiquity, like that of Rhodes and, more recently, Canova's huge nude of Napoleon and Westmacott's Achilles in Hyde Park, inspired him. The committee was unmoved. By March it had approved William Wilkins, architect of the Nelson Column in Dublin, as suitable for the project; his Yarmouth design featured a massive figure of Britannia surmounting a pillar. A sum of £7,500 was now gathered in. However, Wilkins, on inspecting the site, declared that there were inevitable extra costs – namely £2,000 for plank foundations in the deep sand. Work progressed swiftly, despite a fatality on site in mid-construction. The superintendent of works, Thomas Sutton, was on top of the structure making a tour of inspection when he collapsed and died. By 1819 the fluted pillar of County Clare limestone was in place surmounted by coadstone gilded victories, dolphins, a galley and oars and the coadstone figure of Britannia. The whole stood 144 ft high, and within were 217 steps leading upward to give a view out to sea.[14]

An interesting literary footnote appends to this monument during its later life. With the residue of the building fund, the committee constructed a cottage on the South Denes beach, and caretaker for the monument James Sherman was installed there in 1817. At the age of fourteen, while working in the Wrestlers Arms Inn he had been press-ganged into the Navy. The first ship he sailed in was wrecked in 1803. He served in other ships – including the *Victory* under Hardy's captaincy, and on whose recommendation he came back to Great Yarmouth from Greenwich Hospital. During Sherman's occupation of the cottage, he rescued in 1829 a crew member from the brig *Hammond* which was wrecked on the beach. Charles Dickens saw the newspaper reports and, on coming to visit Sherman at his cottage on the beach, he found a perfect original for the character of Ham Peggotty in his novel, *David Copperfield*.

Norwich, as county town, had been one of the strong contenders for the Norfolk monument, but in 1847 it finally obtained its own Nelson memorial in the Cathedral Close, in front of the grammar school. Thomas Milnes, a protégé of E.H. Baily, was paid 700 guineas for a large statue of the Admiral with spyglass and cannon.

Meanwhile, in Scotland, the rival towns of Glasgow and Edinburgh had both raised monuments to Nelson. In Glasgow the foundation stone of an obelisk

A damaged memorial. Lightning strikes the Nelson Tower in Glasgow on 5 August 1810.

designed by David Hamilton was laid on Glasgow Green on the anniversary of the Nile in 1806 before 80,000 spectators. Four years later, on 5 August 1810, disaster struck. *The Scots Magazine* reported:

> On Sunday afternoon we had a most violent storm of thunder and lightning, accompanied by excessively heavy rain. At a 1/4 past 4 the lightning struck the top of Lord Nelson's monument . . . the column is torn open for more than 20 feet from the top, and several of the stones have been thrown down. On the west side the effects of the destructive fluid [i.e. electricity] are visible in more than one place; and on the south side there is a rent in the column, as far down as the head of the pedestal. A number of the stones are hanging in such a threatening posture that a military guard has very properly been placed around the monument to keep at a distance too thoughtless or too daring spectators.

A lightning conductor was installed once repairs had been made. Today it is a grim and unattractive structure which does nothing to redeem the thundering vehicles on the motorway around it.

When the Napoleonic Wars finally ended, the enthusiasm for monuments to victors and victory had a brief following before the post-war economic depression. It was at this time that building of the Nelson monument on Calton Hill in Edinburgh – a scheme which had lain fallow for want of funds since the foundation stone was laid by the Lord Provost in 1807 – was resumed. Robert Burn, an Edinburgh man and architect of Gillespie's Hospital, was the architect of the seamark tower which was designed to be both ornamental and useful. At 106 ft it could be distinguished by shipping in the Leith Roads.

Calton Hill had been intended as the acropolis of the Athens of the north. Other structures included the Observatory House, built by James Craig, the City Observatory, built by W.H. Playfair, and the National Monument, begun in 1823 to celebrate military and naval success, but of which only twelve columns were built. Constructed of Craigleith stone, the Nelson Tower was thought to resemble a collapsible spyglass or even a butter-churn. At the base there were rooms designed by Burn to house two or three wounded seamen, who would act as caretakers to the edifice. The rooms were appropriated to commercial use, however, and leased in 1829 to a vendor of 'soup and sweetmeats'. Inside, 170 steps led the visitor, for the outlay of a shilling, to viewing platforms aloft. The flagpole at the top was designed to enable flags and signals to be hoisted on the anniversaries of Nelson's victories. In practice it signalled the days when the London steamers sailed from and arrived at Leith. In 1852 its use to shipping increased when a time signal was installed on its top, by which captains could set their chronometers.

A Scots memorial. A contemporary engraving of the Nelson Tower on Calton Hill, above Edinburgh.

And what, meanwhile of the *Victory* – that most poignant of all the Nelson monuments? After acting as a funeral car for Nelson's body, she was paid off at Chatham in March 1806. Thereafter she had two spells in the Baltic, flying the flag of Sir James Saumarez, one of Nelson's Band of Brothers, until she was eventually docked for extensive repairs at Portsmouth in 1814, shortly before the peace. She was not undocked until 1816 at the grand age of fifty-one. As Arthur Bugler, the ship's historian, writes: 'Chatham built her, Chatham prepared her for Trafalgar . . . Portsmouth has saved her'.[15] She was never again to leave Portsmouth. In 1824 she was fitted out as the Port Admiral's flagship. While acting as flagship in the 1830s she received a visit from an interested Princess Victoria of Kent. In 1840 the *Victory* was moved to moorings off Gosport: 'for many years afterwards tough old wherrymen ferried thousands of visitors to and from the *Victory* in brightly painted sturdy wherries . . . using the now displaced Gosport hard to embark'. Victoria, now Queen of England, paid an unscheduled visit to the moored ship there on her way back to London from the Isle of Wight on Trafalgar Day 1844. Furthermore she sent to be housed in the ship, as an added attraction, the state barge of Charles II which had carried Nelson's body to Whitehall Stairs and which is now displayed in the Royal Naval Museum.

In the second half of the nineteenth century the ship's fortunes were not so happy. Back to Bugler: 'She endured the indignity of old age and was donated material and equipment no longer required for her younger sisters; on one occasion she suffered the ignominy of being supplied with the second-hand rigging of the fifth rate *Magicienne*. The nation was beginning to forget Trafalgar and HMS *Victory*.' Eventually, in 1922, unable to stay afloat any longer, she was placed in No. 2 Dock in the very heart of the old Georgian dockyard at Portsmouth. The Gosport wherrymen protested at their loss of trade. The Admiralty countered with a suggestion that the wherrymen could show visitors round the *Victory* in her new situation. In this same year King George V arrived at Portsmouth to embark on the Royal Yacht *Victoria and Albert* to visit the Atlantic fleet. The *Victory* was lying very low in the dock, her beauty hidden, and, according to Bugler, 'he gently but expressively motioned with his hands and said "Get her up"'.

A problem arose. The Admiralty could obtain no money for the extensive repair of *Victory* that was needed, as she was no longer a fighting vessel, although she was still – and remains – in commission. 'The *Victory*', says Bugler, 'had . . . become a caricature of the famous flagship of 1805. The hull with its short stumpy masts, wire rigging and many additions was ugly.' To raise the necessary money, the 'Save the Victory Fund' was launched by the Society for Nautical Research. On its committee sat Miss Sybil Thorndike, among others, and the President, Admiral Sir Doveton Sturdee, toured the country. 'Thousands waited hours to see and hear him. Thousands of children in contributing their pennies were rising, as he asked them to rise, to the Nelson standard of duty.'

The greatest memorial. HMS Victory, *surrounded by scaffolding during the great restoration of 1922 to 1927. An etching by Borlase Smart.*

He was once given £65 in pennies. In 1925 Sir Doveton, having induced seventeen railway companies to display Save the Victory placards without charge, died aged sixty-six. Seven years later the fruit of his labour totalled £105,000. The planned recreation of the *Victory*'s 1805 appearance was amply funded.

There was help from unexpected quarters. When the cabins were fitted out with 'bunks, drawers and sea-chest', Mr Wellcome offered to restock the surgeon's cabin and dispensary with medical stores and surgical instruments of the period from his Historical Medical Museum in Wigmore Street. The masts were restored to full size reproductions of those at Trafalgar – but with this important difference: they were hollow metal, and passed through the ship's hull to rest on the dock floor so as not to burden the fragile craft. Similarly, the guns and anchors were made of teak and other wood, rather than iron or lead, and the new steering wheel was hollow. This good work was nearly undone when, in March 1941, a 500 pound high explosive bomb blasted a hole in the *Victory*'s hull 15 ft by 8. Once again, the old ship was patched up, only to fall victim to a new enemy, the death-watch beetle, in the 1960s. Recently, a new and long-term restoration

The new memorial. The monument to Emma Hamilton in Calais, unveiled in 1994 by the donor Mrs Jean Kislak.

project has been initiated, with the aim of making sure that the old lady will be looking her best when she acts as a backdrop for the Trafalgar Bicentenary celebrations in 2005. With any luck she has seen the last of enemy action now and can remain peacefully in No. 2 Dock, a much-loved monument to Nelson and the Navy.

New monuments continue to rise. Emma Hamilton is now remembered in the Parc Richelieu in Calais, close to where she was buried in 1815. The Mayor of Calais and Mrs Anna Tribe, descendant of Nelson and Emma, assisted the donor Mrs Jean Kislak at an inauguration ceremony on St George's Day, 1994. The story of how Jean Kislak from Miami came to honour Nelson's 'bequest to the nation' in the late twentieth century is rich in international adventure, comedy and co-operation. Another key player in the story was The 1805 Club, which provided the sandstone ball from the Wirral, Emma's birthplace, that tops the elegant obelisk of Calais stone. The club has promised to add this new monument to the extensive list of Nelson monuments, and the graves of those associated with him, which it watches over and tends.

'*Si monumentum requiris, circumspice*', 'If you seek his monument, look around'. That tribute to Sir Christopher Wren is set in the floor of St Paul's Cathedral, directly beneath the great dome – and, as it happens, directly *above* the spot in the crypt where Nelson lies. But the many monuments to The Hero in Britain, Ireland, Canada and the Americas prompt the observation: 'If you seek his monument, look everywhere' – on a Highland brae, nude in Liverpool, within a railed perimeter in the West Indies, in allegory in the Guildhall, London. Bronze and marble, granite and coadstone – the materials serve to reflect the wealth and aspirations of those who once remembered Nelson.

References

1. Rodney Mace, *Trafalgar Square Emblem of Empire*, p. 17.
2. Ibid. pp. 42–3.
3. Ibid. pp. 49–50.
4. Sir Nicholas Harris Nicolas, *Dispatches and Letters of Lord Nelson*, Vol. III, p. 139.
5. Countess of Minto (ed.), *The Life and Letters of Sir Gilbert Elliot, First Earl of Minto*, Vol. III, p. 242.
6. Emma Hamilton to Nelson, British Library, Additional MSS. 34,989 f. 4.
7. Yarrington, *The Commemoration of the Hero*, p. 7.
8. Thomas Joseph Pettigrew, *Memoirs*, Vol. II.
9. Robert Southey, *Life of Nelson*, Vol. II (1881), p. 384.
10. Yarrington, op. cit., pp. 79–91.
11. Yarrington, ibid., pp. 92–101.
12. Michael Nash Monument Archive. All the quotations from pamphlets and other ephemera on succeeding pages are taken from the same source; Yarrington, op. cit., pp. 103–15.
13. Joseph Farington, *Diary*, Vol. III, p.124; Yarrington, op. cit., p. 137.
14. Yarrington, op. cit., pp. 140–9.
15. Arthur Bugler, HMS *Victory, Building, Restoration and Repair*.

Nelson at his desk in the Victory in the early morning of 21 October 1805. His famous codicil, leaving Emma Hamilton as a legacy to his country, lies open in front of him. Oil painting by Charles Lucy, 1853.

CHAPTER VII

Nelson the Letter-Writer

by Felix Pryor

H aving her letters by him, Nelson wrote to Lady Hamilton, 'was the next best thing, to being with you'; and we, who have no choice in the matter, have at least Nelson's letters:

> Victory Octr. 19th. 1805 Noon Cadiz ESE 16 Leagues

My Dearest beloved Emma the dear friend of my bosom the Signal has been made that the Enemys Combined fleet are coming out of Port. We have very little Wind so that I have no hopes of seeing them before to-morrow May the God of Battles crown my endeavours with success at all events I will take care that my name shall ever be most dear to you and Horatia both of whom I love as much as my own life, and as my last writing before the battle will be to you so I hope in God that I shall live to finish my letter after the Battle. May Heaven bless you prays your Nelson & Bronte. Octr. 20th. in the morning we were close to the mouth of the Streights but the Wind had not come far enough to the Westward to allow the Combined Fleets to Weather the shoals off Traflagar [*sic*] but they were counted as far as forty Sail of Ships of War which I suppose to be 34 of the Line and six frigates, a Group of them was seen off the Lighthouse of Cadiz this Morng. but it blows so very fresh & thick weather that I rather believe they will go into the Harbour before night. May God Almighty give us success over these fellows and enable us to get a Peace

And at the end Emma, too, had just this unfinished letter. Upon it she wrote a lament which has become as famous as the letter itself: 'This letter was found open on HIS desk & brought to Lady Hamilton by Capn. Hardy/ Oh miserable wretched Emma/ Oh glorious & happy Nelson.'

Nelson's last letter to Emma Hamilton, found open on his desk after the battle. On the right-hand page is her own tragic endorsement, quoted on the previous page.

In the resonant phrase of Captain Mahan, Nelson was the embodiment of the sea power of his age; and in a sense the letters embody Nelson. Another distinguished biographer, Oliver Warner, has expressed the opinion that 'Of the three Nelsons which have been transmitted to posterity – the subject of a legion of biographies, the writer of letters and dispatches, and the author of the sometimes frenzied and always intimate notes to Emma Hamilton, it is the letter-writer who impresses most.'

Warner here identifies two categories of letters: letters and dispatches proper, and the frenzied notes written to Emma Hamilton. This points to one of the distinguishing features of any letter. It has an intended recipient. It is not just a text floating about in the void. It is a message directed at a particular person.

Taking Warner's two categories into account, Nelson's last letter presents something of a special case, a synthesis. Like many of the frenzied notes it is intensely private, intended for the woman he loved ('My dearest beloved Emma the dear friend of my bosom') and yet it also has something of the character of a public utterance ('the Signal has been made that the Enemys Combined fleet are coming out of port'). Its public nature is emphasized by the fact that – as Emma's inscription records – it was left open upon his desk; a valedictory message to be delivered to the world through the woman he loved. It is fitting that it has become a kind of national shrine, a monument to Nelson, displayed in the national museum.

Nelson's love for Emma Hamilton has often been dismissed (not least by his contemporaries) as a kind of aberration; a sort of schoolboy infatuation; a gigantic crush on an increasingly gigantic woman. The frenzied notes he wrote her may not be thought of as impressive; but they do mark him out. There is nothing else quite like them; just as there is – as Emma herself would have insisted – no one else quite like Nelson.

One of the most frenzied of all these notes may well be the first that he ever wrote. In all events it is the first that is known to survive (his earlier letters to her having been more guarded in tone and fit for the eyes of her husband Sir William). It came to light only a few years ago, and was published for the first time in 1988. As its first publication was in a hack anthology intended for the general reader, where hunters after Nelsonian truffles might not be expected to look, it is reprinted here with, it is hoped, fewer errors of transcription.

This first love letter was written nearly a year and a half after the Battle of the Nile, when Nelson was cruising in the Mediterranean. He was chafing under the restrictions placed on him by having to serve under a Commander-in-Chief, Lord Keith:

Wednesday 29th. Janry. [1800]

Seperated from all I hold dear in this world what is the use of living if indeed such an existance can be called so, nothing could alleviate such a seperation but the call of our Country but loitering time away with <u>nonsense</u> is too much, no seperation no time my only beloved Emma can alter my love and affection for you, it is founded on the truest principles of honor, and it only remains for us to regret which I do with the bitterest anguish that there are any obstacles to our being united in the closest ties of this worlds rigid rules, as we are in those of real love. Continue only to love your faithful Nelson as he loves his Emma. Your [*sic*] are my guide I submit to you, let me find all my fond heart hopes and wishes with the risk of my life I have been faithful to my word never to partake of any amusemt. or to sleep on shore. Thursday Janry. 30th. we have been six days from Leghorn and no prospect of our making a passage to Palermo, to me it is worse than death. I can neither eat or sleep for thinking of you my dearest love, I never touch even pudding you know the reason. No I would starve sooner. My only hope is to find you have equally kept your promises to me, for I never made you a promise that I did not as strictly keep as if made in the presence of heaven, but I rest perfectly confident of the reallity of your love and that you would die sooner than be false in the smallest thing to your own faithful Nelson who lives only for his Emma, friday I shall run mad we have had a gale of wind that is nothing but I am 20 Leagues farther from you than yesterday noon. Was I master notwithstanding the weather I would have been 20 Leagues nearer but my Commander In Chief knows not what I feel by absence, last night I did nothing but dream of you altho' I woke 20 times in the night. In one of my dreams I thought I was at a large table you was not present, sitting between a Princess who I detest and another, they both tried to seduce me and the first wanted to take those liberties with me which no woman in this world but yourself ever did, the consequence was I knocked her down and in the moment of bustle you came in and taking me in your embrace wispered I love nothing but you my Nelson. I kissed you fervently and we enjoy'd the height of love. Ah Emma I pour out my soul to you. If you love any thing but me you love those who feel not like your N. Sunday noon fair Wind which makes me a little better in hopes of seeing you my love my Emma to morrow, just 138 miles distant, and I trust to find you like myself, for no love is like mine towards you.

Most of his contemporaries, even more so the Victorians, had they seen this, would have thought the writer had gone mad. At the very least, they would have recoiled in disgust; as they did at Hazlitt's *Liber Amoris*.

But it is not the sexual explicitness that is the most remarkable feature of the letter. It is the sensibility that informs it; the fact that Nelson should have set down this tangle of sensation and consciousness and dreams in the first place. It is astonishing that anyone in 1800 should have felt free to – or even have wanted to – express themselves in this way. It is almost as if Nelson had slipped his century; as if he had leapfrogged the nineteenth, and landed himself in the world of James Joyce and the stream of consciousness with which Molly Bloom ends *Ulysses*.

It is perhaps too simplistic to say that a man who was prepared to break with convention in this way was also a man who was prepared to break with naval precedent and disobey orders; but it would be unwise to dismiss such an extraordinary confession of humanity too lightly.

Nor is this letter entirely irrelevant to Nelson's public career, written as it was so soon after he had refashioned himself into a figure of world renown. The difference between the Nelson of this letter – Nelson after the Nile – and the earlier Nelson can be graphically illustrated by comparing it with one written fourteen years before, on 3 March 1786, to Fanny Nisbet, his wife-to-be.

Like the letter to Lady Hamilton, it is written after a parting and at sea. Indeed, the opening is uncannily similar. The world, though, is that of the eighteenth century:

> Separated from my dearest what pleasure can I feel? None! Be assured all my happiness is centred with thee and where thou art not there I am not happy. Every day, hour and act convince me of it. With my heart filled with the purest and most tender affection do I write this . . .

One imagines that Nelson would have been distressed if even the comparatively conventional letter to his fiancée were to fall into the wrong hands.

Indeed it is a mark of his strong sense that letters were sacrosanct, part of a private person and not to be shared, that he burnt not only his letters from Emma but many of those from his wife as well. According to one account, he called his stepson Josiah into his cabin during preparations for the attack on Santa Cruz in July 1797 'that he might assist in arranging and burning his mother's letters' (although in fact seventy-four have survived). Besides, common prudence dictated that his secret letters to Emma be not exposed to the unforgiving gaze of the world. She was instructed to burn his; something which of course she failed to do. Of her letters to him, less than half a dozen are known to survive, two of these only because they reached the fleet after Trafalgar and were returned undelivered. Viewed in this light, the openness of his last letter appears all the more remarkable.

It seems that the first love letter to Emma was sent by secure messenger, Nelson's trusted servant Tom Allen, together with a more discreetly worded note fit also for her husband's eyes (dated Monday 3 February, the day after the last entry in the love letter). A little later, on 13 February, he wrote her another circumspect letter, explaining that, 'I do not send you any news or opinions, as this letter goes by post and may be opened'. Michael Nash shows in Chapter Eight how the courier Francis Oliver was also used in this way. Other conduits for private correspondence were Nelson's bankers, Messrs Gibbs, Falconet of Naples and Palermo, and the Quaker merchant Edward Gayner of Gibraltar, the latter enclosing notes by Nelson within his business letters.

One of Emma Hamilton's last letters to Nelson. A chatty note about her activities in Canterbury, where she was staying with Nelson's brother William. It also includes stories about their daughter Horatia.

Fear of discovery becomes a recurrent theme in Nelson's letters to Emma. So much so that he is sometimes forced to strip his letters to their bare bones. On 5 July 1803 he tells her: 'Although I have wrote letters from various places, merely to say, "Here I am," and "There I am," yet, as I have no doubt but that they would be read, it was impossible for me to say more than "Here I am, and well".'

Nor was the threat posed merely by his own side. Several times ships carrying his dispatches were captured by the enemy. In the spring of 1804, after the *Swift* was captured, his letters to Emma were sent on to Napoleon in Paris. Nelson told Emma that 'there will be a publication' (19 April), and confessed: 'I wish I had them, but they are all gone . . . But, from us, what can they find out? That I love you most dearly; and hate the French most damnably' (5 May).

Nor was Nelson always the victim. Preserved in the British Library is a letter written by Napoleon, while campaigning in Egypt, to his brother Joseph (his chief confidant) in Paris. It had been intercepted after the Battle of the Nile and is docketed in Nelson's distinctive handwriting: 'found on the person of the Courier'. It was sent by him to the Admiralty eight days after the battle:

> I send you a pacquet of intercepted Letters, some of them of great importance; in particular, one from Buonaparte to his brother. He writes such a scrawl, no one not used to it can read; but luckily, we have got a man who has wrote in his Office, to decipher it. Buonaparte has differed with his Generals here; and he did want – and if I understand his meaning, does want, and will strive to be, the Washington of France. 'Ma mere' is evidently meant 'my Country' . . .

But the bulk of Nelson's correspondence – like the bulk of Napoleon's – deals with public events and public deeds. In this respect he was conspicuously effective, as his contemporaries recognized. In the words of Lord Minto when the Vote of Thanks for the Nile was being moved in the House of Lords:

> The world knows that Lord Nelson can fight the battles of his country; but a constant and confidential correspondence with this great man, for a considerable portion of time, has taught me, that he is not less capable of providing for its political interests and honour, on occasions of great delicacy and embarrassment. In that new capacity I have witnessed a degree of ability, judgement, temper and conciliation, not always allied to the sort of spirit which without an instant's hesitation can attack on one day the whole Spanish line with his single ship, and on another, a superior French fleet, moored and fortified within the islands and shoals of an unknown bay . . .

Quite apart from anything else, Nelson spent a great deal of his time writing official letters. Letter-writing – and sister arts such as memo-drafting, order-giving and signalling – was often his only means of communication; and even when he

Nelson's writing slope. Like many naval officers, Nelson owned a portable desk that could be set up on any convenient flat surface. Special compartments contained supplies of paper, ink, pens, seals and wax.

did have the opportunity to explain his ideas verbally, as before Trafalgar, they would often subsequently be embodied in a memorandum.

Indeed he wrote so many official letters that it sometimes made him ill. On 1 October 1805, soon after joining his fleet before Trafalgar, he told Emma:

> It is a relief to me, to take up the pen, and write you a line; for I have had, about four o'clock this morning, one of my dreadful spasms, which has almost enervated me . . . I had been writing seven hours yesterday; perhaps that had some hand in bringing it upon me [indigestion was diagnosed]. . . .

The letter continues:

> I joined the Fleet late on the evening of the 28th of September, but could not communicate with them until the next morning. I believe my arrival was most welcome, not only to the Commander of the Fleet, but also to every individual in it; and, when I came to explain to them the 'Nelson touch,' it was like an electric shock. Some shed tears, all approved – 'It was new – it was singular - it was simple!'; and, from Admirals downwards, it was repeated – 'It must

succeed, if ever they will allow us to get at them! You are, my Lord, surrounded by friends whom you inspire with confidence.'

In this private description of a public event, Nelson the private lover of Emma, and Nelson the admiral once more merge.

Nowhere more strongly than in his letters to Emma does his perception of himself come through. He sees himself as the stuff of legend; as public hero, or – with that mordant sense of the absurd with which he sometimes punctures even his own self-esteem – as object of ridicule, fit for the burin of a Gillray or Cruikshank: 'How I should laugh, to see you, my dear friend, rowing in a boat; the beautiful Emma rowing a one-armed Admiral in a boat! It will certainly be caricatured . . .'. It is this slip from the first person ('How I should laugh') to the third ('a one-armed Admiral') that is so arresting, and which distinguishes Nelson's writing style: the remark tradition ascribes to him on his leaving Emma for the last time – 'Brave Emma! Good Emma! If there were more Emmas there would be more Nelsons' – is utterly typical of this vein.

Another example of this self-projection is contained in the well-known letter, dated 4 August 1804, to Admiral Kingsmill, an old friend whom he had not seen for many years:

> Can I forget all your former kindness to me? No, Horatio Nelson is (all that is left of him) the same as you formerly knew him . . . I am sorry to tell you that my health, or rather constitution, is so much shook, that I doubt the possibility of my holding out another winter . . . but my dear Kingsmill, when I run over the undermentioned wounds – eye in Corsica, Belly off Cape St Vincent, Arm in Teneriffe, Head in Egypt – I ought to be thankful that I am what I am . . .

With this awareness of his own physical self and public persona came an awareness of the physical presence of letters, which the bluffing note sent during the Battle of Copenhagen – discussed below – so graphically illustrates.

It is perhaps the mark of a great letter-writer that something of this physical immediacy, this sense of the living presence, survives even when the letter has been stripped of its physical attributes, robbed of much of the eloquence given to it by handwriting, address-panels, seals – stains, even – and reduced merely to a printed text; a block of type amid a sea of text.

This sense of physical immediacy can be seen in Nelson's letter to Emma written after the birth of their daughter Horatia, when he was in agonies of jealousy over approaches being made to her by the future Prince Regent. It is dated 'Friday night, 9 o'clock' (itself an immediate evocation), 14 February 1801; and is probably best skipped by anyone contemplating a life in the modern academic community:

Do you know how I am amusing myself this evening? Troubridge is gone to bed, and I am alone with all your letters except the cruel one, that is burnt, and I have scratched out all the scolding words, and have read them 40 times over, and if you were to see how much better & prettier they read I am sure you would never write another scolding word to me. You would laugh to see my truly innocent amusement, therefore, again I entreat you never to scold me, for I have NEVER deserved it from you, you know . . .

The immediacy is such that it is almost as if we had stumbled across a film of the living, talking, breathing Lord Nelson.

This self-awareness finds something of a literal embodiment in the name by which Nelson signed himself. His earliest surviving letter – written, like his last, from the environs of Cadiz, dated 20 February 1777 (and for some reason not printed in Nicolas's *Dispatches and Letters*) – is signed 'Horatio Nelson'. But even at this early stage matters are not entirely straightforward. Within his family circle Nelson was known as 'Horace', not 'Horatio'. And although one would expect any eighteenth-century gentleman when signing himself to opt for the more formal version of his name, Horace Nelson could perfectly well have dodged the issue. His relation and namesake the connoisseur Horace Walpole, who disliked his given name of Horatio, used to sign himself 'Hor' or simply with initial, a compromise followed by Nelson's father who usually addressed his son as 'H' or 'Hor'. Nelson's 'Horatio' implies a measure of conscious choice. The family diminutive was not for him.

Up until 1798 Nelson's signature remained 'Horatio Nelson', being of course unaffected by the knighthood conferred on him after the Battle of Cape St Vincent. The first change to his signature was made after the Battle of the Nile, when he was granted a barony under the style 'Baron Nelson of the Nile, and Burnham Thorpe'. He now took to signing himself 'Nelson', as was conventional for a peer. The news of his elevation appears to have reached him on 17 or 18 November 1798, so letters written after this date bear this signature.

A year later, on 1 November 1799, King Ferdinand of the Two Sicilies granted him the dukedom of Bronte. This ushered in a bewildering sequence of changes to Nelson's signature that was to cover the space of just over a year. The first alteration to accommodate his Sicilian honour occurs on 24 October 1799, when he signs himself 'Bronte Nelson' (Emma having given him advance notice of the grant). From then until 21 March the following year his signature varies between 'Bronte Nelson' and 'Nelson', with two letters (dated 21 and 22 December 1799) signed 'Nelson & Bronte'.

On 21 March 1800 matters become further complicated. That day Nelson issued a memorandum to the fleet under his command: 'By my Patent of Creation, I find that my Family name of Nelson has been lengthened by the words, "of the Nile". Therefore, in future my signature will be, "Bronte Nelson of the Nile" . . .'. So, until near the end of 1800, he signs himself, 'Bronte Nelson of the Nile'.

Nelson's signatures (from top to bottom): right-handed signature; one of his very first attempts at a left-handed signature (within hours of the amputation); eventual left-handed signature; signature after being created Baron Nelson; signature after being created Duke of Bronte; signature after learning his full English title; final signature.

At the end of that year he returned at last to England. On his arrival there in November 1800 he dropped his foreign title. First he tried signing himself 'Nelson of the Nile'. This must be accounted the rarest of his signatures, only two letters using it appearing in the *Dispatches and Letters*, both dated 18 November 1800 (another, dated 17 November, was in the Wolf Collection, sold at auction in 1990). Unhappy with this, he switches back again to the simpler 'Nelson'. The first letter with the reappearance of this signature in the *Dispatches and Letters* is dated 21 November, the day after he took his seat in the House of Lords. This is of course the form anyone else would have used all along.

But he clearly still hankered after his Sicilian honours. Royal licence for him to use the Bronte title was granted that January. He once more set out to sea and on 26 January 1801 we find him signing himself 'Nelson & Bronte', the formula he had toyed with back in December 1799. For a few days he hesitates, alternating his signature between 'Nelson' and 'Nelson & Bronte'. He signs himself 'Nelson' for the last time on 4 February 1801. For the rest of his life he remains 'Nelson & Bronte'.

These changes in his name can partly of course be attributed to vanity, fanned by Lady Hamilton. It was she who had written to him on 26 October 1798, after the Nile: 'If I was King of England I would make you the most noble puissant DUKE NELSON, MARQUIS NILE, EARL ALEXANDRIA, VISCOUNT PYRAMID, BARON CROCODILE, and PRINCE VICTORY, that posterity might have you in all forms . . .' And both of his real-life titles must have been closely associated in his mind with her. She was chief celebrant of his victory at the Nile and had, he always maintained, enabled him to fight the battle by securing supplies for his fleet. Her links with the Bronte title were, if anything, even closer. She was the chief adornment at the court which gave it to him and, with the Queen's sanction, was the first to tell him about it. Indeed one suspects that she may even have had some hand in choosing it.

At the same time these labyrinthine changes to his signature seem to run beyond mere vanity. They seem also to reflect something of his own very conscious process of transformation into a figure of fame and legend: the transformation of Horace Nelson from 'Horatio Nelson' – via 'Nelson', 'Bronte Nelson', 'Nelson & Bronte', 'Bronte Nelson of The Nile', 'Nelson of the Nile' and 'Nelson' – into 'Nelson & Bronte'.

Although his Bronte estates were practically worthless, the name itself held extraordinary power. His dukedom lay on the slopes of Mount Etna, and it was here that the Cyclops Brontes – one-eyed like Nelson himself – had forged Neptune's trident and Jove's thunderbolt. The name Bronte in Greek signifies thunder (as in Brontosaurus, the thunder lizard); so Emma dubbed Nelson 'My Lord Thunder' and 'Great Jove'. His new signature perfectly fitted the apotheosis of the hero: Britannia's one-eyed Admiral, forger of her trident, and master of her thunder.

This meddling with names and signatures had one unexpected consequence. The use by Nelson of his Italian title prompted one of his many admirers, an Irish clergyman by the name of Patrick Brunty (a name possibly derived from the Gaelic O'Prunty), to adopt the spelling favoured by Nelson. Literature has thus been deprived of the Brunty or O'Prunty sisters. The Italian origin of their adoptive spelling is revealed by the famous diaeresis over the final 'ë', which while it no doubt adds greatly to their romantic appeal was in fact only put there to save them from the embarrassment of having an Italian word pronounced in the English fashion.

The Brontë sisters' diaeresis is often used in rendering Nelson's signature in print; sometimes, even, an acute accent is used. He himself, knowing it to be an Italian name, did not bother. Typographical convention causes further confusion by expanding the ampersand Nelson habitually used in linking his two titles, which means that the original form, 'Nelson & Bronte', often ends up on the printed page expanded to a rather unwieldy 'Nelson and Brontë'.

'Nelson & Bronte' does not in fact mark quite the last word as regards Nelson's shifting identity. No sooner had he settled on 'Nelson & Bronte' in the early months of 1801 than he temporarily shifted his flag to another name altogether. His new persona was designed for very different ends. The purpose this time was not to seek glorification, but to avoid it.

Nelson received the news that Emma had given birth to their daughter Horatia on 1 February 1801. Fearful of public exposure, he fashioned the pretence when writing to her that his real name was 'Thomson' or 'Thompson'. As with the English incarnation of Hergé's detective twins, use of the 'p' was strictly optional.

Mr Thom(p)son, a sailor in Nelson's ship, was the child's father. The mother was Mrs Thom(p)son, who was being looked after by Emma. Mr Thom(p)son was not in fact married to Mrs Thom(p)son: an irascible uncle stood in their way. The Thom(p)son child had two devoted godparents in Vice Admiral Lord Nelson and Emma, Lady Hamilton.

This charade resulted in a series of extraordinarily confusing letters, which reach their apogee on 5 February 1801 when Emma is instructed to register the child as 'Horatia, daughter of Johem and Morata Etnorb'. Immediately after writing this Nelson tells her to 'read the surname backwards, and take the letters of the other names'. This is tantamount to a confession that he delighted in the switching of names and identities for their own sake, and makes nonsense of any serious attempt at disguise (which anyway would have been rendered useless by his highly distinctive handwriting).

The famous last codicil to his will, written on the morning of Trafalgar, provides a touching postscript to this affair: 'I also leave to the beneficence of my Country my adopted daughter, Horatia Nelson Thompson; and I desire she will use in future the name of Nelson only.'

The letter to Kingsmill, quoted above, in which Nelson lists his wounds,

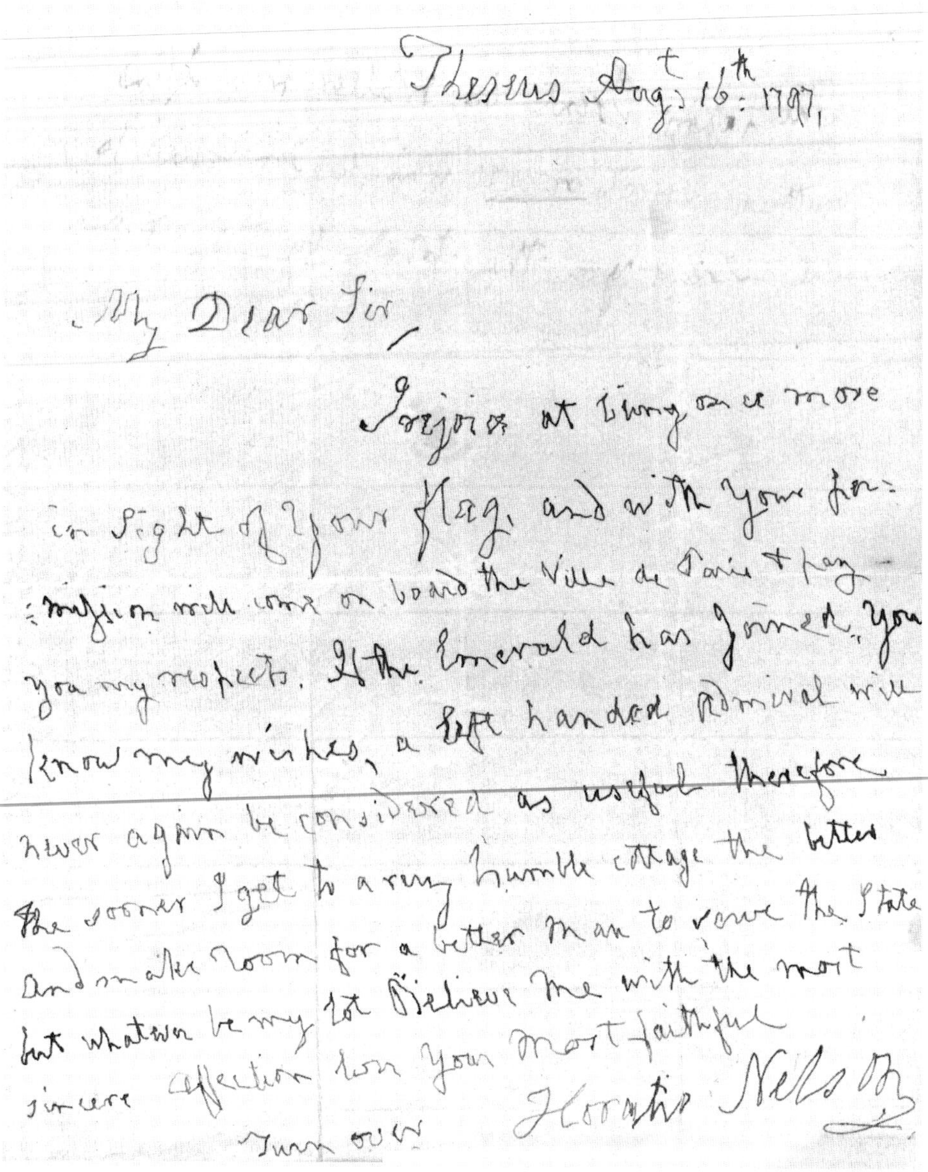

Theseus, Aug: 16th 1797,

My Dear Sir,

Rejoice at being once more in sight of your flag, and with your permission will come on board the Ville de Paris + pay you my respects. If the Emerald has joined, you know my wishes, a *left* handed Admiral will never again be considered as useful therefore the sooner I get to a very humble cottage the better and make room for a better man to serve the State but whatever be my lot Believe me with the most sincere affection I am your most faithful

Turn over

Horatio Nelson

One of Nelson's first left-handed letters, addressed to his Commander-in-Chief Lord St Vincent. He reflects sadly that 'a left-handed admiral will never again be considered as useful' – one of his less accurate predictions!

including his Cyclopean eye and 'the Arm in Teneriffe', begins: 'It gave me a twitch of pleasure to see your handwriting again . . .'. And it is handwriting, above all other things, that gives a letter its immediacy, that surge of electricity that can trigger what Nelson so tellingly describes as a 'twitch' of pleasure. The 'Arm in Teneriffe' forced a more radical change to the physical appearance of his letters than did any alteration to the wording of his signature.

Nelson's right arm was amputated in the early hours of the morning of 25 July 1797. With it he lost, in Keats's phrase, 'this warm scribe, my hand'. One would expect some change of writing with a change of hand. Apart from anything else, the angle and mechanics of propelling the pen along the paper are altered. But the alteration in Nelson's case was dramatic. Perhaps this, too, links in with the other changes that were soon to happen to him.

Before the amputation, his handwriting was a fairly conventional one for the time, being a fluid cursive, sloping to the right. Afterwards, when forced to write with his left hand, his writing becomes squarish with a tendency to slope backwards. It would be difficult to confuse it with any other hand of the period. Nelson's new handwriting is as distinctive as his new name.

Nelson appears to have written out a huge quantity of his letters himself. When one comes across an original it is more often than not autograph (meaning, in this sense, in his own handwriting). And this is despite the fact that the physical act of writing clearly caused him considerable effort. His propensity to suffer seasickness certainly did not help. Nor did the fact that he was forced to write left-handed, without having another hand with which to steady the paper. Furthermore he had only one good eye to write by; and that was an eye often subjected to considerable strain and liable to infection. It can come as no surprise therefore to find him making complaints in his letters such as 'my head will be turned with writing', or to read of the 'spasm' that assailed him when writing dispatches before Trafalgar.

Of course for many of his routine or duplicated dispatches (such as the orders to 'the Respective Captains' before Trafalgar) Nelson employed secretarial help. Perhaps his most prominent assistant in civilian life was his long-standing friend Alexander Davison, who was sole prize-agent after the Battle of the Nile and who looked after his business interests. Among his secretaries at sea were John Tyson and the two Scotts. Tyson was appointed his secretary at Naples, although he had known Nelson much longer, and was afterwards to serve as a Page at his installation as a Knight of the Bath. The two Scotts both served with Nelson on board the *Victory*. John Scott held the post of Admiral's Secretary, and it was he who was cut down on the ship's quarter-deck an hour or so before his master met with the same fate on the same spot. The Revd Alexander John Scott, known as Dr Scott, was the ship's Chaplain. He helped Nelson, who was a poor linguist, with his foreign correspondence (Nelson's foreign letters were usually written in English, with a translation enclosed). It was he who held Nelson as he lay dying and who afterwards wrote to Emma (8 January 1806): 'When I think, setting

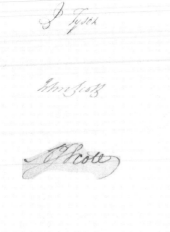

The signatures of Nelson's secretaries: John Tyson – personal secretary in the Mediterranean, 1799–1800; John Scott – personal secretary in the Victory, *1803–5; Alexander Scott – Chaplain of the* Victory *and Nelson's interpreter, 1803–5; Alexander Davison – Nelson's close friend, from when they met in Quebec in 1782, and later his agent.*

aside his heroism, what an affectionate, fascinating little fellow he was, how dignified and pure his mind, how kind and condescending his manners, I become stupid with grief for what I have lost . . .'.

It was also the secretary's job to copy Nelson's outgoing correspondence into letter books; examples of these, sprinkled with annotations in Nelson's instantly recognizable hand, can be seen in the British Library. Latterly Nelson had copies made by means of the copying-press patented by James Watt in 1780. By this process the original letter was pressed against dampened absorbent see-through paper. The impression left on the see-through paper could then be read from the other side, thus reversing what would otherwise have been a mirror-image. These press-copy books are also among the Nelson Papers in the British Library.

If the handwriting of a letter belongs to a secretary and stumps the recipient, he or she will often turn to examine the seal before ripping the letter open. A seal served, before the introduction of gummed envelopes, to hold a letter together once it had been folded and addressed. They came in two types: the traditional seal, consisting of a blob of wax impressed with a device; or the wafer-seal, consisting of a small disc of gum and flour, coloured to look like wax, which merely needed dampening to be used. A wafer could also have a device impressed upon it.

Nelson was very particular about such things. During the Battle of Copenhagen, realizing that although he was victorious it was going to be practically impossible for him to withdraw, he sent ashore under flag of truce his famous letter 'To the

Brothers of Englishmen, the brave Danes', threatening dire retaliation unless they ceased firing. His early biographers, Clarke and M'Arthur, repeat the story told to them by an eyewitness, Colonel Stewart, of how the letter was sealed:

> In order to show that no hurry had ensued upon the occasion, he sent for a candle to the cockpit, that he might affix a larger seal than usual. The letter being written and carefully folded, he sent for a stick of sealing wax: the person dispatched for the wax had his head taken off by a canon-ball; which fact being reported to the Admiral, he merely said, 'Send another messenger for the wax.' It was observed to him, that there were wafers on his table. 'Send for the sealing wax,' he repeated. It was done, and the letter sealed with a large quantity of wax, and a perfect impression. 'May I take the liberty of asking, why, under so hot a fire, and after so lamentable an accident, you have attached so much importance to a circumstance so apparently trifling?' 'Had I made use of a wafer,' he replied, 'the wafer would have been still wet when the letter was presented to the Crown Prince; he would have inferred that the letter was sent

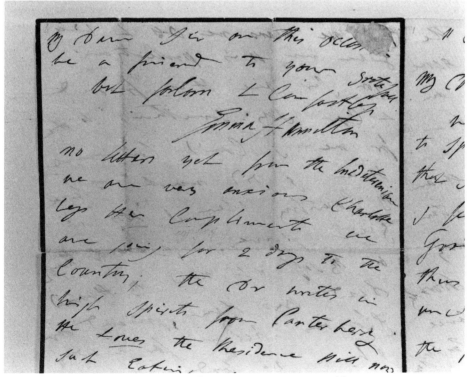

A letter from Emma Hamilton to the Prime Minister Mr Addington, written on black-edged mourning paper following the death of her husband Sir William.

off in a hurry; and that we had some very pressing reasons for being in a hurry. The wax told no tales.'

Such a communication would have been sealed with a coat of arms, the bigger and more exalted the better; and when serving as representative of one's country the royal arms could come into play.

For more routine correspondence Nelson favoured a simple peer's seal of an 'N' surmounted by a coronet. This was a fairly conventional form for the time (Byron for example used a coronetted 'B'). When writing to Emma, he would often use her profile modelled in imitation of a classical gem; a mode that had been popularized by the glass paste intaglios of James and William Tassie (see Chapter Four). Sometimes his seals were more exotic. In one of his letters to Emma after the Nile he used a design incorporating a palm tree, birds and torches. But when it came to extravagance of design it was, as always, she who outdid him. Her seals can be found inscribed with mottoes such as 'Lord Nelson God Bless Him Amen Amen Amen', 'Nelson Victorious First of August', 'Nelson the Baltic April 2nd' and 'Emma'. When in less flamboyant mood, she used his peer's monogram.

After the death of Sir William Hamilton (with Emma at his bedside and Nelson

Two examples of Nelson's visiting cards: one dating from when he was a captain and the other from his days of fame.

holding his hand) on 6 April 1803, both used black wax instead of the more usual red to seal their letters. Sir William's death also prompted Nelson to use paper printed with a thin black mourning border. This shows him once more to be ahead of his times. Mourning stationery did not become generally popular in England until a few decades later when ready-made and printed-up envelopes became available. It is possible that, like his early use of the engraved visiting card, Nelson picked up the fashion in Italy. The most conspicuous of later users of such stationery was Queen Victoria, who in mourning for Albert favoured small octavo sheets dwarfed by three-quarter inch borders. One wonders what she would have made of the precedent set by Nelson in mourning for his mistress's husband.

Sometimes a Nelson letter can be found which is as much scarred as the man. In his letter of 1 April 1805, quoted above, he tells Emma that he knows 'that all the Mediterranean letters are cut and smoked, and perhaps read'. This refers to the practice, dating from the seventeenth century, of disinfecting letters brought by ship to the United Kingdom from countries infected by the plague. Methods used included exposing letters to the air, heating them in a fumigating box, splashing them with disinfectant (normally vinegar), or slashing them so as to allow the bad air out and the fumigant or good air in.

This threat to Nelson's secret enclosures – this attempt to purge what is hidden – provides a curiously literal example of censorship at work. It might be thought of as the enactment of a metaphor; certainly no other good purpose was served, as letters do not carry infection anyway.

Very often, having been carried by messenger or dispatch-boat, Nelson's letters show no evidence of having been through the posts. Of those that have, many bear the Foreign Office datestamp or, more frequently, his Free Frank. As a member of the House of Lords, Nelson was allowed the privilege of sending ten letters a day, so long as he signed, dated and wrote from where it was sent on the address panel. If sent from or through London, such Free Franks were stamped with a crowned 'Free' postmark in red ink. Although it was strictly speaking an abuse of privilege, Members of Parliament used to frank letters sent by friends and relations; and Nelson used his frank to secure free postage for Emma and members of his family.

In the 1820s and '30s a craze developed for collecting Free Fronts (franked address panels) and pasting them into albums; one which vanished overnight when the privilege was abolished with the introduction of the Universal Penny Postage on 10 January 1840. More often than not the 'Nelson & Bronte' encountered in such albums is Nelson's brother, the first earl, who died in 1835.

The fad for collecting Free Fronts coincided with the growth of what A.N.L. Munby has called 'the cult of the autograph letter'. And it is a measure of Nelson's fame that he has been forged more often than even the Brunty sisters.

Probably the most deceptive of Nelson forgeries belong to a group of letters purporting to have been written with his right hand when on board the *Albemarle*

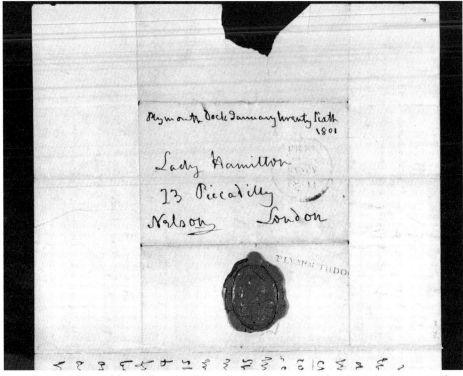

Envelope addressed by Nelson. It bears his signature, or 'frank', which meant that the letter was carried free of charge.

stationed at New York in November 1782. Naturally the fact that a letter is written with his right hand gives it rarity value; and its New York address is calculated to appeal to a particular market.

There is in fact only one genuine Nelson letter written from New York printed in the *Dispatches and Letters*. This is dated 17 November 1782 and is to his old commander William Locker. In the genuine letter Nelson mentions a promising young officer called Charles Pilford whose name does not appear in the Navy Lists and who may have died or left the service before receiving promotion.

The forger has cunningly chosen the mysterious Pilford as his addressee. In one forgery Pilford is told: 'I hardly know where my ambition would land me but if I die Admiral suppose must be satisfied'; in another: 'My interest at Home you know is next to nothing the name of Nelson being little known, it may be different one of these days.' Surely only the flintiest-hearted of collectors could fail to respond to such appeals. There are many other forgeries in circulation, but these are by-and-large generally no more competently executed than the Hitler Diaries, and should deceive nobody.

Bath Jan'y 29th 1788

My Dear Lloyd

There is nothing You can desire me to do that I shall not have the greatest pleasure in complying with, for I am sure you can never hopes a thought that is not most strictly honorable, I was much flattered by the Marquis's kind notice of Me, and I beg you will make my respects acceptable to him, tell him that I hopes his place in Mr. Palmers Box but his Lordship did not tell me all its charms, that generally some of the handsomest Ladys at Bath are partakers in the Box, and was I a Bachelor I would not answer for being tempted, but as I am hopebed of every thing which is valuable in a Wife I have no occasion to think beyond a pretty face, I am sorry the King is so poor had he been worth what those Vile Dogs of oppossition think, what a vast Sum would have been given to the Nation, but I now hope all the nation will Subscribe liberally, you will believe that I do not urge others to give and to withold myself but my mode of Subscribing will be novel in its manner. and by doing it I mean to debar myself of many com=

A Nelson facsimile. This excellent facsimile of Nelson's letter to Thomas Lloyd is so good that it has passed for the real thing.

Fame also brings facsimiles. The most commonly encountered is a very well-etched facsimile of a letter written with his left hand from Bath on 29 January 1798 to Thomas Lloyd. It was originally published in T.O. Churchill's *Life of Nelson*, 1808. Writing in 1910, A.M. Broadley remarked: 'Some years ago I saw it in a catalogue priced at several pounds! . . . The original would be worth quite ten guineas.' The ten-guinea original did eventually come to light, and was sold at auction in 1979 for about a hundred times the price quoted in 1910.

Genuine letters may be seen in many places. Their present whereabouts reflects the history of the dispersal of Nelson's effects (as outlined by John Munday in Chapter Three) and of the letters' publication (as outlined by Michael Nash in Chapter Eight). The standard guide to the history and location of Nelson manuscripts is Katherine Lindsay-MacDougall's article, 'Nelson's Manuscripts at the National Maritime Museum', published in *The Mariner's Mirror* for 1955.

The three main repositories are the British Library, which holds the Nelson and Bridport Papers inherited by Nelson's niece, the National Maritime Museum, which holds part of the Hamilton Papers, and the Nelson Museum, Monmouth, which holds the Lady Nelson Papers. These museums of course hold other material besides; and many museums and libraries – including the Royal Naval Museum, Portsmouth – have acquired smaller but none the less interesting holdings.

The earliest love letter, published here, is at present in a private collection in New York. The last letter, written as the Combined Fleet was preparing to weather the shoals off Trafalgar – or, as Nelson spells it, 'Traflagar' (Dr Scott was always to insist that the emphasis should be placed on the last syllable) – has come to rest in the British Library.

Other letters, including those from the Morrison Collection, are scattered: official dispatches, love letters to Emma, routine business notes; the whole paraphernalia of a life which is as vividly etched in his letters as those of his younger contemporaries, Byron and Keats. In the words of Clemence Dane:

There are many accounts of Nelson, written from many points of view. Men of his own profession, contemporaries and moderns, rivals and friends, hero-worshippers, grave official white-washers, flippant unofficial blackeners and gossips, all have had their fling. But there is only one portrait in all the vast collection which seems to me perfectly unbiased and consistent, only one portrait which shows the heroic virtues, the theatrical faults, the genius, the passion and the sweet, humane foibles of the man clear and duly proportioned, and that is the portrait which Nelson unconsciously painted of himself in his dispatches and correspondence. In spite of the vast differences in character and literary style, Nelson's devastating frankness when he gets a pen into his hand always recalls Pepys.

References

Quotations from Nelson's letters are taken from Nicolas, *Dispatches and Letters*, Morrison, *Hamilton and Nelson Papers*, and Naish, *Nelson's Letters to his Wife*; except for the first love letter to Emma, which was previously published in *The Faber Book of Letters*, edited by Felix Pryor (1988), the present text having been corrected from a photocopy of the original supplied by Mr and Mrs Harry Spiro, by whose generous permission the letter is published.

Nelson's first surviving letter, left unpublished by Nicolas, is among the Nelson Papers in the British Library, Add. MS. 34,988. The original of the letter to Thomas Lloyd was sold at Sotheby's on 23 July 1979, lot 17; the letter signed 'Nelson of the Nile' in the second part of the Wolf Sale, Christie's, 20 June 1990, lot 218.

The quotation near the beginning by Oliver Warner is from his *Portrait of Lord Nelson*, pp. 356-7; the concluding quotation is from Clemence Dane's introduction to *The Nelson Touch*. Other references are to Bradley's *Chats on Autographs* (1910), p.78, and A.N.L. Munby, *The Cult of the Autograph Letter in England* (1962).

The quotation from Clarke and M'Arthur's account of Copenhagen is taken from Morrison; other facts and information are taken from the foregoing (principally Naish) and from the standard biography by Carola Oman.

The authority for believing that Scott pronounced Trafalgar in the Spanish fashion (which we here suggest prompted Nelson's own pronunciation as reflected in his spelling) is Gatty's *Life of the Rev A.J. Scott*, 1842, pp. 220–1.

Sotheby's and John Wilson kindly provided examples of forgeries; and Alan Rawlings invaluable help on disinfected mail and franking.

THE

LIFE

OF

THE RIGHT HONOURABLE

HORATIO

LORD VISCOUNT NELSON:

BARON NELSON OF THE NILE,

AND OF BURNHAM-THORPE AND HILBOROUGH IN THE COUNTY OF NORFOLK;

KNIGHT OF THE MOST HONOURABLE MILITARY ORDER OF THE BATH;

DOCTOR OF LAWS IN THE UNIVERSITY OF OXFORD;

VICE-ADMIRAL OF THE WHITE SQUADRON OF HIS MAJESTY'S FLEET;

DUKE OF BRONTE, IN FARTHER SICILY;

GRAND CROSS OF THE ORDER OF ST. FERDINAND AND OF MERIT;

KNIGHT OF THE IMPERIAL ORDER OF THE OTTOMAN CRESCENT;

KNIGHT GRAND COMMANDER OF THE EQUESTRIAN, SECULAR, AND CAPI-
TULAR, ORDER OF ST. JOACHIM OF WESTERBURG;

AND

HONORARY GRANDEE OF SPAIN.

BY MR. HARRISON.

IN TWO VOLUMES.

VOL. I.

Lord Viscount Nelson's transcendent and heroic services will, I am persuaded, exist for ever in the recollection of my people; and, while they tend to stimulate those who come after him, they will prove a lasting source of strength, security, and glory, to my dominions.

*The King's Answer to the City of London's Address
on the Battle of Trafalgar.*

LONDON:

Printed, at the Ranelagh Press,

BY STANHOPE AND TILLING;

FOR C. CHAPPLE, PALL MALL, AND SOUTHAMPTON ROW,
RUSSELL SQUARE.

1806.

CHAPTER VIII

Building a Nelson Library

by Michael Nash

Few people in history have been more written about than Horatio Nelson. The most comprehensive list available[1] features well over a thousand titles, both British and foreign, and new titles still come to light on a regular basis. Some of these books are of major importance; many are of comparatively little value; all are of interest to the Nelson enthusiast. They include full-scale biographies, brief sketches, collections of his correspondence, poetry, fiction, catalogues of exhibitions, juvenile works; in short, whatever the form of published material, Nelson has featured therein.

Naturally so vast a subject cannot be covered fully in a brief essay. Instead, the aim here is to provide a guide to the most notable titles, aimed at those who wish to build their own Nelson Library: a 'Top Twenty', as it were, of the Nelson biographies and collections of published correspondence.

Nelson lived in an age before autobiography was fashionable and, in any case, had little leisure in a duty-packed life for such an indulgence. But he did leave a brief personal memoir, written in 1799 for the *Naval Chronicle*, a magazine aimed at naval officers and their relatives and published in forty six-monthly editions between 1799 and 1818. One of the editors was John M'Arthur, who had himself served in the Royal Navy. Starting as a clerk, he was promoted to Purser in 1779 for his gallantry in boarding a French privateer. He wrote a treatise on *The Principles and Practice of Naval Courts Martial* and another on fencing. He also drew up a code of signals and later claimed that Lord Howe's famous code had been based on his ideas. A gifted linguist, he translated or edited books in several languages and this gift was put to a more warlike use when, during the opening stages of the French Revolutionary War, he was secretary to Lord Hood, the commander-in-chief of the Mediterranean fleet. In the course of his duties he came into regular contact with Horatio Nelson, captain of the 64-gun ship of the line HMS *Agamemnon*, and one of Hood's protégés. In 1799 M'Arthur used his professional connections with the new hero to acquire a 'scoop' for the third volume (1800) of the magazine: a 'biographical memoir', based on Nelson's own words. This original text, entitled *A Sketch of my Life*, was later printed in facsimile in the official biography which M'Arthur published in collaboration with James Clarke in 1809 (see below). It is a terse, factual account of the many actions in which Nelson had taken part with occasional characteristic flourishes, such as the naïvely vainglorious conclusion: 'Thus may be exemplified by my life that perseverance in any profession will most probably meet its reward . . . and I may say to the reader, "Go thou and do likewise!" '

Biographies of Nelson first began to appear during the sudden rise in interest that followed the victory of the Nile and which led to the demand for portraits and commemorative material examined in Chapters Two and Four. The first published details of his life that can be traced appeared in the first volume of what was to become an annual publication, *British Public Characters* (1798), and the first biography to appear between its own covers, and to deal with Nelson exclusively, was a pamphlet entitled *A Memoir of the Life of Admiral Lord Nelson*, published by a Norwich printer called J. Payne. The exact date is uncertain but internal evidence from the text itself suggests 1801. An even earlier biography, bound in with other related material, was published in Southampton in 1799.

It was not until the great surge of interest in 1805/6 that the first full-length biographies were published. One of the first in the field, although not in quality of content, was the colourful and extremely fanciful memoir written by Francis William Blagdon for Orme's *Graphic History of the Life, Exploits and Death of Horatio Nelson* (1806). Although the text was poor, the book featured a fine set of engravings, many of them coloured, which earn it a place in our Top Twenty. These include an early depiction of Nelson's famous encounter with the polar bear (see colour plate 10); a charming vignette of him explaining The Nelson Touch to his captains before Trafalgar; and some beautifully coloured views of the funeral. Although both text and engravings were dismissed as without merit by Nicolas – that acerbic critic of almost every Nelson biography that preceded his own great work – the book is still eagerly sought after for its plates. As many of them appear individually nowadays in print shops, it is obvious that a large number of the original books have been broken up. As a result, they are now both scarce and expensive.

So far, all the descriptions of Nelson's life have been based on public accounts; the next to be published had the advantage of inside information. James Harrison, whose book, *The Life of Horatio Lord Viscount Nelson*, was published in 1806, was a hack writer, down on his luck, who had been befriended by Emma Hamilton. At this time she was making increasingly desperate attempts to obtain a Government pension and, in particular, to draw attention to the scandalous way in which Nelson's last codicil, leaving herself and Horatia as 'a Legacy to my King and Country', was being ignored by the Government. It appears that she paid for the publication of the book by C. Chapple of Pall Mall and, clearly, she hoped that a book extolling her own part in Nelson's life might further her cause. As a result of her involvement, Harrison was able to include some anecdotes that are clearly based on Emma's own stories and which make the book a valuable source. It must, however, be used with care; for she was perfectly prepared to be creative with the truth when it suited her – for example in the very unfair allusions the book makes to Lady Nelson.

Out of London there was a similar demand for lives of The Hero of Trafalgar and numerous pamphlets or short biographies were produced. Among them was *An Accurate and Impartial Life of the late Lord Viscount Nelson* by Frederick Lloyd, published by J. Fowler in the Lancashire town of Ormskirk, which found its way in the Liverpool packet to Boston, USA, where it was pirated by one William Bolton and published in March 1806. The US version had only forty-six pages but it did boast a folded copper engraving of the battle formation at Trafalgar and a portrait frontispiece. As the first transatlantic Nelson biography, it wins a place in the Top Twenty for its curiosity value.

Two years later, in 1808, *The Life of Lord Viscount Nelson, Duke of Bronte Etc* by T.O. Churchill was published by Robert Bowyer of Pall Mall, and was so

The frontispiece of the biography by Frederick Lloyd, published in Ormskirk, Lancashire.

popular that it went through a second edition in 1810 and a third in 1811. The first edition is distinguishable from its successors by its larger format and an edition de-luxe was printed with proof plates on India paper. Once again, the text is hardly memorable but the plates have a contemporary charm all of their own. Based on a delightful set of pen and ink sketches by W. Bromley (now in the Royal Naval Museum) the series, for the first time, illustrated more minor incidents in Nelson's career – such as the boarding of the American privateer, the loss of the sight of his eye at Calvi and of his arm at Tenerife. Even the views of the great set-piece battles concentrate on Nelson's part in them, whether leading the boarding party at St Vincent, or collapsing into Sergeant Secker's arms at Trafalgar. The series concludes with a charming close-up of the group around the coffin at the climax of the great funeral service that looks very much as if it was done by an eyewitness (see illustration on p. 13). The book is also notable for the inclusion for the first time of a facsimile Nelson letter, this one written to Thomas Lloyd and dated 29 January 1798. So good is the reproduction that copies are frequently removed from the book and turn up on the market masquerading hopefully as an 'original' letter. Nicolas, true to character, dismissed it as 'A wretched compilation intended as the vehicle of some equally wretched engravings'.[2] Posterity has been rather kinder and, as with Orme's work, the book now deserves a place in the Top Twenty.

So, by 1808 there were already numerous biographies available, but none had yet been fully worthy of their subject. Recognizing the need, John M'Arthur joined forces once again with the Chaplain to the Prince of Wales, Revd James Stanier Clarke, and devised a plan for producing a massive 'official' biography that would be based so far as possible on Nelson's own papers. At that time there was of course no central collection of such papers: most of them were still lovingly treasured as keepsakes by his many relatives, friends and naval colleagues. So the first task of the authors was to track down the material they wanted and to copy it. They were remarkably successful in their quest and their massive two-volume work, published in 1809 by Cadell & W. Davis of the Strand, contains copies of many important letters from sources such as Earl Nelson, George Rose, Emma Hamilton, Dr Beatty and Captain Hardy – although the authors could not resist the temptation to 'improve' the style and occasionally in places even falsified evidence to protect reputations. To add further to the book's appeal, they commissioned an impressive set of illustrations from some of the leading artists of the day, including Benjamin West (whose allegorical frontispiece to Volume One is examined in Chapter One), and the great marine artist Nicholas Pocock, who contributed vivid views of Nelson's four great actions which have become among the most popular and well known of all the battle scenes associated with him. A series of studies of famous Nelsonian incidents was contributed by Westall and it is his versions of events, such as the encounter with the polar bear, that have become most familiar through being constantly reproduced in subsequent biographies; while Bromley's versions of the same incidents are now much less well known.

Hardly surprisingly, such a massive and lavishly produced book was expensive. Those who had subscribed before publication (and there is an impressive list of them at the beginning of volume one, including just about everybody of any consequence connected with Nelson still living) paid eight guineas for a copy with proof illustrations and six guineas for the ordinary copy. After publication the cost went up still further 'on account of the expenses having so very much exceeded the calculation'. As a result it could only be obtained by the wealthy and so an octavo abridged version, illustrated with a simple portrait frontispiece only, was published in 1810. A second edition proper appeared in 1839/40, divided into seven parts that could be bound up into three octavo volumes. They contained some additional biographical notes of the main characters and also the recollections of Nelson's servant Tom Allen and memoirs of Hardy and Collingwood. The text has not stood the tests of time or later scholarship, being full of what Professor John Knox Laughton described as 'irrelevant and doubtful matter' (for example, a number of rather histrionic tales of childhood prowess); and the original edition, although handsome in appearance, is cumbersome to read because of its size and weight. None the less, 'Clarke and M'Arthur', as the work is always called, must stand as one of the great Nelson biographies and no Nelson Library worth its name can be without it.

Close on its heels came one of the greatest and certainly by far the most popular biographies: Robert Southey's *Life of Nelson*. A masterpiece of literary style by a

Robert Southey, Poet Laureate and author of one of the great Nelson biographies published in 1813.

poet at the height of his powers (he was appointed Poet Laureate in 1813), it first appeared on 1 May 1813 in two slim volumes and has hardly ever been out of print since. In excess of one hundred editions have been published in England alone and it has been translated into numerous languages.

Southey's association with Nelson's life had begun in February 1810, when he published an article in the *Quarterly Review*, based on the main existing biographies by Harrison, Charnock, Churchill and Clarke and M'Arthur. His publisher John Murray was delighted with the article and immediately commissioned him to extend his study into a full-length book, but Southey found it a formidable task mainly because of his lack of knowledge of nautical affairs. He wrote: 'I am such a sad lubber that I feel half ashamed of myself for being persuaded ever even to review THE LIFE OF NELSON much more to write one. . . . I walk among sea terms as a cat does in a china pantry, in bodily fear of doing mischief, and betraying myself'.[3] In the end his sailor brother Thomas helped him to avoid the worst maritime pitfalls and the result was a work that has inspired generations of sailors – as Southey hoped it would. His command of language puts the book on a higher plane than any of its competitors and gives to Nelson's life the aura of a great Greek tragedy. Nowhere is this better seen than in the famous passage where Southey recalls the mood in England when the news of the death of Nelson arrived:

The death of Nelson was felt in England as something more than a public calamity: men started at the intelligence, and turned pale; as if they had heard of the loss of a dear friend . . . The people of England grieved that funeral ceremonies, public monuments, and posthumous rewards, were all that they could now bestow upon him, whom the king, the legislature, and the nation, would have alike delighted to honour; whom every tongue would have blessed; whose presence in every village through which he might have passed would have wakened the church bells, have given school-boys a holyday, have drawn children from their sports to gaze upon him, and 'old men from the chimney corner', to look upon Nelson ere they died. The victory of Trafalgar was celebrated, indeed, with the usual forms of rejoicing, but they were without joy.[4]

The book is not without its faults. Chief among these was Southey's repetition of the accusations made against Nelson of misconduct during the Neapolitan Revolution in 1799: accusations which have been, very largely, refuted by subsequent research. Like its predecessors, therefore, it should be read with care and, for this reason, one of the best editions available is the version published by J.M. Dent in 1922 with invaluable footnotes by the first director of the National Maritime Museum, Sir Geoffrey Callender, which corrects Southey's mistakes and provides useful background on the main characters and events. None the less,

Frontispiece of the anonymous edition of Nelson's letters to Emma Hamilton published in 1814.

even as it stands, it is a matchless work; a worthy tribute to a great man by one of his great contemporaries. Sir Humphrey Davy, who knew and admired both Nelson and Southey, described it as an 'immortal monument raised by genius to valour'.[5]

No sooner was that monument raised, however, than it began to be spattered with mud. Less than a year after the publication of Southey's *Life*, the first shot was fired in what was to become an extended battle over the parentage of Horatia Nelson. It came in an anonymous book published in two volumes by Thomas Lovewell & Co., *The Letters of Lord Nelson to Lady Hamilton; With a Supplement of Interesting Letters by Distinguished Characters*. For the first time the true, passionate nature of Nelson's involvement with Emma Hamilton was revealed to the general public and it caused a revulsion of feeling against him. *The Quarterly Review* began its review of the book with:

> It is with great regret that we undertake to give to our readers some account of these volumes. The only cloud which has obscured the bright fame of the immortal Nelson was generated by the fatal atmosphere of Naples. His public honour and his private faith have been sullied by, to say no worse of it, a foible, of which these volumes are a fresh, and, we must add, a shameless record.[6]

In fact, not all of the letters were completely genuine. When some of the originals came into Nicolas's hands in the 1840s, he was able to show that the anonymous editor had in places deliberately falsified them in order to make his book more spicy. But by then the damage was done. The exact nature of the Nelson/Hamilton relationship had become a matter of public debate and the irascible old Earl St Vincent summed up the feelings of many of his contemporaries when he wrote of the book: 'It will reflect eternal disgrace upon the character of Lord Nelson, which will ultimately be stripped of everything but animal courage, of which he certainly had an abundant share.' Strong words; but then 'Old Jarvie' never really understood or fully sympathized with his colourful and more brilliant subordinate.

Who then was responsible for 'leaking' these key documents? At the time blame fell on poor Emma. She strenuously denied having had anything to do with their public appearance, but she was not believed and the scandal surrounding the book probably did much to hasten her descent towards an early grave. She died, a sad and lonely figure, in Calais just a few months after its publication. Another possible candidate was thought to be Harrison, because of his known close ties with Emma. He was even accused of having stolen the letters from Merton. However, modern research has shown that a far more likely candidate is a shadowy bit-player in the Nelson story known as Francis Oliver.

Oliver is first mentioned as a secretary to Sir William Hamilton in Naples, around the time that the young Emma Lyons arrived to stay with her lover's uncle. Later, when Nelson and the Hamiltons reached Vienna during their triumphal tour of Europe in 1800, they re-encountered Oliver who had settled there earlier and was clearly an accomplished linguist. He appears to have acted as a confidential courier and we know that later, at the time of the birth of Horatia, he carried between Nelson and Emma the very letters that were later published with such damning effect. Indeed, the most famous one, beginning, 'Now my own dear wife, for such you are in my eyes and in the face of heaven', which shows so clearly that the two were lovers, actually contains the phrase 'I daresay that Oliver will faithfully deliver this letter'. Later still, after Nelson's death, he resurfaces again as Emma's secretary and it is clear from surviving correspondence that they had a bitter and long-standing quarrel. Indeed, it appears that Oliver had threatened to publish something defamatory about Emma as early as 1808 for, in that year, another of her protégés, Dr Lawrence, wrote to Nelson's brother-in-law George Matcham: 'Oliver has expressed much gratitude for your kindness and promises not to publish anything. I hope you have written to Lady Hamilton, as it might be the means of making her happy on that head.'[7] By July matters were clearly getting worse for Lawrence again wrote to Matcham: 'I would advise Lady H. to desire an Attorney to write a letter threatening [Oliver] with an action for defamation, which will fully put a stop to this nonsense.'[8]

Whether Oliver's 'nonsense' actually extended as far as the publication of these damaging letters cannot be proved beyond doubt; on the other hand, their actual existence was never disputed. They passed into the hands of the publisher of the book, Lovewell, and when he became bankrupt in 1817 were bought in a sale of his effects by the Secretary to the Admiralty, John Wilson Croker. He made them available to Nicolas who, significantly, made very little use of them in his great collection of Nelson's letters. When Croker died in 1858, they again came up for sale, this time at Sotheby's and were bought by Sir Thomas Phillipps of Middle Hill. They remained in his family until 1946, when they were purchased by the National Maritime Museum. As will be seen later, other compilers of Nelson letter anthologies have made use of them, but the original, 1814, edition deserves its place in any Nelson Library as much for its effect on Nelson's reputation as for its actual content.

The extent of that effect may, perhaps, be seen in the fact that a thirty-year gap now intervened before the publication of the next book in our list. The editor, Sir Nicholas Harris Nicolas (1799–1848), has already appeared a number of times as a stern critic of other men's efforts to capture the life of Nelson for posterity. He had served in the Royal Navy, joining as a First Class Volunteer in 1808, when he was just nine and was frequently in action, mainly in boat actions on the coast of Calabria. He became a lieutenant by 1815 but, with the ending of the war, he found himself on half-pay along with many of his contemporaries and decided to follow a career as a barrister instead. An acknowledged antiquary and historian, he published a number of works, but it is for his massive and scholarly *magnum opus, The Dispatches and Letters of Vice Admiral Lord Nelson*, published in seven volumes between 1844 and 1846 that he is chiefly remembered – and, indeed, honoured. No Nelson collection is complete without them.

Nicolas used his extensive social contacts and his personal reputation to gain access to many collections and individual letters, including the mass of papers

The gilt decoration on the original binding of Sir Nicholas Harris Nicolas's seven-volume Dispatches and Letters, *published in 1844–6.*

inherited by Nelson's niece, Lady Bridport, and now in the British Museum, having been purchased from her son in 1895. Although it is at first sight simply a collection of letters, Nicolas took care to arrange his material in strict chronological order, adding extensive and very helpful footnotes where necessary to give biographical details of everyone who appears in the text, and also backing up the letters with additional documents relating to Nelson's career. As a result it is as good as a biography. The reader can follow Horatio Nelson from the proud teenager writing jocularly to his brother William announcing his promotion to lieutenant (or 'master of arts' as he jokingly calls it), written from the Navy Office on 14 April 1777; to the peer of the realm and commander-in-chief penning the words of his incomparable prayer in the half-cleared Great Cabin of HMS *Victory* on the morning of 21 October 1805. As Felix Pryor points out in Chapter Seven, Nelson was a remarkably vivid letter-writer and the careful editing (*without* the 'improvements' Nicolas so deplored in other people's work) enables him to speak directly to posterity with a freshness and an immediacy that are at once both striking and extremely moving.

However, not even the magisterial Nicolas was infallible. By 1846 no one, not even Horatia herself, had any doubt but that she was Nelson's daughter – one only has to look at the photographs that have survived of her in old age to see how remarkably like her father she became as she grew older. But she believed passionately – so passionately that she convinced Nicolas – that Emma was not her mother and he published a special appendix in his seventh and final volume attempting to support her belief. And, as we have seen, he failed to make full use of the very revealing Nelson/Emma letters which Croker had made available to him – possibly out of chivalrous desire to spare Horatia any further distress.

This, however, was a rare slip and every subsequent Nelson biographer has acknowledged their debt to Nicolas. Laughton, writing in the *Dictionary of National Biography* in 1894, said that it is 'the only work treating of Nelson's professional career which is to be implicitly trusted'[9] and, more recently, Carola Oman, in the introduction to her own major biography in 1946, called it 'the Bible of the Nelson student'.[10] The greatest of all the twentieth-century Nelson scholars, Oliver Warner, said that it was the foundation for all serious study of Nelson and his life.

Remarkably, however, there have not been any further editions. Nicolas himself started work on a second edition but only managed to complete the first volume (which includes a transcription of the original manuscript of Nelson's *Sketch of My Life*) before his untimely death in Boulogne in 1848. The publisher, Henry Colburn, hoping to reach a wider audience, planned a cheap reissue of the work to be completed in fourteen monthly parts at five shillings each, with the first issue intended for publication on 1 January 1847. It was never completed. So the first edition stands alone; complemented by subsequent smaller collections of other Nelson letters compiled by later authors, but never superseded. The last word can

The frontispiece of the biography by Dr Thomas Pettigrew published in 1849. This is an engraving of the portrait by the Neapolitan artist Guzzardi, mentioned in Chapter Two.

be left to *The Standard* for 1847, which remarked haughtily: 'The family that shall want this book must be ungrateful to the memory of Nelson.' Mr Colburn could not have asked for more!

A work which followed close behind Nicolas's last volume, and was partly inspired by the question of Horatia's parentage, was *The Memoirs and Life of Vice Admiral Lord Nelson*, published in two volumes in 1849 by T. and W. Boone. It came from the pen of Dr Thomas James Pettigrew, the son of a naval surgeon, who himself practised surgery, first at the new Charing Cross Hospital and then as surgeon to the Duke and Duchess of Kent, in which capacity he had vaccinated the future Queen Victoria. He became librarian to the Duke of Sussex and although he published a number of medical, literary and antiquarian works, he seems also to have had a strong taste for controversy. In the case of Horatia he had the advantage of knowing for certain that Nicolas was wrong; for he had in his possession many of Nelson's letters to Emma – probably purchased from the widow of Alderman Joshua Smith, the benefactor who had purchased a number of Nelson relics, including the Trafalgar coat, from Emma. Pettigrew later sold the majority of his Nelson papers at Sotheby's in 1853 for the princely sum of £501 6s 6d.

Despite the apparently convincing evidence of the letters, Pettigrew's book did not end the controversy. Nicolas was dead but his friends rushed to his defence in *The Times* where, among others, Samuel Phillips attempted to demolish Pettigrew and his theories. Truths and myths about Emma were dragged from cupboards and, in almost hushed whispers, aired in the press. Some thought Pettigrew ought to be snubbed; others clearly enjoyed the scandal. Most important of all, allegations were made that Pettigrew had actually forged the damning 'Thompson' letters, and even the infamous 'Now my own dear wife' letter. Despite the assaults on his reputation, Pettigrew remained calm, contenting himself with occasional return volleys in *The Times* and no doubt privately delighted that, largely as a result of the controversy, his book was rushed into a second edition within months of its first publication! The advertisement for this edition made the point of claiming that 'upwards of Six Hundred Letters and Documents, which have never before been printed, and the existence of which was scarcely known, will appear in these Memoirs'. Even though Pettigrew's book owes its success more to the scandal it aroused than to any great literary or historical merit, it none the less deserves a place in the Top Twenty because of the fascinating and revealing material it contains.

So long as Horatia lived, and continued to deny that Emma Hamilton was her mother, no final settlement of the question of her parentage was possible. However, she died, true to the end to her version of events, in 1881; and within a few years, two important books were published which removed any lingering doubts. The first, entitled *Lady Hamilton and Lord Nelson*, was by John Cordy Jeaffreson (1831–1901). A novelist and inspector of manuscripts for the Royal Historical Manuscripts Commission, Jeaffreson had already published two investigative books, *The Real Lord Byron* and *The Real Shelley*. In the course of his work he had encountered a large set of Nelson letters, many of them unpublished, in the collection of autograph letters amassed by Alfred Morrison

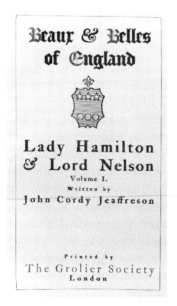

The title page of the de-luxe edition of the biography by John Jeaffreson.

and he used these to present a reasoned and balanced analysis of the complicated questions surrounding the Emma/Nelson relationship. First published in two small, unillustrated volumes in 1888 by Hurst and Blackett, *Lady Hamilton and Lord Nelson* was reprinted in a 'new and revised edition containing additional facts, letters, and other material' in 1897 with a frontispiece portrait of Emma. There was also a limited edition de-luxe, published in both England and America, with a number of additional illustrations.

Before Jeaffreson's second edition appeared, the letters themselves were published in 1893 and 1894, under the rather unwieldy title of *The Collection of Autograph Letters and Historical Documents formed by Alfred Morrison (Second Series 1882–1893) – The Hamilton and Nelson Papers* – usually referred to tersely in Nelson biographies as 'Morrison'. The son of a politician, and a man of considerable wealth, Alfred Morrison (1821–97) spent his life assembling a large and comprehensive collection of autograph letters. During the 1880s he managed to acquire a considerable number of Nelson and Hamilton papers from various sources and so, for the first time, was able to bring together in one work a very large proportion of the material that had been used to fuel the controversies of the previous seventy years. Edited by Morrison himself, the book was printed in two quarto volumes for private circulation among his friends – although, judging by the number of 'unopened' copies that still appear on the market, it would appear that many of those friends did little more than dip into the book. Had they explored further, they would have found a veritable mine of Nelsonian material, described by Laughton a few years later as 'a work of the highest possible value'

THE COLLECTION

OF

AUTOGRAPH LETTERS

AND

HISTORICAL DOCUMENTS

FORMED BY

ALFRED MORRISON

(Second Series, 1882–1893).

THE HAMILTON & NELSON PAPERS.

VOLUME I.

1756–1797.

PRINTED FOR PRIVATE CIRCULATION.
1893.

The title page of the edition of Nelson's letters to Emma Hamilton published by Alfred Morrison in 1893–4.

and by Warner as 'a primary source, since it amplifies Nicolas' collections of 1844–46 and illuminates the history of Lady Hamilton'. The book is the more valuable since Morrison's huge collection has since been dispersed. He died in 1897 and, in May 1919, his collection was auctioned at Sotheby's in a sale lasting eighteen days and including some 3,300 lots. It raised the enormous sum for those days of £50,654 17s 6d.

Now that the true nature of the famous love affair had finally been settled, it began to lose its fascination and, as a result, succeeding biographies were able to deal in a more balanced way with Nelson's public life instead of concentrating so heavily on his personal affairs. As the Trafalgar centenary approached, there was a predictable spate of new biographies, many of them simply rehashes of existing material, but three stand out from the rest as offering new and interesting insights into the now familiar story.

The first, in 1896, was by one of the leading Nelson authorities of the day, Sir John Knox Laughton (1830–1915). He wrote a number of Nelson books but his best was undoubtedly *The Nelson Memorial: Nelson and his Companions in Arms*, published by George Allen. It contains an excellent bibliography, some of whose judgements have already been quoted here, and is a very balanced and useful introduction to Nelson's life. However, its main value lies in its original approach to the subject. Instead of concentrating almost exclusively on Nelson and on his exploits, Laughton also features many of his fellow-officers and so, for really the first time, Nelson is placed within the context of his very gifted generation, instead of being isolated on a pedestal. The book is also valuable for its many good illustrations; but the frontispiece is a piece of history in its own right (see colour plate 11). Specially commissioned for the work, it contains a view of the stern of the *Victory* surrounded by coloured flags spelling out the famous 'England Expects' signal. However, the signal is wrong. In common with all his contemporaries – including those who hoisted the signal in the *Victory* and all over the Empire on Trafalgar Day – Laughton took the flags from the wrong signal book. The error was not corrected, and the right flags allocated, until Perrin made his discovery at the Admiralty in 1908.

No such errors marred the next biography to appear, *The Life of Nelson: The Embodiment of the Sea Power of Great Britain*, which still ranks, along with Southey and Nicolas, as one of the greatest. The author, Alfred Thayer Mahan (1840–1914), was a serving officer in the United States Navy. From an early age he had been interested in naval history and was President of the US War College from 1886 to 1889. In 1890 he published his first great work, *The Influence of Sea Power upon History*, a penetrating study of the British use of sea power during the Seven Years War, following it in 1892 with *The Influence of Sea Power upon the French Revolution and Empire*. Both books had a profound effect upon naval thinking since they demonstrated the indirect and yet decisive way in which sea power can influence world events. Having examined the events of the great wars themselves, Mahan then turned his attention to Nelson for, as the subtitle of his book emphasized, he saw in his career the summation of all his theories.

Predictably, reactions in England to the idea of an American writing a life of Nelson were not, at first, particularly favourable, however high the reputation of the author. But Mahan had approached the work with his customary thoroughness and was supported by established Nelson scholars such as Laughton and Professor Thursfield; by members of the Nelson family, including the third Earl Nelson and Nelson Ward (one of Horatia's sons); and by the descendants of some of Nelson's band of brothers who opened their family archives to him. He also benefited from being the first major author to write with the works of Nicolas, Jeaffreson and Morrison before him and so was able to penetrate the mind of his subject in an unprecedented way. Additionally, he was the first senior naval officer to approach Nelson from the point of view of a fellow-professional. Published in England by Sampson Low and Marston, the resulting book is an authoritative and impressive work which still offers valuable insights both on Nelson's professional career and on his private life.

The book was extremely popular and was widely recognized as a work of major importance. It appeared in two handsome blue-bound volumes: the English edition bearing a gilt vignette of Nicholas Pocock's painting of Nelson's five main ships on the front; while the American edition sported a semi-profile of the subject. The illustrations are not particularly notable, being in the main

The gilt decoration on the original bindings of Captain A.T. Mahan's biography: (left) the American edition; (right) the English edition.

reproductions of portraits of some of the main characters. But there is one small surprise: the first appearance in any Nelson biography of a portrait of Horatia, a delightful miniature of her aged twenty-two and obviously contributed by Nelson Ward, since the original is now in the Nelson-Ward Collection at the Royal Naval Museum. A second edition, this time in a single volume, was published in 1899 and a much abridged paperback version, with an introduction by A.V. Alexander, First Lord of the Admiralty, was published by Penguin in 1942 as a wartime morale-booster.

It was also used as an inspiration by the other side in the same war. When an Italian squadron paid a goodwill visit to Malta in the spring of 1938, the British second-in-command of the Mediterranean fleet, Vice Admiral Sir Andrew Cunningham, noticed that the Italian commander-in-chief, Admiral Riccardi, had a copy of *The Life of Nelson* on the table by his bed. Remembering later the way in which Riccardi had proudly pointed the book out to his hosts, Cunningham commented dryly: 'His subsequent actions during the war rather showed that he had not greatly profited by his nightly reading.'[11]

The last of the turn-of-the-century biographies was another study by a naval officer, this time an Irishman, Lord Charles Beresford (1846–1919), who collaborated with Herbert Wilson (1866–1940) to produce *Nelson and His Times*. First issued by the *Daily Mail* in fortnightly parts, it is usually found nowadays in one of the special very handsome bindings offered by the publishers Eyre & Spottiswoode. Beresford had first come to fame in 1882 when, in a piece of classically Nelsonian gallant effrontery, he had engaged a huge fort in single combat with his tiny gunboat HMS *Condor* during the bombardment of Alexandria by the British Mediterranean fleet. His subsequent career was equally colourful – both at sea and ashore, where, as an MP, he constantly argued for a stronger Navy. As a result of his personal agenda, the text of *Nelson and His Times* occasionally reads like a political tract: 'If we look for Nelson's true monument we shall find it in the British Empire of our day . . . We can best do him honour and repay the debt which we owe him, by remembering his teaching, by refusing to sacrifice duty to comfort, and by persistently strengthening the great force which he led to victory.'[12]

If the text is sometimes rather dated, the interest of the illustrations can never pall. The advent of reasonably good quality photographic reproduction meant that this was the first – and still one of the best – of the pictorial biographies. There are over 450 illustrations ranging from reproductions of famous battle paintings to portraits of nearly every significant person with whom Nelson was associated. But by far the main value of the book lies in its remarkable series of photographs of Nelson relics – many of which were at that time still in private hands and were photographed specially for the publication. They make the book an invaluable source for curators of the modern Nelson collections.

Like Mahan's book, *Nelson and His Times* reached some influential places. At the end of the Second World War, when the British entered Potsdam, they discovered a special presentation copy bearing the inscription 'To the German Emperor with respectful compliments from Lord Charles Beresford, June 1898.' The book, with the Kaiser's bookplate, was given by Winston Churchill to Admiral Sir Andrew Cunningham (he who had observed Admiral Riccardi's bedtime reading) and after his death it was presented to the National Maritime Museum, where it is still preserved.

Surprisingly the centenary celebrations did not produce any biography of note. Possibly it was felt that Mahan's monumental work more than met the need and there was no requirement for another full-length study. Instead, as the twentieth century progressed, historians concentrated on studying particular aspects of the Nelson story in greater depth. Emma Hamilton received sympathetic treatment at last from Walter Sichel in 1905. Detailed studies of Trafalgar were produced by a Frenchman, Edward Desbrière, in 1907 and by the leading English naval historian of the day, Julian Corbett, in 1910. Mary Eyre Matcham, granddaughter of Nelson's favourite sister Kitty, produced a charming study of the Nelson family in 1911, and the first biography of Lady Nelson made its appearance in 1939. Horatia had to wait until 1970 for her own biography and Emma was again properly treated, and brought to vivid life, by Mollie Hardwick in 1969 and Flora Fraser in 1986. Moreover, there were further collections of Nelson letters to add to the enormous body of material already available in printed form, including *Nelson's Letters from the Leeward Islands*, edited by Geoffrey Rawson in 1953, which sheds fascinating new light on Nelson's controversial activities in the West Indies in the 1780s by publishing the Shirley-Nelson correspondence for the first time; and George Naish's *Nelson's Letters to his Wife and Other Documents, 1785–1831*, published by Routledge and Keegan Paul in conjunction with the Navy Records Society in 1958.

Between the wars the pattern began to be established for at least one biography of Nelson to be published in each decade and this trend has continued ever since. In the 1930s there was another sailor's account by Admiral Mark Kerr, entitled simply *The Sailor's Nelson* (Hurst and Blackett, 1932) and *Nelson* by Clennell Wilkinson (1888–1936), published by George G. Harrap and Co. the previous year. Of the two, Wilkinson's has the most merit and deserves a place in the Top Twenty as a first-rate introduction to the Nelson story, treating the great love affair with sympathy and understanding.

In the 1940s there were two more notable books. One, *New Chronicles of the Life of Lord Nelson* by Charles Britton (Cornish Brothers Ltd, Birmingham, 1946), is really little more than a compendium of interesting facts although it has some useful lists of some of the most important portraits, monuments and places visited by Nelson. The other is a major masterpiece and a worthy successor to Southey, Nicolas and Mahan: *Nelson* by Carola Oman, published first in America in 1946 and then in England in 1947 by Hodder and Stoughton Ltd.

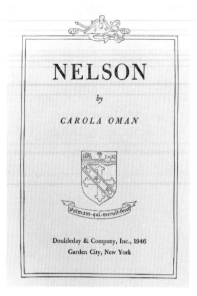

NELSON

by

CAROLA OMAN

Palmam qui meruit ferat

Doubleday & Company, Inc., 1946
Garden City, New York

*The title page of the American edition of
Carola Oman's biography, 1946.*

The daughter of the great historian of the Peninsular War, and Chichele Professor of Modern History at Oxford, Sir Charles Oman, Carola Oman (Lady Carola Mary Anne Lenanton 1897–1978) was the first biographer to study Nelson's life in the light of all the new material that had appeared since Mahan's great work. Drawing particularly on the Nisbet Papers in the Llangattock collection, housed in Monmouth Museum, she was able to give a far more balanced view than had earlier been possible of Nelson's marriage to Fanny Nisbet and showed that it had been both happy and fulfilled until very close to its end. At last, both the women in Nelson's life were allowed to emerge from the shadows and take their place on the stage alongside him, in a book that did not seek to take sides. It is an intensely personal view of Nelson, distilled from a faithful reading of many thousands of letters and gives by far the most detailed, intimate and vivid picture available of the man himself – a hero still, but human and fallible. At over seven hundred pages, it was longer even than Mahan and yet was contained within one volume. Sadly, however, post-war austerity printing standards meant that both the binding and the paper were poor and, worst of all, the illustrations were scanty and disappointing. None the less it still stands, nearly fifty years after its publication, as incomparably the best modern biography and has gone through several editions, including one as recently as 1987.

In the 1950s two men emerged as Nelson experts. George Naish, a curator at the National Maritime Museum (possessed of an encyclopaedic knowledge of Nelson and his associates that, sadly, he rarely committed to paper), published the excellent edition of Nelson's letters to his wife already referred to. But even his

Oliver Warner – one of the great twentieth-century Nelson experts.

knowledge was eclipsed by that of Oliver Warner – acknowledged by all Nelsonians until his death in 1976 as the leading Nelson expert of the post-war period. He wrote numerous books on Nelson-related subjects – in particular, a fine biography of Collingwood and a series of first-rate studies of Nelson's battles for the *Great British Battles* series published by Batsford. He was also an expert on the Nelson portraits. In 1958 he distilled his considerable knowledge into a slim volume, *A Portrait of Lord Nelson*, published by Chatto and Windus.

Although only 372 pages long, it is a masterly work. It features some new material – for example an excellent account of the Baltic campaign; a vivid account of Nelson's visit to Naples and, most fascinating of all, the discovery that he had at least one mistress before Emma, a 'dolly' whom he kept at Leghorn. It ends with a most useful list of the main portraits – although our knowledge of this subject has been very greatly increased since then by the meticulous researches of Richard Walker. Highly readable and balanced in all its judgements, it is by far the best introduction to Nelson's life and has been very successful ever since its first appearance. There are also two editions in paperback. It is certainly worthy of a place in the Top Twenty.

So, too, is another short life, this time by a more modern sailor, Captain Geoffrey Bennett, who had served for some thirty-five years in the Royal Navy and had seen much action in the Second World War. Entitled *Nelson the Commander* and published by Batsford in 1972, it is very much a seaman's account and wins its place in the Top Twenty by being by far the best of this particular type of Nelson biography. It contains little in the way of new material except that, for the first time, details are given of Nelson's failure to act with the Russian Admiral Ushakov in the Mediterranean in 1799, based on papers that had been published in Moscow shortly before the book appeared.

So to the 1980s and, once again, two biographies appeared within months of each other: *The Immortal Memory* by the father and son team David and Stephen Howarth (Dent, 1988), and *Horatio Nelson* by Tom Pocock (The Bodley Head, 1987). Both books are excellent; although it is Tom Pocock who has inherited Oliver Warner's mantle as the recognized leading Nelson expert. Like Warner, he had previously published works on Nelson and related subjects, including a study of Nelson's early career based on the new material that had been discovered, and a biography of one of his most beloved protégés, Captain Sir William Hoste. He then concentrated his extensive expertise in a warm and highly readable book that introduces the reader to yet more new Nelsonian material: his love for an older officer's pretty and sophisticated young wife in the West Indies; his plans for a new career in politics during his frustrating years ashore; and a delightful glimpse of life at Merton seen through the eyes of his young niece. Shrewd in its understanding of its subject and searching in its judgements, it will be a long time before *Horatio Nelson* is overtaken, and, as a measure of its continuing success, it has recently been reissued in paperback.

To sum up then, Nelson has suffered at the hands of the biographers – perhaps more than most other historical figures of comparable stature. And yet, he has survived the troubled waters of the nineteenth century and now commands an international admiration and a world-wide following. He owes his pre-eminent position not just to his professional skill and innovative thinking, outstanding though they were; nor just to his remarkable personal courage and apparent lack of fear, reinforced by his strong Christian faith. What marks Horatio Nelson out, and obviously still fascinates biographers, is the fact that, in an age known for its cruelty, and in a profession dedicated to warfare, he stands out as a humane and caring figure. Of few other great war leaders has it been said, as was said of Nelson by one of his captains, that he was a man to *love*.

'Many lives of Nelson have been written: one is yet wanting', wrote Southey in 1813.[13] Little did he know that he was seeing not the end, but the beginning of a trend that is with us yet. As this book goes to press, another biography, this time by Christopher Hibbert, has just been published; the Royal Naval Museum is currently putting together plans for a major Nelson Biography Project to mark the bicentenary of his death and there will doubtless be many other, less ambitious lives published as 2005 approaches. So the list of Nelson titles is still expanding and modern collectors are more spoiled for choice than any of their predecessors.

The riches that have been hinted at here may seem daunting to a newcomer; but no one can do very wrong if they base their library on the twenty main titles that have been highlighted. One note of caution must, however, be sounded. The field of Nelsonian literature is rich and endlessly varied and the thrill of collecting thoroughly addictive. Before long, all collectors worth their salt find that, for them, there is *always* one more life of Nelson 'yet wanting'.

References

1. Unpublished list prepared by the author.
2. Sir Nicholas Harris Nicolas, *The Dispatches and Letters of Lord Nelson* (1844–6), Vol. 1, p. viii.
3. Jack Simmons, *Southey* (1945), p. 142.
4. Robert Southey, *The Life of Nelson* (1813), Vol. 2, pp. 272–3.
5. Sir Geoffrey Callender, *Southey's Life of Nelson* [with an Introduction and Critical Notes] (1922), pp. xxv–xxvi.
6. quoted in: *Analectic Magazine*, 1814, p. 452.
7. M. Eyre Matcham, *The Nelsons of Burnham Thorpe* (1911), p. 267.
8. Ibid., p. 269.
9. *Dictionary of National Biography*, Vol. XL, p. 207.
10. Carola Oman, *Nelson* (1947), p. vii.
11. A.B. Cunningham, *A Sailor's Odyssey* (1951), p. 190.
12. Lord Charles Beresford and H.W. Wilson, *Nelson and his Times* (1897–8), p. 232.
13. Southey, op. cit., Vol. I, p. ix.

A Nelson Chronology

1758	29 September, Horatio Nelson born at Burnham Thorpe, Norfolk.
1767	26 December, Catherine Nelson, Nelson's mother, dies.
1771	Nelson joins HMS *Raisonnable* as a midshipman.
	August, sails to the West Indies in a merchant ship.
1773	June to September, joins Arctic expedition.
	Joins HMS *Seahorse* and sails to East Indies.
1775	Invalided from his ship suffering from malaria. Returns to England.
	War of American Independence begins.
1777	9 April, passes examination for lieutenant. Appointed to
	HMS *Lowestoffe* for service in the West Indies.
1778	September, appointed first lieutenant of HMS *Bristol*.
	December, appointed commander of HMS *Badger*.
1779	June, promoted to post captain, appointed to command
	HMS *Hinchinbrooke*.
1780	Takes part in the Nicaraguan expedition (capture of Fort San Juan).
	Falls ill and returns home to England.
	Sits for portrait by John Rigaud.
1781	Appointed to command HMS *Albemarle*.
1782	Joins North American Squadron. Visits Quebec and New York.
1783	War of American Independence ends. Returns home. Visits France.
1784	Appointed to command HMS *Boreas*. Sails for West Indies.
1785	May, meets Frances Nisbet.
1786	Appointed ADC to Prince William Henry.
1787	11 March, marries Frances Nisbet at Nevis.
	Returns to England. Placed on half-pay. Lives at Burnham Thorpe with his wife.
1793	Beginning of the French Revolutionary War.
	26 January, appointed to command HMS *Agamemnon*.
	June, sails for the Mediterranean.
	September, visits Naples. Meets Sir William and Lady Hamilton.

1794	January to August, Corsican campaign.
	12 July, right eye injured at Calvi.
1795	14 March, Hotham's Action. HMS *Agamemnon* in action with the *Ça Ira*.
1796	March, appointed Commodore.
	Joins HMS *Captain*.
1797	14 February, BATTLE OF ST VINCENT. Created Knight of Bath.
	Promoted Rear Admiral. Hoists flag in HMS *Theseus*.
	24 July, failure of attack on Santa Cruz, Tenerife. Loses right arm.
	Returns home and goes to Bath to recover.
	Sits for portrait by Lemuel Abbott.
1798	March. Hoists flag in HMS *Vanguard* and joins fleet off Cadiz.
	April, enters Mediterranean in command of a detached squadron.
	July, in pursuit of the French Toulon fleet with Napoleon on board.
	1 August, destroys the French fleet at Aboukir Bay, BATTLE OF THE NILE, badly wounded in the head.
	Created Baron Nelson of the Nile.
	22 September, arrives at Naples.
	23 to 26 December, rescues Neapolitan royal family from advancing French army and takes them to Palermo.
1799	23 January, the French capture Naples.
	Sits for portrait by Guzzardi.
	Begins relationship with Emma Hamilton.
	8 June, transfers his flag to HMS *Foudroyant*.
	June, assists in the recapture of Naples. Orders the execution of Admiral Carracciolo.
	Created Duke of Bronte by King of Naples.
1800	June, recalled home. Returns overland with the Hamiltons.
	August, in Vienna. Sits for portrait by Füger.
	Life-mask taken for bust by Thaller and Ranson.
	6 November, arrives at Great Yarmouth.
	Sits for portraits by Hoppner and Beechey.
1801	Publication of first biography to appear between its own covers.
	Separates from his wife.
	1 January, promoted to Vice Admiral.
	13 January, hoists flag in HMS *San Josef*.
	5 February, Emma Hamilton gives birth to their first daughter Horatia.
	12 March, sails, with Hyde Parker, to the Baltic.
	2 April, THE BATTLE OF COPENHAGEN. Flies flag in HMS *Elephant*.
	Created Viscount.
	6 May, succeeds Parker as Commander-in-Chief.
	June, returns home.

	27 July, appointed to command anti-invasion forces in the Channel, hoists flag in HMS *Medusa*.
	15 August, failure of attack on Boulogne.
	September, buys Merton Place, Surrey.
	1 October, armistice signed between Britain and France.
	22 October, returns home to Merton.
1802	25 March, Treaty of Amiens (end of the French Revolutionary War).
	26 April, his father, Revd Edmund Nelson dies.
	July and August, tours South Wales and the Midlands with the Hamiltons.
1803	6 April, Sir William Hamilton dies.
	16 May, Napoleonic War begins. Appointed C-in-C Mediterranean.
	18 May, hoists flag in HMS *Victory*.
	6 July, joins the fleet off Toulon.
1804	Blockades French in Toulon.
1805	April to July, chases French fleet to West Indies and back.
	18 August, arrives back in England. To Merton on leave.
	14 September, rejoins the *Victory* at Portsmouth.
	28 September, takes command of the fleet off Cadiz.
	21 October, THE BATTLE OF TRAFALGAR
	6 November, news of Trafalgar arrives in England.
	First monuments erected (in County Cork and Taynuilt, Argyllshire).
	4 December, HMS *Victory* arrives at Portsmouth with Nelson's body on board.
	5 December, Day of Thanksgiving for Trafalgar.
1806	8 January, funeral procession on the River Thames.
	9 January, funeral service in St Paul's Cathedral.
	Effigy by Catherine Andras installed in Westminster Abbey.
	Orme's *Graphic History* published.
1807	7 July, foundation stone laid of monument on Portsdown Hill, Portsmouth, paid for by Nelson's comrades at Trafalgar.
1808	Montreal monument erected.
1809	Clarke and M'Arthur's *Life* published.
	Birmingham monument erected.
1813	Southey's *Life* published.
	Liverpool monument erected.
1811	Braham's song 'The Death of Nelson' first performed.
1814	Launch of the first HMS *Nelson*, a 120-gun battleship.
1842	Nelson, New Zealand, founded.
1843	Trafalgar Square column and statue completed.
1844	First volume of Nicolas' *Dispatches and Letters* published.
1845	Prince Albert purchases Nelson's Trafalgar coat and presents it to Greenwich Hospital.

1867	Maclise's 'Death of Nelson' mural in Houses of Parliament completed. Nelson monument in Trafalgar Square finally completed by addition of Landseer's lions.
1891	The Navy Exhibition, Chelsea. Many Nelson relics included.
1895	The Navy League founded.
1897	Mahan's *Life* published.
1905	Trafalgar centenary celebrations.
1918	*Nelson* released – first full-length Nelson film.
1922	HMS *Victory* placed in dry-dock, launch of the 'Save the *Victory* Fund'.
1925	Launch of seventh HMS *Nelson*, a battleship.
1927	Restoration of HMS *Victory* completed.
1937	National Maritime Museum opened. Nelson relics on display.
1939	Victory Museum opened. Nelson relics on display.
1942	*Lady Hamilton* (film) released.
1947	Carola Oman's *Nelson* published.
1951	Statue erected in Portsmouth.
1966	*Nelson: A Study in Miniature* by Terence Rattigan, performed on ITV. Dublin monument blown up by IRA.
1972	Lambert McCarthy Gallery opened at Royal Naval Museum, to contain Nelson memorabilia collection of Mrs Lily McCarthy, CBE.
1981	The Nelson Society founded.
1982	*I Remember Nelson*, TV series shown by ATV.
1990	The 1805 Club founded.
1994	Monument to Emma Hamilton erected in Calais.
1995	Beginning of 'The Nelson Decade'.

A Nelson Gazetteer

A brief guide to the main places in Great Britain where the material mentioned in this book may be seen.

1. HMS *Victory*

HM Naval Base, Portsmouth, P01 3NU. Tel. and fax: 01705 819604

Regular tours by experienced guides to all key parts of the ship, including Nelson's cabin and the cockpit, where he died. Special interest tours available.

Open daily (except 25 Dec.). Admission charge (which includes admission to the Royal Naval Museum).

2. The Royal Naval Museum

HM Naval Base, Portsmouth, PO1 3NU. Tel.: 01705 727562. Fax: 01705 727575

Major collection of Nelson relics and commemoratives – due to be redisplayed in new exhibition in 1998. Regular events and lectures. Small Nelson archive and library.

Open daily (except 25/26 Dec.). Admission charge. (HMS Victory ticket-holders admitted free).

3. The National Maritime Museum

Romney Road, Greenwich, London, SE10 9NF. Tel.: 0181-858-4422. Fax: 0181-312-6632

Major new exhibition of Nelson relics and commemoratives. Regular lectures and seminars on Nelson and Nelson-related subjects. Large Nelson archive and library.

Open daily (except 24–26 December). Admission charge.

4. The Nelson Museum, Monmouth

Priory Street, Monmouth, Gwent, NP5 3XA. Tel.: 01600 713519

Collection of relics and commemorative material. Large Nelson archive. Displays currently being upgraded.

Open daily (except Christmas Day and New Year). Sundays: afternoons only. Admission charge.

5. Lloyd's Nelson Collection

Lloyd's, Lime Street, London, EC3M 7HA. Tel.: 0171-327-6260. Fax: 0171-623-8238

Fine collection of Nelson silver and other relics and commemorative items. Some Nelson letters.

*Admission free **by appointment only.***

6. The British Library

Great Russell Street, London, WC1B 3DG

A large collection of Nelson manuscripts, which is available to researchers in the Manuscripts Reading Room on presentation of a readers ticket. The famous last letter to Emma Hamilton is on display in the British Library Gallery of the British Museum.

Museum: Open daily (Sundays, afternoons only). Reading Room Mon–Sat. Admission free.

7. Castle Museum, Norwich

The Castle, Norwich, Norfolk, NR1 3JU. Tel.: 01603 223624. Fax: 01603 765651

A small collection of Nelson material is displayed in the main history gallery.

Open daily (except Christmas Day). Sundays: afternoons only. Admission charge.

8. Burnham Thorpe, Norfolk

Nelson's father's church of All Saints survives (although much restored), as does the old village inn (now The Lord Nelson). A plaque in the wall marks the site of the Old Parsonage.

9. Maritime Museum for East Anglia, Great Yarmouth

25 Marine Parade, Great Yarmouth, Norfolk, NR30 2EN. Tel.: 01493 842267

A small collection of Nelson material forms part of the permanent displays.

Open: May–September. Admission charge.

10. St Paul's Cathedral

St Paul's Churchyard, London, EC4M 8AD. Tel.: 0171-236-4128

The Flaxman statue stands in the south transept; the crypt, where Nelson's tomb is situated, is open to the public.

Open Monday to Saturday. Admission charge to the cathedral.

11. Westminster Abbey Undercroft Museum

Westminster Abbey, London, SW1P 3PA. Tel.: 0171-233-0019

Catherine Andras' splendid effigy of Nelson has been recently restored and is on display.

Open daily (except 25 Dec.). Admission charge.

12. National Portrait Gallery

St Martin's Place, London, WC2H 0HE. Tel.: 0171-306-0055. Fax: 0171-306-0056

Portraits of Nelson form part of the permanent displays. Others are held in the reserve collections.

Open daily (except 1 Jan., Good Friday, May Day and 24–6 Dec.). Admission charge.

The Authors

Flora Fraser is the author of *Beloved Emma: The Life of Emma, Lady Hamilton*, and lives in Bayswater with her daughter Stella. Her biography of Queen Caroline, estranged wife of George IV, will be published autumn 1995. She enjoyed studying ancient sculpture at Oxford, and brings an equal enthusiasm to her discussion of the Nelson monuments.

John May is an antique dealer, specializing in eighteenth- and early nineteenth-century objects, author of *Commemorative Pottery 1780–1900* and *Victoria Remembered* and contributor of articles to many magazines, including, 'The Nelson Silver', 'Antique Collecting', 'An Eye for Nelson', 'Antiques and Art Monitor'. Member of The 1805 Club and the Nelson Society.

Timothy Millett is a fifth generation member of the old established firm of A.H. Baldwin & Sons Ltd, founded in 1872. He has contributed several articles to numismatic journals and regularly gives lectures to local numismatic societies throughout the UK on his specialist subject, British Commemorative Medals from the Seventeenth to Nineteenth Centuries.

John Munday, MA, FSA was born in Portsmouth and worked as a junior assistant, Public Libraries & Museums, there during the Blitz. He served in the Royal Navy between 1942 and 1946 and actually slung his hammock in HMS *Victory*. Devoted to drawing and painting, some of his work was acquired by the War Artists' Advisory Committee. After reading Fine Arts at Durham, he joined the staff of the National Maritime Museum, Greenwich, in charge of the Library and Reading Room. He then became Curator of Presentation and was latterly Head of Weapons and Antiquities. He is now Curator Emeritus.

Michael Nash spent twenty-five years in shipping before becoming a bookseller and now runs Marine Books of Hoylake. A Founder, and Honorary Life Member of the Nelson Society (1981), he was the editor of their journal *The Nelson Dispatch* between 1981 and 1986. A Founder Member and Chairman of The 1805 Club (1990), he edited their first yearbook, *The Trafalgar Chronicle*.

Tom Pocock is an author and journalist specializing in naval affairs and history. A former war correspondent and Naval Correspondent of *The Times* and Defence Correspondent of the London *Evening Standard*, he is the author of fifteen books, five of them about Nelson and his time. His biography, *Horatio Nelson*, was runner-up for the Whitbread Biography Prize and subsequently has twice been published in paperback.

Felix Pryor is manuscript consultant to Phillips, as well as a cataloguer for Sotheby's, Christie's and other auctioneers. He acts as advisor to several public and private collections, including Burghley

House and the Royal Pavilion, Brighton. He is editor of *The Faber Book of Letters* (1988) and author of a study of Shakespeare, *The Mirror and the Globe* (1992).

Richard Walker is picture cataloguer (miniatures) for the National Trust. Author of *Regency Portraits* (1985), *Miniatures in the Collection of Her Majesty the Queen* (1992) and *The Portraits of Nelson* (unpublished).

Colin White is Chief Curator of the Royal Naval Museum. An expert on the Victorian Navy, he has produced two major exhibitions on the subject and two books, *The End of the Sailing Navy* (1981) and *The Heyday of Steam* (1983). However, his first love has always been Horatio Nelson, and he is now concentrating on him, with a series of articles and lectures exploring aspects of the Nelson Legend. He is currently working on an extensive new Nelson exhibition for the RNM.

Bibliography

What follows is intended only as a guide to works specifically mentioned in this book, or consulted in its preparation. For fuller lists of books relating to Nelson the reader should refer to:

Cowie, Leonard W., *Lord Nelson 1758–1805: A Bibliography*, Meckler, 1990
Warner, Oliver, *Lord Nelson: A Guide to Reading with Notes on Contemporary Portraits*, Caravel Press, 1955

There is also a very good bibliography in *The Nelson Memorial* by Sir John Knox Laughton (for details see no. 12 below)

1. THE BIOGRAPHIES

The full details of the 'Top Twenty' biographies mentioned by Michael Nash in Chapter Eight.

(1) Blagdon, Francis William, *Orme's Graphic History of the Life, Exploits, and Death of Horatio Nelson, Viscount and Baron Nelson of the Nile, and of Burnham-Thorpe in the County of Norfolk. . .* (For undated edition:) *Embellished with a Series of Engravings, Illustrative of his Heroic Achievements* (For dated edition:) *. . . Containing Fifteen Engravings; and intended as an Accompaniment to the Three Celebrated Whole-Sheet Plates of His Lordship's Splendid Victories, viz. The Battles off St Vincent's, the Nile and Trafalgar, which are explained by References and Keys.* London: printed for, and published and sold by Edward Orme, 59 Bond Street, the corner of Brook Street; and by Longman, Hurst, Rees, and Orme, Paternoster Row, 1806.

(2) Harrison, James, *The Life of Horatio Lord Viscount Nelson, of the Nile . . .* 2 vols. London: printed at the Ranelagh Press, by Stanhope and Tilling, for C. Chapple, Pall Mall, 1806.

(3) Lloyd, Frederick, *An Accurate and Impartial Life of Viscount Nelson, Duke of Bronte in Sicily, . . . Comprehending Authentic and Circumstantial Details of his Glorious Achievements: together with Private Anecdotes, . . . never before published.* Printed for, and published by J. Fowler, Market-Place, Ormskirk; J. Lang, Printer, Water Street, Liverpool, 1806.

(4) Churchill, T.O., *The Life of Lord Viscount Nelson, Duke of Bronte, &c. Illustrated by Engravings of its most Striking and Memorable Incidents.* London: printed by T. Bensley, Bolt Court, for J. and W. MacGavin, 107 New Bond Street; and sold by R. Bowyer, 80 Pall Mall; etc. 1808 (2nd ed. 1810; 3rd ed. 1811).

(5) Clarke, James Stanier, and M'Arthur, John, *The Life of Admiral Lord Nelson, K.B. From His Lordship's Manuscripts,* 2 vols. London: printed by T. Bensley, Bolt Court, Fleet Street, for T. Cadell and W. Davies in the Strand, and W. Miller, Albemarle Street, 1809 (abridged edition, single octavo volume, 1810; 2nd ed. 3 vols, 1839/40).

(6) Southey, Robert, *The Life of Nelson,* 2 vols. London: printed for John Murray, Bookseller to the Admiralty and to the Board of Longitude, 50 Albemarle Street, 1813. (For details of further editions see Michael Nash, 'Southey's Nelson: Early and Collectable Editions', *Trafalgar Chronicle,* No. 1, 1991, pp. 36–54.)

(7) Anonymous, *The Letters of Lord Nelson to Lady Hamilton; with a Supplement of Interesting letters by Distinguished Characters,* 2 vols. London: printed by Macdonald and Son, Smithfield, for Thomas Lovewell & Co., Staines House, Barbican; and sold by all booksellers, 1814.

(8) Nicolas, Sir Nicholas Harris, *The Dispatches and Letters of Vice Admiral Lord Viscount Nelson, with notes,* 7 vols. London: Henry Colburn, publisher, Great Marlborough Street, 1844–6.

(9) Pettigrew, Thomas Joseph, *Memoirs of the Life of Vice-Admiral Lord Viscount Nelson, K.B. Duke of Bronte, etc. etc. etc.,* 2 vols. London: T. and W. Boone, 29 New Bond Street, 1849 (2nd edition same year).

(10) Jeaffreson, John Cordy, *Lady Hamilton and Lord Nelson: an Historical Biography based on the letters and other documents in the possession of Alfred Morrison Esq. of Fonthill, Wiltshire,* 2 vols. London: Hurst and Blackett, Limited, 13 Great Marlborough Street, 1888 (2nd 'New and Revised' edition, single volume, 1897. Also, same year, limited edition in two volumes, published by The Grolier Society).

(11) Morrison, Alfred, *The Collection of Autograph letters and Historical Documents formed by Alfred Morrison (Second Series 1882-1893): The Hamilton & Nelson Papers*, 2 vols. Printed for private circulation, 1893 and 1894.

(12) Laughton, Sir John Knox, *The Nelson Memorial: Nelson and his Companions in Arms*. London: George Allen, 156 Charing Cross Road, 1896 (also large paper edition limited to 100 copies, and an abridged edition for the Centenary in 1905).

(13) Mahan, Captain A.T., *The Life of Nelson, the Embodiment of the Sea Power of Great Britain*, 2 vols. Boston: Little, Brown and Company. London: Sampson, Low, Marston & Company Limited, 1897 (2nd edition, revised, single volume, Boston & London, 1899).

(14) Beresford, Lord Charles, and Wilson, H.W., *Nelson and His Times*. London: printed by Eyre and Spottiswoode, Her Majesty's Printers; published by Harmsworth Brothers Limited, 24 Tudor Street, E.C. No date (1897–8) (published in ten parts between October 1897 and March 1898 and bound into one volume).

(15) Wilkinson, Clennell, *Nelson*. London, Bombay & Sydney: George G. Harrap & Co. Ltd, 1931.

(16) Oman, Carola, *Nelson*. New York: Doubleday & Company Inc., Garden City, 1946. London: Hodder and Stoughton Limited, 1947 (other editions followed).

(17) Naish, George P.B. (ed.), *Nelson's Letters to his Wife and other documents, 1785–1831*. London: published in conjunction with the Navy Records Society by Routledge and Kegan Paul, 1958.

(18) Warner, Oliver, *A Portrait of Lord Nelson*. London: Chatto & Windus, 1958.

(19) Bennet, Geoffrey, *Nelson the Commander*. London: B.T. Batsford Ltd, 1972.

(20) Pocock, Tom, *Horatio Nelson*. London: The Bodley Head, 1987.

2. GENERAL WORKS

Beatty, Sir William, *The Authentic Narrative of the Death of Lord Nelson* (London, 1807).

Brown, Laurence, *British Historical Medals*, 2 vols (London, 1980).

Bugler, Arthur, *HMS Victory: Building, Restoration and Repair*, 2 vols (London, 1966).

Callender, Sir Geoffrey, 'His Guardian Angel', *Illustrated London News*, 20 March 1943.

Chamberlain, W.H., *Reminiscences of Old Merton* (London, 1923).

Crook, J. Mordaunt, and Port, M.H., ed., *The History of the King's Works*, 6 vols (1973).

Cunningham, A.B., *A Sailor's Odyssey* (London, 1951).

Dawson, Warren R., ed., *The Nelson Collection at Lloyd's* (London, 1932).

Forder, Charles, *A History of the Paston School* (North Walsham, 1975).

Fraser, Edward, *Greenwich Royal Hospital and the Royal United Service Museum* (London, 1911).

Gatty, Mrs and Dr, *Recollections of the Life of the Rev. A.J. Scott* (London, 1842).

Gill, Edward, *Nelson and the Hamiltons on Tour* (Gloucester, 1987).

Harries, Richard, with Cattermole, Paul, and Mackintosh, Peter, *A History of Norwich School* (Norwich, 1991).

Isaacson, Cecil J., *Nelson's 'Five Years on the Beach' and the Other Horatio Nelson of Burnham Thorpe* (Fakenham, 1991).

Jenkinson, H., *Practical Guide to North Wales* (London, 1878).

Jowett, Evelyn M., *An Illustrated History of Merton and Morden* (London, 1951).

Keigwin, K.P., 'Lord Nelson's Journey Through Germany' *The Mariner's Mirror*, Vol. XXI).

Kemble, James, 'The Medical Life of Lord Nelson', *Idols and Invalids* (1933).

Locker-Lampson, F., *My Confidences* (London, 1896).

MacDougall, Lindsay, 'Nelson's Manuscripts at the National Maritime Museum', *The Mariner's Mirror*, 1955.

Mace, Rodney, *Trafalgar Square, Emblem of Empire* (London, 1976).

Matcham, E, Eyre, *The Nelsons of Burnham Thorpe* (London, 1911).

May, W.E., and Annis, P.G.W., *Swords for Sea Service*, 2 vols (London, 1970).

Milford Haven, Marquess of, *British Naval Medals* (London, 1919).

Minto, Countess of, ed., *The Life and Letters of Sir Gilbert Elliot, First Earl of Minto*, 3 vols (1874).

Moorhouse, E. Hallam, *Nelson in England* (London, 1913).

Nash, Michael, ed., *The Nelson Masks* (Hoylake, 1993).

Nelson, Rt Hon, Horatio [third] Earl, 'Nelson Relics and Relic Hunters', *The Windsor Magazine*, 1904.

Pocock, Tom, *The Young Nelson in the Americas* (London, 1980).

——, *Nelson and the Campaign in Corsica* (Hoylake, 1994).

Pollard, J.G., 'Matthew Boulton and Conrad Heinrich Kuchler', *The Numismatic Chronicle*, Vol. X (1970).

Pope, Dudley, *The Great Gamble* (The Copenhagen Campaign), (London, 1972).

Pugh, P.D. Gordon, *Nelson and His Surgeons* (London, 1968).

——, *Naval Ceramics* (Bath, 1971).

Rathbone, Philip, *Paradise Merton: The Story of Nelson and the Hamiltons at Merton Place* (Windlesham, 1973).

Robinson, Charles, 'The Engraved Portraits of Nelson', *The Print Collector's Quarterly* XVII (1930).

Shaw, Lachlan, *The History of the Province of Moray* (1883).

Taylor, G.L., *Autobiography of an Octogenarian* (1870–2).

White, Arnold, and Moorhouse, E. Hallam, *Nelson and the Twentieth Century* (London, 1905).

Yarrington, Alison, *The Commemoration of the Hero* (London, 1988).

Additionally, both *The Nelson Dispatch* (Journal of The Nelson Society) and *The Trafalgar Chronicle* (Journal of The 1805 Club) are rich sources of Nelsonian information.

For details of these societies, and the addresses of their current secretaries, contact: The Chief Curator, Royal Naval Museum, HM Naval Base, Portsmouth, P01 3NU.

Index

Page numbers in italic refer to illustrations. Numbers in bold refer to colour plate numbers. Continuous text references ignore intervening illustration pages.
N = Horatio, Lord Nelson
Emma = Lady Emma Hamilton